Here, horror is dissected into all its terrifying parts. Inside, you'll discover:

THE ORIGINS OF HORROR:
The ancient mythology, folklore, and religious traditions that have shaped the genre since the dawn of humanity.

THE CHARACTERS OF HORROR:
The stories behind horror's most iconic characters—the vampires, witches, and werewolves that have bled into our hearts.

THE SCIENCE OF HORROR:
What happens in our brains when we're scared—and why we can't get enough of it.

HORROR THROUGH THE DECADES:
How history, culture, and catastrophe have shaped the genre from the turn of the twentieth century to today.

and more!

With seek-and-find puzzles, quizzes, and hidden surprises throughout, *The Illustrated Compendium of Horror* is a fun and interactive guide to one of the world's most enduring genres.

Enter . . . if you dare.

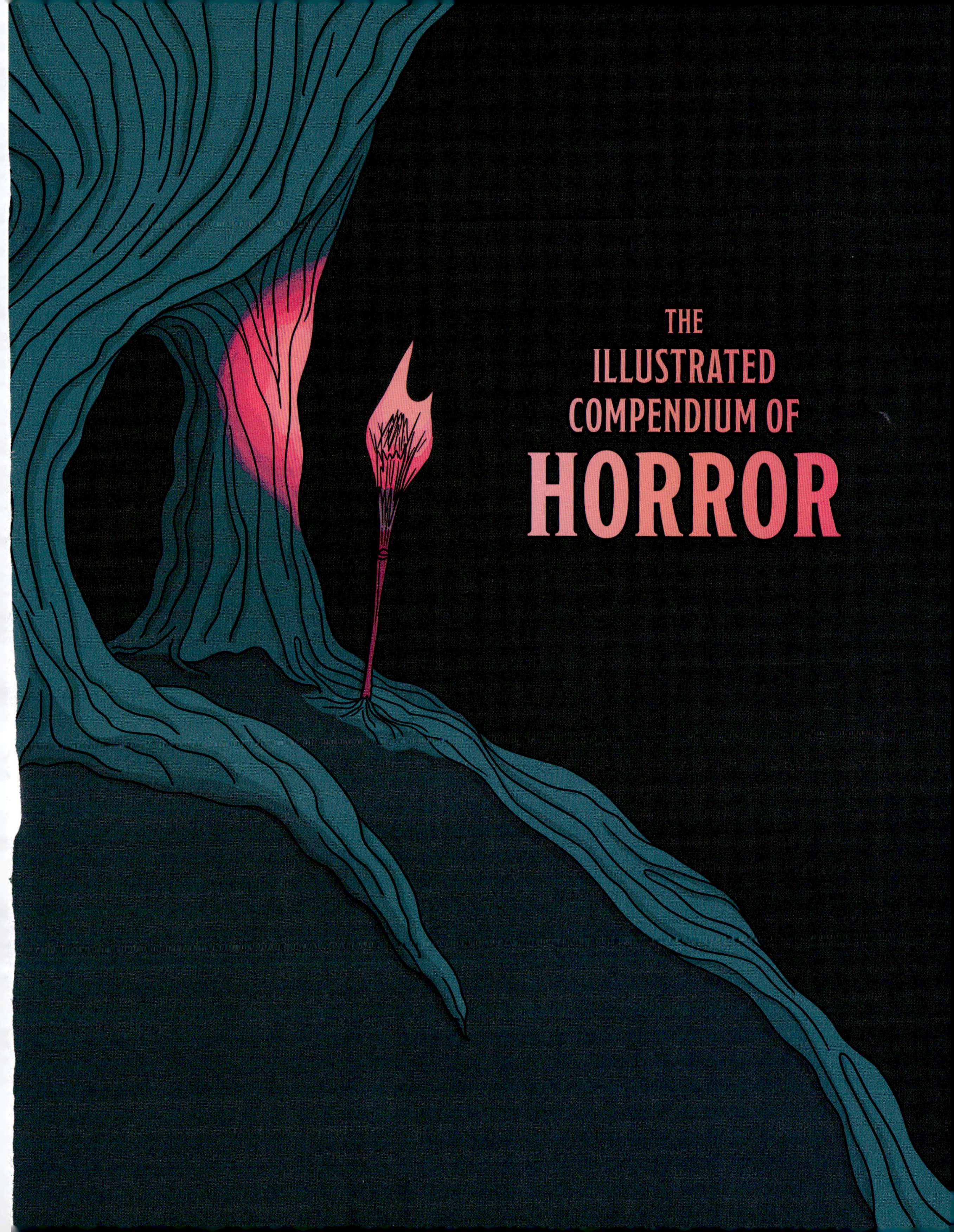
THE
ILLUSTRATED
COMPENDIUM OF
HORROR

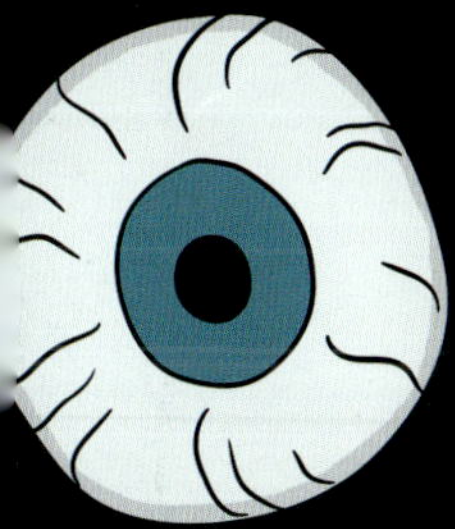

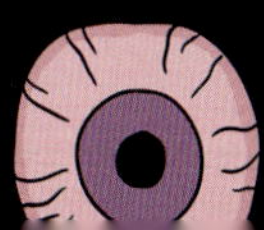

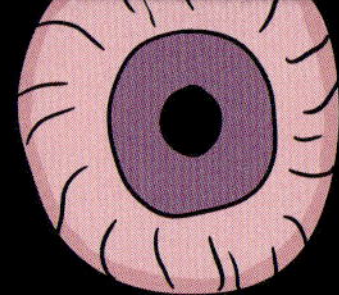

THE ILLUSTRATED COMPENDIUM OF

HORROR

1

THE ORIGINS OF HORROR

WELCOME IN, WANDERER. SHALL WE BEGIN? The origins of horror can be traced back to the dawn of human existence, for the first horror tales weren't told to scare for fun but constructed to warn and protect primitive beings from the dangers of nature and the unknown.

Telling horror stories was once essential to human survival, and despite our evolution, we've never stopped. Through ancient mythology, folklore, and religion, we have continually harnessed fear as a powerful tool for motivation and control. This has led to a vast collection of terrifying stories from cultures around the world, ultimately giving rise to the genre we now call horror.

Whether we like it or not, fear it or not, the genre of horror was born with us, and will continue to reflect, help, and haunt us until the end.

Grab a lantern, turn the page, and follow me through the origins of horror . . . if you dare.

Folklore and Mythology

Why did we tell folktales, and why were they so scary?

Myths and folktales were humanity's first horror stories, originating centuries ago as depicted in prehistoric cave art and continuing globally through indigenous and ancient shamanic traditions. During these early times, before the advent of written language, much of life was unknown and therefore threatening. With limited understanding of natural forces, early humans crafted stories to make sense of the dark forests, wild animals, storms, and the mysteries of nature. Their innate drive to explain and understand life's wonders, death, and the afterlife led to the weaving of cautionary tales filled with evil entities like spiteful gods and soul-stealing spirits. ✦

THE ROLE OF NATURE IN HORROR

With limited understanding of natural forces, early humans crafted stories to make sense of the mysteries of nature. These tales personified and deified the elements, portraying them as monsters or gods, which in turn had a profound impact on future horror narratives.

Can you imagine witnessing an eclipse without having any basic knowledge of astronomy? Lava pouring toward you from a volcanic eruption, the ground spontaneously shaking beneath you, or cloud tunnels expelling frozen water from the sky?

Mountains were likened to frost giants by the Norse. In ancient Greece, wind and storms were personified as gods who brought cold and ice. In West Africa it was Shango who brought thunder and lightning, and in the Plains tribes of North America it was the Thunderbird. Volcanoes were personified by Pele in Hawaiian cultures, Agni in Hindu cultures, and the sun god Ra in Egyptian cultures.

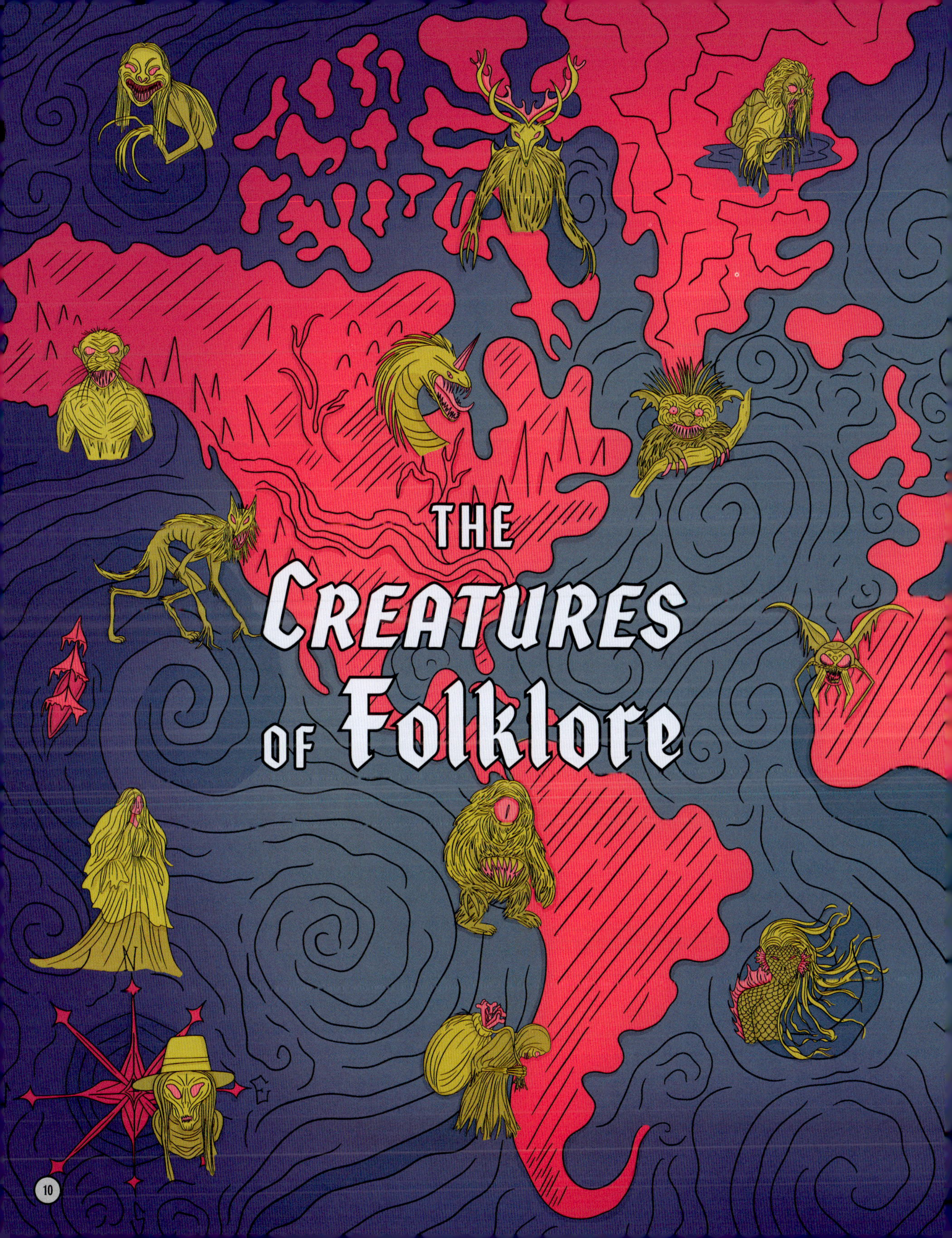
THE
CREATURES
OF Folklore

Folktales weren't created just to explain natural phenomena. They were survival stories crafted to help humans navigate danger, morality, and even the darkest emotions. Across the globe, cultures discovered that one of the most effective ways to protect their communities was to shape their fears into creatures that lurked in forests, rivers, and mountains—beings that embodied their deepest warnings, beliefs, and taboos. These creatures weren't arbitrary. They were cautionary, and terrifying on purpose. Fear was the point. A story powerful enough to make someone hesitate before wandering alone into the woods, stepping too close to the water's edge, or breaking a serious taboo like incest, cannibalism, or unchecked greed could mean the difference between life and death. These are the creatures that scared us into safety.

THE CREATURES OF Folklore

MAHAHA

INUIT - ARCTIC

Those who shirked their responsibilities were warned of this frozen demon with a nasty smile who tickled its victims to death.

WENDIGO

ALGONQUIN-SPEAKING PEOPLES - NORTH AMERICA

An emaciated creature with insatiable hunger for human flesh. Said to be the result of a person who committed acts of deceit, greed, or cannibalism.

QALUPALIK

INUIT - NUNAVUT, ARCTIC

A monstrous sea creature said to live beneath the Arctic ice whose terrifying reputation kept children away from the dangerous sea.

KUSHTAKA

TLINGIT - PACIFIC NORTHWEST, UNITED STATES

A half-man, half-otter trickster said to lure victims toward the water, frightening people away from dangerous shores.

UKTENA

CHEROKEE - SOUTHEASTERN UNITED STATES

A massive horned serpent covered in glittering scales whose terrifying reputation kept people away from dangerous waters and sacred places.

PUKWUDGIE

WAMPANOAG - NORTHEASTERN UNITED STATES

These devilish little forest spirits who set traps, threw rocks, and mimicked voices to lure people into the woods were created to warn about the consequences of not respecting the forest.

SKINWALKER

NAVAJO - SOUTHWESTERN UNITED STATES

A malevolent shapeshifting witch said to stalk the night in animal form. In Diné tradition, Skinwalkers were believed to be those who broke moral taboos.

LA LLORONA

MEXICO, NORTH AMERICA

A grief-stricken mother who drowned her children and died of sorrow, eternally haunting rivers and frightening people away from dangerous waters at night.

PISHTACO

THE ANDES, PERU, BOLIVIA, SOUTH AMERICA

A vampiric figure who drained the life from human victims and whose legend reflected colonial exploitation and warned of outsiders who profited from Indigenous people.

MAPINGUARI

AMAZON RAINFOREST, BRAZIL, SOUTH AMERICA

A jungle-dwelling giant with one large eye and a gaping mouth in its stomach whose horrific description kept people from entering the dangerous jungle alone.

EL SILBÓN

COLOMBIA, VENEZUELA, SOUTH AMERICA

A wandering ghost carrying a sack of bones whose haunting whistle kept people from venturing out alone at night.

YACURUNA

AMAZON RAINFOREST, BRAZIL, SOUTH AMERICA

Water spirits said to ride giant black crocodiles and pose as humans to lure victims into the water. Their terrifying tales deterred people from treacherous jungle rivers.

TROLLS

SCANDINAVIA, NORTHERN EUROPE

Monstrous, ugly creatures who dwelled in mountains, caves, and forests whose fearsome tales kept people from wandering too deep into the wilderness.

LESHY

SLAVIC - EASTERN EUROPE

Ancient spirits who led hunters astray, never to be seen again. Their legends warned of the dangers of the forest.

JIANGSHI

TAOIST - WESTERN HUNAN, CHINA

Reanimated corpses known as "hopping vampires" that fed on the living, reinforcing the importance of proper burial rites.

YUREI

JAPAN

Restless, vengeful spirits of those who died harboring powerful negative emotions, reinforcing the importance of resolving grievances in life.

LEMURES

ANCIENT ROME, ITALY, EUROPE

Restless spirits of the dead believed to return when wronged in life, whose legends explained illness and misfortune within families.

DJINN

MIDDLE EAST

Wrathful and dangerous spirits who dwelled in deserts and mountains. When disturbed or angered they would bring illness or misfortune to your home. Created to make people fear the consequences of committing immoral acts such as pride and disobedience.

RAKSHASA

BUDDHIST, HINDU - INDIA

Demonic beings with sharp teeth and clawed hands who embodied sins like lust and greed, their stories cautioning against moral corruption.

ADZE

EWE - GHANA, TOGO, AFRICA

A vampiric spirit guised as a firefly that slipped through keyholes to possess a person. Its legend explained sudden illness and misfortune.

SASABONSAM

ASHANTI - GHANA, WEST AFRICA

A vampire-like creature that hung from trees by hooked feet and attacked with iron teeth, its legend warning against wandering the forest alone.

YARA-MA-YHA-WHO

INDIGENOUS PEOPLES - AUSTRALIA

A small frog-like creature that slowly sucked the life from you if you were lazy, eventually transforming you into a yara-ma-yha-who yourself.

AMMIT

ANCIENT EGYPT, NORTH AFRICA

A creature who was part lion, part crocodile, and part hippo, who would await souls in the afterlife and eat their hearts if they lived an immoral life.

TOKOLOSHE

ZULU - SOUTH AFRICA

A malevolent imp-like creature said to cause illness and misfortune, cautioning against the use of witchcraft.

TUREHU

MĀORI - NEW ZEALAND

Unexpected disappearances or illness were often attributed to encounters with the turehu, fairylike beings said to dwell in misty forests and mountains.

THE FLORA OF HORROR

Whether because of their mysterious nature, toxic properties, or strange forms, we see recurring plants, flowers, and mushrooms used as symbols commonly associated with dark themes and the supernatural. To this day, we use the same scary flora to poison the pages of our horror tales. Welcome to the garden of the deadliest plants of horror . . . Be careful what you touch.

BELLADONNA

Also known as deadly nightshade and beautiful death, this flower is the queen of the poison garden. Its fatally toxic berries reinforce the belief that it was created by the devil himself.

DEVIL'S TRUMPET

Also known as datura or moonflower, devil's trumpet is pollinated by moths and known for its glowing white flowers that only bloom at night. It is a highly toxic plant with hallucinogenic properties. In folklore, it's often linked to shape-shifting and thought to open gateways to the spirit world.

WOLFSBANE

Also known as aconite, devil's helmet, and monkshood, wolfsbane is a highly poisonous plant not only used to kill in horror stories but also to ward off werewolves, who are rumored to be repelled by it.

CASTOR

Known as the evil twin of the poison garden, this plant has two uses: one medicinal, and one deadly. In horror, the castor plant's lethal ricin is ground into a powder and put in food.

FOXGLOVE

As poisonous as they are beautiful, in folklore, these deadly plants are said to grow in places where the veil between our world and others thins, sometimes acting as portals to the fairy realm.

VENUS FLYTRAP

The queen of carnivorous plants with a taste for flesh. What's scarier than being caught and slowly digested alive by a pretty little plant with teeth?

HEMLOCK

This plant is synonymous with death and is often associated with witches, necromancy, and betrayal. Its toxic properties cause a silent paralysis and eventual death.

YEW

Because these trees are most often found in cemeteries, they act as the guardians of spirits and portals to the underworld. Yew trees' leaves and berries carry fatal levels of taxine, a poison slipped into food or drinks in horror tales.

HENBANE

Because of its toxic and hallucinogenic properties, henbane is associated with witches and oracles who use its dark magic to induce visions, trances, and madness.

FUNGI

Because of exotic varieties like dead-man's-fingers and bleeding tooth, lethal toxicity, phosphorescent glow, and deep underworld web of creeping, fruiting fingers, mushrooms are often used as symbols to represent the deadliest entities of "sporror."

BAD Omens

OWLS

In some cultures, the hoot of an owl at night is a sign that death is near.

Bad omens are the harbingers of horror—they act as dark foreshadowing devices that tell us where we're headed is certainly not safe. The bad omens from our earliest stories, like black cats and broken mirrors, have now evolved into some of the most iconic symbols of the entire horror genre.

BATS

If a bat flies into your home, they are said to bring evil spirits and bad luck with them.

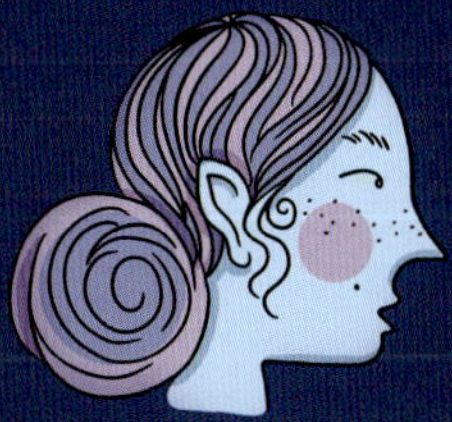

THE MOON AND WOLVES

The full moon is not only known as a bad omen, but one of the most powerful symbols in horror. Each of its phases holds a different meaning, and many beings in folklore—good or evil—draw strength from it. To double up on bad omens, add the howl of a wolf and you probably won't live to see the morning.

BLACK CATS

Black cats have long been associated with dark magic, for if one crossed your path, you were sure to be cursed by a spiteful witch. Cats are also associated with the Black Death. In the peak of the outbreak in the fourteenth century, cats were deemed "unholy animals." Ironically, this belief led to many cats being slaughtered, making the rat population grow, and the plague grow with it.

BROKEN MIRRORS

Regarding broken mirrors as bad omens originated in ancient Rome, where they believed your reflection was a continuation of your soul. Breaking a mirror was thought to harm the spirit within it and even release other evil spirits in the process.

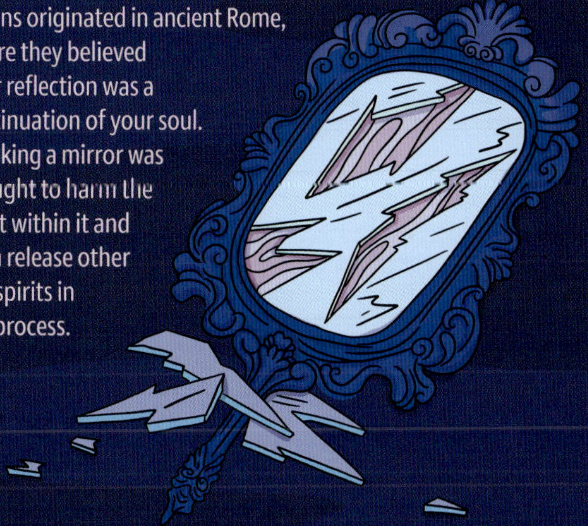

UNLUCKY NUMBERS

Numbers like 4, 13, 17, and 666 are seen as bad omens because of their association with biblical betrayals, religious fears of the coming of the Antichrist, or even sounding similar to something sinister, like the number 4 in Chinese.

SPILLING SALT

One of the most ancient superstitions, the act of spilling salt, became a bad omen because salt was once a valuable and rare substance, even thought to have protective qualities. Spilling salt, or wasting it, was seen as a great offense that would attract misfortune. In Leonardo da Vinci's *The Last Supper*, Judas is shown knocking over a saltcellar, representing his impending betrayal of Jesus.

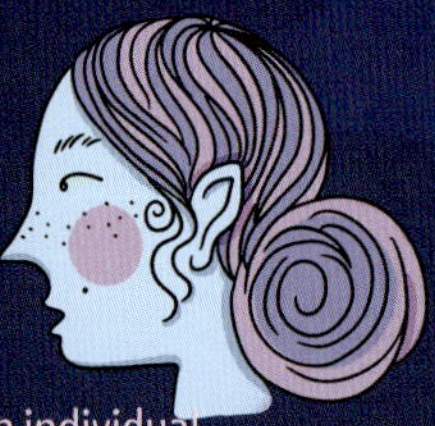

DOPPELGÄNGERS

Originating in Germany, a doppelgänger ("double of a person") is thought to symbolize a split soul; a malevolent shadow self that mirrors an individual. Many cultures believe that seeing your doppelgänger signifies a fracture in the natural order and that death is not far behind.

MOTHS

Almost every culture has attached their own beliefs and negative associations to the moth—they are seen as a manifestation of death itself, messengers from the spirit world, and because of their attraction to flame, metaphors for irresistible temptation and sin.

BIRDS

From Norse mythology to Indigenous peoples' beliefs, European folklore to Middle Eastern tales, birds—particularly ravens, blackbirds, crows, and owls—are believed to be bad omens. Their dark colors, unique sounds, and penchant for live or rotten flesh, have forever tied them to the afterlife, leading humans to believe that death, even if you can't see it, could be looking right at you.

The Autopsy of Death

The folklore and mythology we've encountered in this chapter have illustrated that the foundation of horror is human's innate, ferocious desire to explain the unexplainable and to understand what we cannot. Now, many of our mysteries have been solved and we no longer question weather events, illness, or the dangerous properties of plants. We even have explanations for many of the strange noises we hear at night. But no matter what we can now explain, rationalize, and understand, there is one thing, the biggest thing, life's ultimate mystery, and the perpetrator of fear that will forever remain unsolved: death.

Death and the afterlife is the ultimate question and therefore the ultimate fear for humans. It is the only question we'll never be able to answer until we ourselves have, passed through the veil. We fear death the most, that's why we talk about it the most. There's no reasoning with it, no true understanding of it, and death, our inevitable fate, is coming for us all no matter how scared we are.

Death is why the horror genre exists. We have been obsessed with death since we were given life, and our stories surrounding it, trying to make sense of it, grapple, appease, bargain, control and outsmart it, will continue to be the central theme of our horror stories for the rest of our existence. And maybe even beyond.

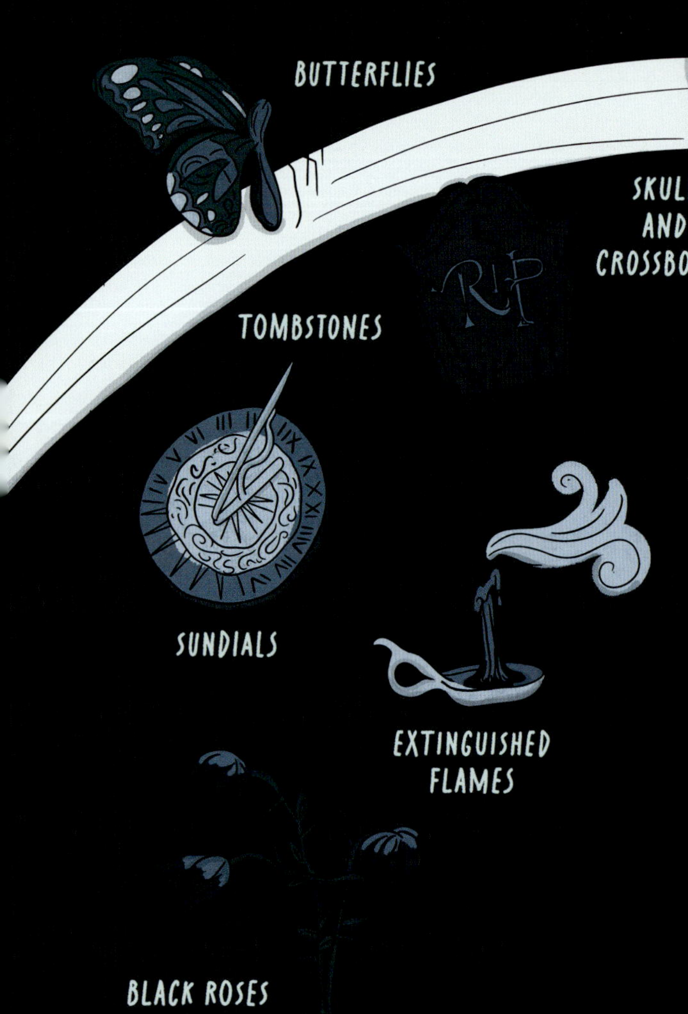

Symbols of Death and Memento Mori

Just like our ancestors' attempted rationalizations of the unexplainable, we've created symbols, warnings and even personifications to confront our greatest fear. Many of us keep these creepy keepsakes near to us as daily reminders that our fate is inescapable. These are what we call memento mori.

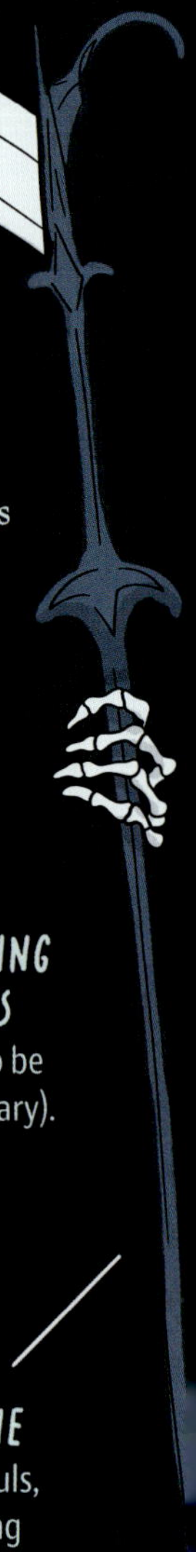

GLOWING EYES
(just to be extra scary).

The Literal Anatomy of Death

The ultimate symbol of death we've created is death itself, death incarnate, the personification of death—The Grim Reaper.

LARGE BLACK WINGS
suggesting he is a fallen angel, personifying our fear that even if we ascend to heaven, our sins will deny us entry and land us in hell.

A SCYTHE
to reap souls, harvesting them for the afterlife.

A BONY PHYSIQUE
to indicate that our bones are all that remain after death.

GOTHIC FASHIONS
via his uniform of a dramatic black shroud, cloaking him in darkness.

Ashes to Ashes, Dust to Dust

Many cultures believe that death is the process in which a soul transitions from this life to the next—that it's the start of another journey, not the "final resting place." Horror stories have adopted a lot of these rituals meant to reassure us, because what's better fodder for a scary story than death rituals going wrong? What would happen if a spirit wasn't properly contained, unable to move on, or find peace in the afterlife?

Curiously, all human burial practices involve one of the four natural elements—air, fire, earth, and water. These elements symbolize the cycle of rebirth, and while these methods can be beautiful in their own right, many include unsettling practices, like being picked to the bone, burned, cured in bogs, embalmed, and even stuffed with spices. Let's dig open the grave to see what the horror genre refuses to keep buried.

AIR: In a sky funeral, the body is respectfully laid out and exposed to animals and birds as food. This act aligns with the core Buddhist value of compassion for all creatures. Denying living wildlife a life source that is no longer useful would be considered a wasteful act. Another sky burial of sorts is the practice of hanging coffins off cliff faces, intended to bring the bodies of the dead closer to the heavens. Some say this has caused the mountains and cliff sides to be haunted by spirits

FIRE: Since the beginning of time, cultures have used fire not only as a way of disposing of our remains, but as a process of transition, purification, and fertilization. Whether it's via a funeral pyre, Viking funeral boat, or a traditional crematorium, using fire to release the spirit from the body is believed to be a final and effective way to detach the soul from the body.

EARTH: Being sealed within a coffin, tomb, crypt, mausoleum, or sarcophagus has been the primary practice used for the dead since antiquity due to religious traditions, cultural customs, and the desire for a physical resting place. Major faiths like Islam, Judaism, and Christianity have traditionally favored burial because it's viewed as a sacred duty that honors the body's dignity.

THE ANCIENT EGYPTIANS: These ancient humans are known for their grand and elaborate burial customs, and their burials didn't involve body disposal, but *preservation*.

During the process of mummification, all the body's vital organs were removed except for the heart, which was kept intact for judgment by Anubis in the afterlife. To judge someone's character, ancient Egyptians believed that the heart was placed on a scale and weighed against the "feather of truth." If the heart balanced the feather, the person was allowed to proceed into the afterlife. If the soul had lived an impure life, and the heart outweighed the feather, Anubis would feed it to the monster Ammit, and the soul would be cast eternally into darkness.

Additionally, Egyptians were ceremonially entombed with food, pets, possessions, and even ancient board games, all of which they could carry into the afterlife.

WATER: Many cultures have considered water as a passage to the afterlife and have therefore used bodies of water to ferry their dead to the beyond. Vikings set warriors adrift on burning ships, symbolizing their journey to Valhalla. Hindus release ashes into the Ganges River to aid the soul's liberation. Some Native American tribes, like the Ojibwe, placed bodies in canoes to drift away. Pacific Islanders and Celts viewed water as a link to ancestors, sometimes casting remains into the sea or sacred lakes, and ancient Greeks and Egyptians also saw rivers as pathways to the next world.

BOG FUNERALS: These ancient funeral practices, used for over seven thousand years, consisted of placing the bodies of the dead into peat bogs. The uniquely cold, acidic, and virtually oxygen-free environment of a bog would almost perfectly preserve dead bodies in their living form. Legends say that these "bog bodies" were sacrifices to appease the gods and that spirits of the sacrificed would forever linger to haunt the swamp.

SCARY
Buries

Many of our burial customs are based on our beliefs of what will happen to the deceased's body and soul in the afterlife. These practices are rooted in the fear that if the dead aren't properly put to rest, they will rise again. This idea has not only dictated our behavior but also enriched our horror narratives. Because let's be honest . . . besides death itself, what's scarier than a corpse coming back to life? These are some of the methods we've created throughout history to keep the dead, *dead*, and appease spirits so they won't return to haunt us!

TRAPPING

Placing heavy objects on graves like large stones was thought to hold the dead inside if they became reanimated. In the Victorian era during the vampire panic, even completely bricking over a grave was commonplace.

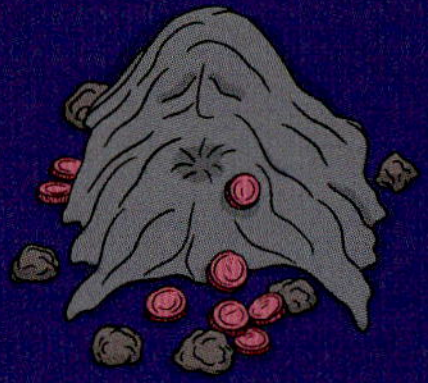

FACIAL COVERINGS

It was once thought that when a person dies, the soul would escape through the mouth and remain in the living world, thus beginning the practice of placing cloth coverings on the faces of the dead. Other items like rocks and coins would also be placed over the mouth or on the eyes to keep their soul contained.

LOCKDOWN

Another method born during the hysteria of vampire fear was placing padlocks on the feet and sickles across the neck of the dead.

BODY ORIENTATION

The practice of facing the deceased's feet in the direction of the rising sun to guide them toward heaven, or on their right side to direct them toward Mecca, is still used to help the dead arrive in the afterlife properly. Some cultures even buried their dead face down for it was thought to trap the spirit in the ground.

EXTRA PRECAUTIONS

Driving stakes or iron rods through the heart of a corpse was sometimes used to make sure the dead were going to stay, well, dead, especially if that person had lived an impure life or died under sinful circumstances.

RAPID BURIALS

Some believed that once the dead were dead, if they weren't quickly buried within hours, the spirits would stay on earth forever.

TURNING OF THE BONES

In some cultures, families periodically exhume the bodies of deceased loved ones to clean them, dress them in new clothes, and sometimes even perform dances for them. This is done out of the fear of offending their dearly departed, and to avoid provoking them into becoming angry vengeful spirits.

MOVING OUT

To this day we leave flowers and gifts on graves. This ancient custom of grave offerings originated from the belief that by providing the deceased with their belongings, the spirit would not return to earth to retrieve them.

COFFIN BELLS

This is not a custom to keep the dead *dead*, but to save the accidentally buried alive! Whether due to a coma or any type of unidentifiable unconsciousness, the dead, primarily in the nineteenth century, were buried with a rope threaded into their coffin, tied to a bell aboveground to ring if they awoke. Grave keepers would stand watch and listen for bells in the night. This happened so often that it originated the phrase saved by the bell. Oops.

THE HISTORY OF Halloween

All Hallows' Eve, the night of ancient rituals, magic, and mischief, the night to celebrate and walk among the dead, is a night we have celebrated for over three thousand years. Known today as Halloween, its historical and cultural significance is rooted in themes of death, fear, and the supernatural, making it one of the most influential traditions on the horror genre.

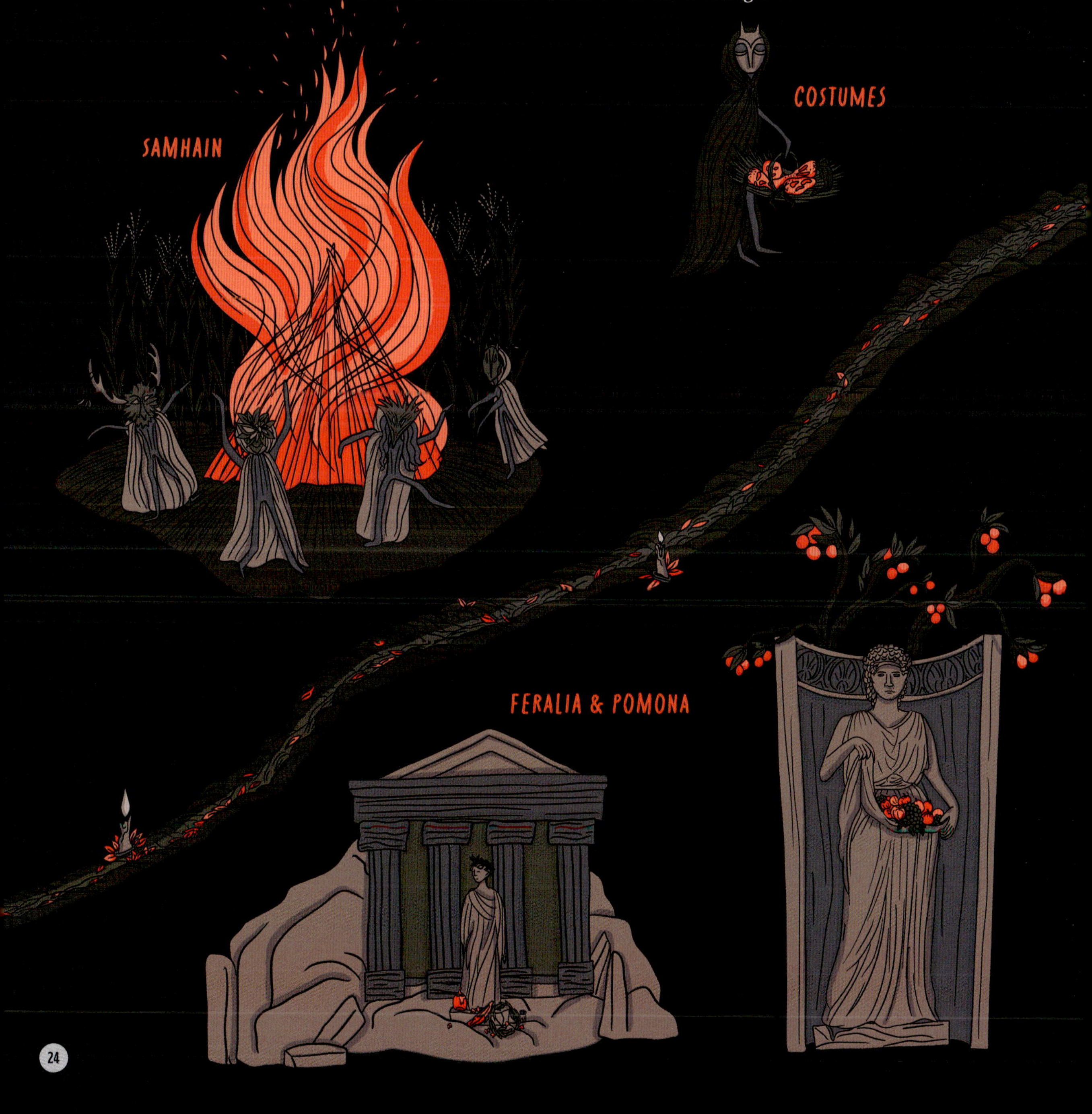

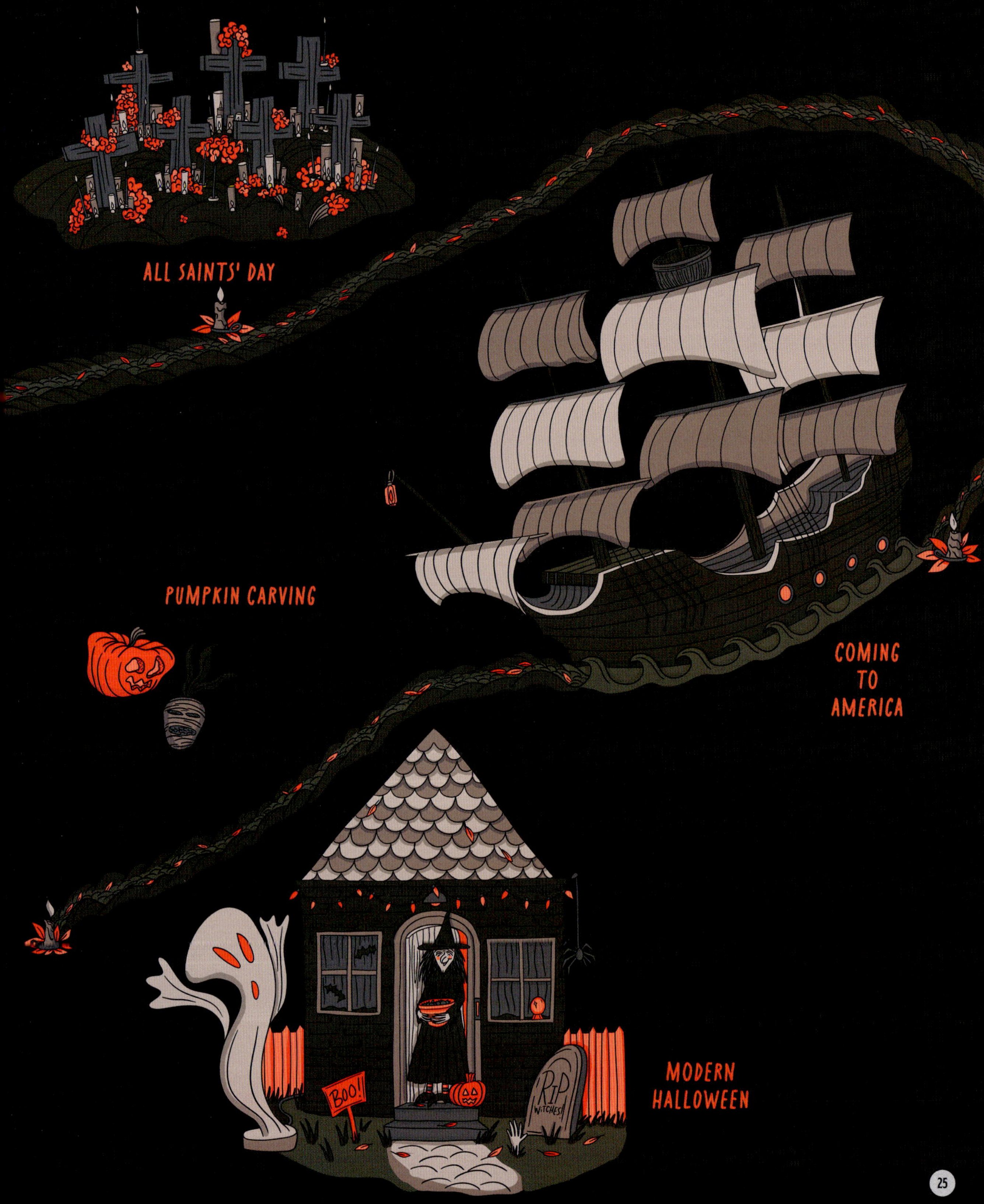
ALL SAINTS' DAY
PUMPKIN CARVING
COMING TO AMERICA
BOO!
RIP
WITCHES!
MODERN HALLOWEEN

SAMHAIN - CA. 1200 BCE

The ancient Celtic festival of Samhain, pronounced "SOW-in," is where the tradition of Halloween began. A pagan new year celebration, October 31 marked the end of the harvest and beginning of the darker half of the year. Samhain was a celebration to honor this change in season but also to honor the dead, for it was believed to be the time of year where the boundary between the living and deceased was thinnest, and that spirits could easily roam among us. To honor this cycle of life and death in all living things, pagans celebrated by dancing around bonfires to scare away evil spirits, making offerings for blessings and protections through the winter, building altars, fortune-telling, and "guising."

HALLOWEEN COSTUMES

Because people feared the presence of angry spirits during Samhain, they created elaborate masks, often in the shapes of animals, out of materials from that year's harvest. This process of disguising, or "guising," oneself to confuse malicious spirits began the tradition of dressing up for Halloween.

FERALIA AND POMONA - CA. 43 CE

When the Roman Empire moved into Celtic territory, they brought their own traditions of honoring the dead and giving gratitude for nature's bounty. Over the course of their four-hundred-year occupation, their celebrations, Feralia and Pomona, slowly blended with the Celtic rituals of Samhain.

The celebration of Pomona, the goddess of fruit and trees, was the Roman version of honoring the harvest. Because Pomona was celebrated during the fall season, the apple became the symbol of the celebration. This is thought to be the reason why bobbing for apples became part of our Halloween tradition.

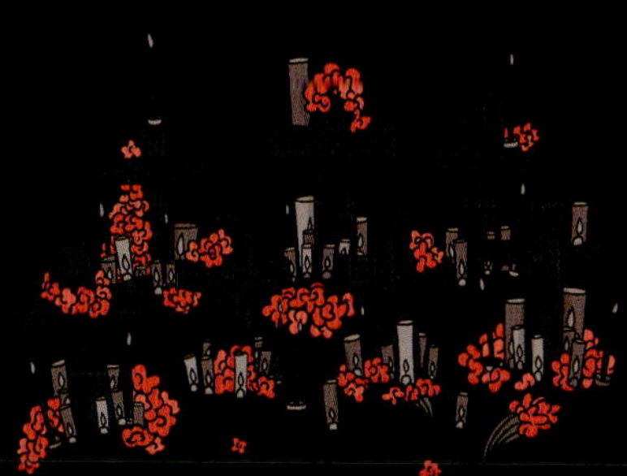

ALL SAINTS' DAY - 609 CE

The creation of All Saints' Day by Pope Boniface IV shifted the practice of honoring the dead away from the ancient Celtic traditions, rooted in pagan, secular beliefs, into more church-sanctioned traditions. All Saints' Day is when our focus started to shift away from honoring the cycle of life and death in nature and became more focused on memorializing martyrs and saints.

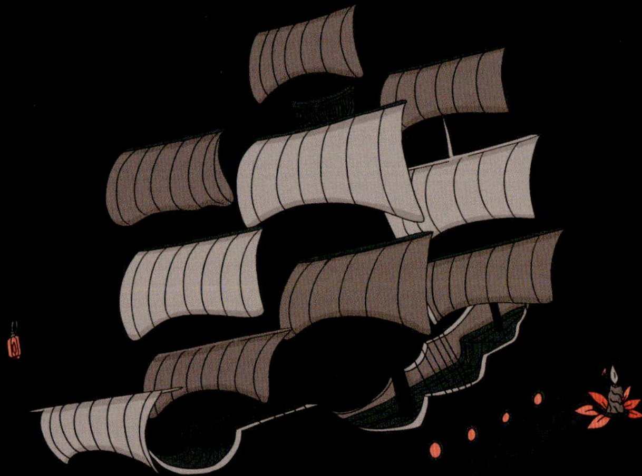

COMING TO AMERICA - 1620-1640

Halloween didn't start to develop in America until European immigrants settled in New England and their traditions began to blend with American Indians' harvest celebrations.

PUMPKIN CARVING

Crafting lanterns from crops has been a Halloween tradition since Samhain, but it wasn't until Irish immigrants came to America, where pumpkins were much larger than the previously carved turnips or potatoes, did we start carving them instead.

THE JACK-O'-LANTERN

The name *jack-o'-lantern* originated from the legend of Stingy Jack, a deceptive man who trapped the devil with tricks and was later denied access into heaven because of it. As punishment, Satan gave Stingy Jack an ember of hellfire in a turnip and condemned him to eternally roam the earth with nothing else to light his way.

MODERN HALLOWEEN

In the 1920s and 1930s, Halloween became the modern celebration we know today. The traditions of trick-or-treating and dressing up in costume evolved away from their superstitious and religious roots and became more festive, community-based customs.

TRICK OR TREAT!

Dressing up to confuse spirits was introduced into our Halloween celebrations during Samhain, but the next iteration, mumming, didn't evolve until the Middle Ages when people would don costumes and put on dances and plays in exchange for treats. Later, with All Saints' Day came the tradition of baking soul cakes, a soft spiced cake exchanged for alms and prayers while going door to door. There's even an eighteenth- and nineteenth-century Christmas tradition called Belsnickling, where kids would dress up and perform tricks in exchange for food. All these traditions are the origins of our modern-day tradition of trick-or-treating.

EPIC HORROR

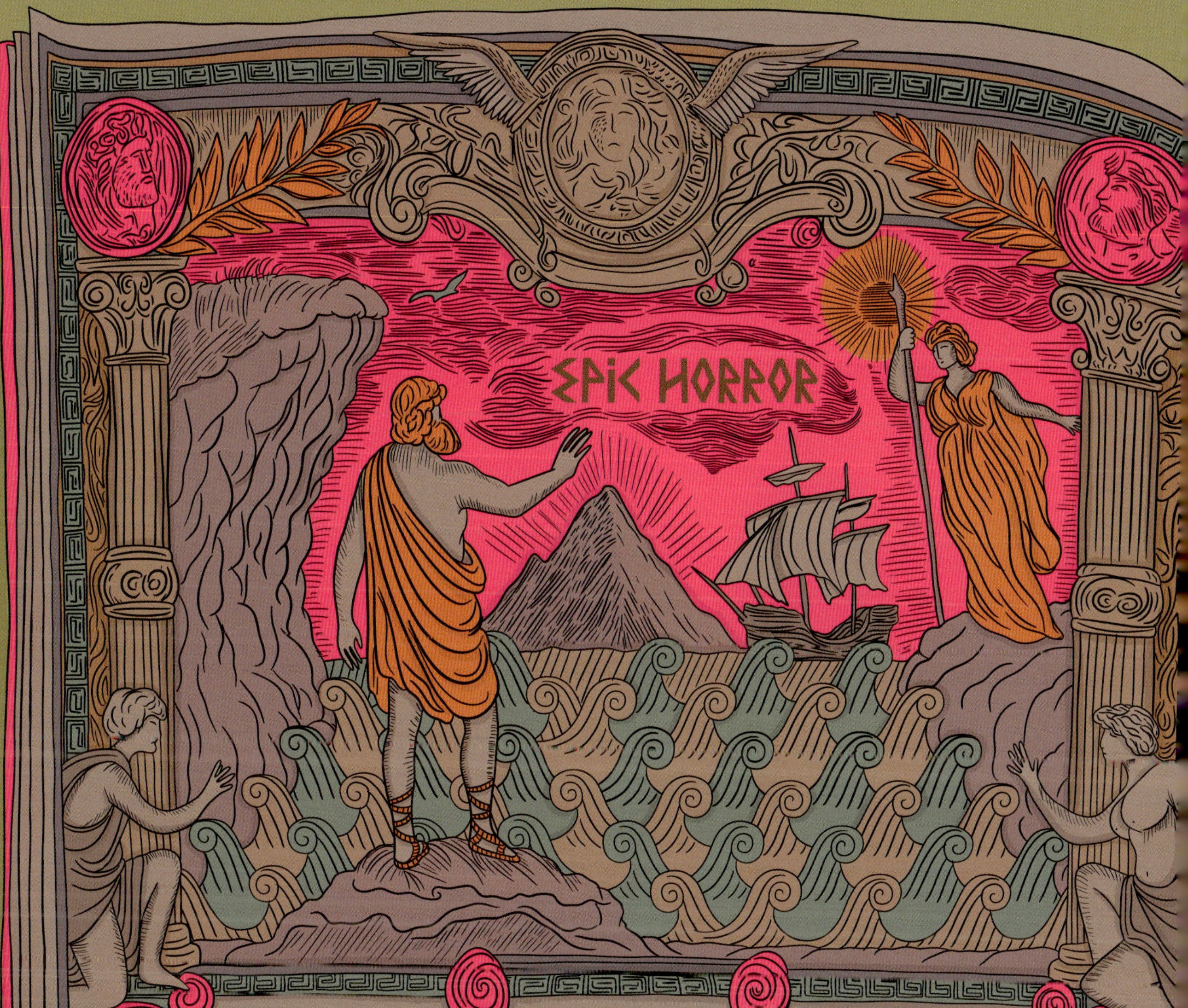

When the folktales we told for centuries evolved from being relayed orally to written down, horror really began to take shape as a distinct genre. With the advent of writing, the mythological monsters, gods, and spirits we spoke of in local communities were cemented permanently on the page, allowing them, for the first time, to be shared across cultures and generations.

Some of our oldest recorded stories are those written by the ancient societies of Mesopotamia and Greece. These early literary works, most notably the *Epic of Gilgamesh* (ca. 2100 BCE) and Homer's *Odyssey* (ca. 725 BCE), were elaborate mythologies that combined both religious and horror elements such as death, the underworld, and supernatural creatures like the cyclops, sirens, and Medusa.

Because of these themes that are pillars of the genre, these works, regarded as epic poetry, can also be regarded as horror.

HAPPILY NEVER AFTER

Grimms' Fairy Tales, collected by brothers Wilhelm and Jacob Grimm in early nineteenth-century Germany, are often thought of as whimsical bedtime stories full of princesses and happily ever afters. However, they are actually among the earliest and most gruesome horror stories created. The brother Grimms' collections of tales were harvested from the darkest elements of the oldest European folklore then translated from cautionary oral tales into written moral lessons. Unlike the sterilized modern adaptations, these original fairy tales were filled with horrific punishments to scare disobedient children. The morals of stories we know and love like "Snow White," "Cinderella," and "Sleeping Beauty" weren't gleaned through gleeful interactions with woodland animals but through acts of murder, gruesome death, deception, rape, self-mutilation, and A LOT of cannibalism, making the morbid and macabre collection of over two hundred tales from the Brothers Grimm foundational to the horror genre

Religion

So far, we've discovered that the primary motive of early storytelling was to teach moral lessons and uphold social norms. Religious narratives are the ultimate, most powerful, and scariest example of this yet.

Through demonic possession, eternal damnation, hellfire, the supernatural, and more, scare tactics are the most prominent theme among all religious narratives, used to incite fear and instill obedience among followers. This central theme of divine retribution, intended to control and frighten potential heretics into submission, has inherently made all religious narratives *horror* narratives.

Fear of the Divine: Religious Scripture or Horror Anthology?

Most religions, particularly three out of the "big five," Christianity, Judaism, and Islam, have their own versions of judgment day, apocalypse, and realms of eternal darkness within their scriptures. Some stories are less fear-based, and even intended to be hopeful, while others use cosmic-scale retribution to intentionally scare sinners into obeying God. These apocalyptic tales of existential warning have been some of the most influential stories both on human behavior and the genre of horror. The most prominent religious texts horror has borrowed from are the following:

THE BOOK OF ENOCH

An ancient Jewish text containing visions and revelations of a cataclysmic end-times such as the sun and moon changing course creating earthly destruction, the wicked being thrown into a fiery abyss, and demonic fallen angels being unleashed on those who reject righteousness.

THE BOOK OF DANIEL (HEBREW BIBLE)

The Book of Daniel is filled with terrifying prophecies of the winds of heaven churning up seas with four great beasts arising from them, and the Ancient of Days taking its seat upon a river of fire.

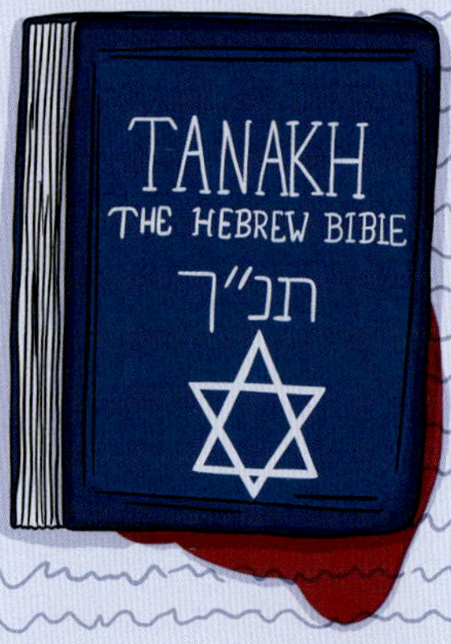

THE QURAN

The verses of the Quran describing the end-times contain frightening images of the moon splitting, the sun folding in on itself, and stars falling from the sky.

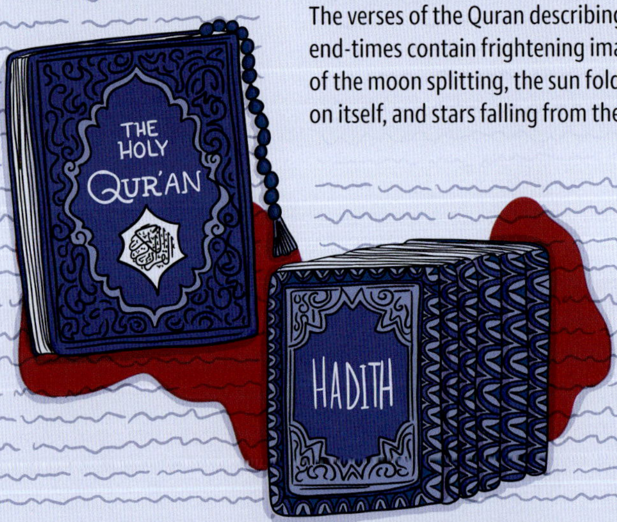

THE BOOK OF REVELATION (HOLY BIBLE)

The four horsemen, war, famine, plague, Satan, fiery lakes of sulfur, a black sun made of goat hair, and a bloodred moon are the most recognized images of the apocalypse, and some of the most used in horror narratives.

BOOK OF TRIBULATIONS (THE HADITH)

Equal in importance to the Quran, the Hadith is a collection of sayings and teachings of the prophet Muhammad. The Book of Tribulations describes the Islamic version of the apocalypse and the rise of the Antichrist, Dajjal, with imagery of incredible landslides, smoke-filled blackened skies, and the sun rising in the west.

Hell and the Underworld

Consider me your Virgil, grab your lantern, and follow me down, down, down into the depths of hell. For centuries, the concept of hell has been a powerful tool in religious traditions, used to instill fear and threaten the punishments of sin. Images of raging fires, endless suffering, and separation from God encourage followers to maintain a virtuous moral code. By creating hell to use as the ultimate consequence, religions aim to control human behavior, uphold social order, and perpetuate spiritual rule. The terrifying depictions of hell, often seen in scriptures, sermons, and art, are burned into the collective's mind and serve as a warning to those who stray from God's path. Religious theology took our innate human fear of death and the afterlife and turned the terror up to eleven.

The horror genre borrows heavily from this tradition, with depictions of literal and symbolic underworlds. From Dante's *Inferno* to modern horror like *Hellraiser*, the idea of a satanic realm full of demons and inescapable suffering speaks to humanity's innate fear of pain and an unending death. The horror genre perpetuates the terror of hell, eternally using it as a stage to explore existential fears and the human condition.

The Inhabitants of Hell

In religious narratives, we see characters like ghosts and witches represent dark and dangerous entities, but the most common of all, and scariest of all, is the religious personification of evil and sin itself: the demon. Almost all religions and cultures' mythology contain demons, but the ones that most commonly appear in our horror stories are associated primarily with Christian theology—most notably, Lucifer, the most powerful, notorious demon of all.

Though demons appear frequently in horror, we rarely see them in the flesh. More often than not, demons enter the chat by possessing others (wait, does that count as in the flesh)? Demonic possession has become one of the most commonly used horror tropes of all time and is a big reason why religion is cited as a major contributor to the genre. Since demons are personifications of evil, they are brilliantly and metaphorically used in religious horror to depict evil entering an unclean or religiously weak soul, only exercisable by a priest. Possession is an effective tactic to drive home the point that evil is always ready to take over from within and that religion is the soul's only hope for salvation.

Paradise and Paradiso

Religious fear isn't found just in scripture. Two of the most famous horror stories of all time are religiously themed epic poems, each with rich, vivid, dramatic, and absolutely horrific depictions of hell and eternal damnation. And both with concepts and characters that have been the backbone of innumerable horror stories. John Milton's *Paradise Lost* and Dante Alighieri's *Inferno* are two examples of how we've created and consumed horror stories unconsciously for centuries. These works aren't traditionally classified as horror—you wouldn't even find them in the horror section of a bookstore. Yet both have shaped our existence, behavior, beliefs, and religions with their use of fear and scary imagery.

Paradise Lost: The Genesis of Fear

One of the most famous poems in the English language, John Milton's *Paradise Lost*, is a retelling of the biblical story of Genesis in which Satan rebels against God and is banished to hell. As a fallen angel determined to destroy God's new creation of man, Satan tempts Adam and Eve to eat from the tree of knowledge of good and evil, which leads to their fall from grace and expulsion from the Garden of Eden.

Although Milton's reframing of the creation story isn't traditionally considered a horror story, the elements of corruption, Satan's power, and a nightmarish hell easily mistake it as one. *Paradise Lost* is the perfect reminder that, with the genesis of life, came the genesis of fear.

The Inferno

The first of three books that make up Dante Alighieri's *Divine Comedy* is titled *The Inferno*, and is the most vivid and detailed depiction of hell man has ever conceptualized. Through Dante's eyes, we journey through the nine circles of hell and witness each circle's poetic punishments for sinners. From limbo to treachery, we observe souls being tortured in boiling pools of blood, flaming pits, infinite darkness, and some of the most unimaginable accounts of suffering ever written. The visceral language of *The Inferno* makes it not only one of humanity's greatest works of art, but also one of humanity's greatest horror stories. One so impactful on people's image of hell that it's said to have shaped the concept within the Christian religion more than the Bible itself.

The Autopsy of Alighieri's Hell

Dante Alighieri's hell is laid out differently than the biblical hell. Instead of a bottomless pit, Dante organizes the realm in nine concentric circles in the shape of a well, with each circle corresponding to a different sin. The circles range from limbo, the largest and least sinful outer circle, to treachery, the smallest and most severe ninth circle. Every circle's punishment is eternal. Turn the page to descend.

ABANDON ALL HOPE YE WHO ENTER HERE
DANTE'S INFERNO

CIRCLE I - LIMBO

CIRCLE II - LUST

CIRCLE III - GLUTTONY

CIRCLE IV - GREED

CIRCLE V - ANGER

CIRCLE VI - HERESY

CIRCLE VII - VIOLENCE

CIRCLE VIII - FRAUD

CIRCLE IX - TREACHERY

CIRCLE I - LIMBO: A watered-down version of heaven for unbaptized Christians and virtuous pagans.

CIRCLE II - LUST: The circle of violent wind and storms that endlessly ravages the souls of adulterers and those easily swayed by lust.

CIRCLE III - GLUTTONY: The third circle is covered in a freezing layer of slush gluttonous souls are condemned to lie in under an icy black rain.

CIRCLE IV - GREED: The fourth circle is filled with the souls of those who have hoarded wealth or possessions. Those here are forced to joust one another with large weapons and boulders protruding from their chests.

CIRCLE V - ANGER: The fifth circle is set on the swampy river Styx where angry souls are condemned to eternally fight one another upon the putrid, slimy surface, or worse, watch from beneath it.

CIRCLE VI - HERESY: The sixth circle is for the souls of heretics who are trapped in fiery torture tombs.

CIRCLE VII - VIOLENCE: The seventh circle is divided into three rings. The first ring is for murders and those who have committed acts of violence upon others. Their punishment is to forever float in a river of boiling blood. The second is the Wood of the Suicides for those who inflicted violence upon themselves. These souls are transformed into gnarled trees and fed on by harpies. The third ring is for those who committed violence against God, nature, or art. These souls are cast out onto a blistering desert of sand under a scorching flame-filled sky.

CIRCLE VIII - FRAUD: The eighth circle is shaped as an amphitheater with ten concentric ditches for the souls of the fraudulent to be punished. Each ditch has its own punishment and increases in severity depending on your crime. Punishments include being whipped by demons, doused in excrement, set on fire, or having one's head turned backward.

CIRCLE IX - TREACHERY: Considered by Dante as the worst sin because to him betrayal was the ultimate violation of trust and order, both essential to human relationships and divine justice. The ninth circle of hell depicts the committers of treacherous acts trapped in a frozen lake to represent the cold-hearted nature of their betrayal. In the center of the frozen lake stood Satan chewing on the worst of the perpetrators, which in Dante's case, were Brutus, Judas, and Cassius.

WHERE'S DANTE?

ALL HOPE IS LOST TO YE WHO ENTER THIS ETERNAL SEEK-AND-FIND.

- 6 copies of Dante's *Inferno*
- Charon's boat
- 6 bags of coins for Charon
- 1 hellevator and its 9 floors
- 5 pitchforks
- 94 lost souls
- Dante
- 1 throne of judgment
- 2 fallen angel harps
- 6 fallen angel feathers
- 6 little demons
- 3 gluttonous candy bar wrappers
- 1 lava lamp

GOING DOWN
LIMBO 1
LUST 2
GLUTTONY 3
GREED 4
ANGER 5
HERESY 6
VIOLENCE 7
FRAUD 8

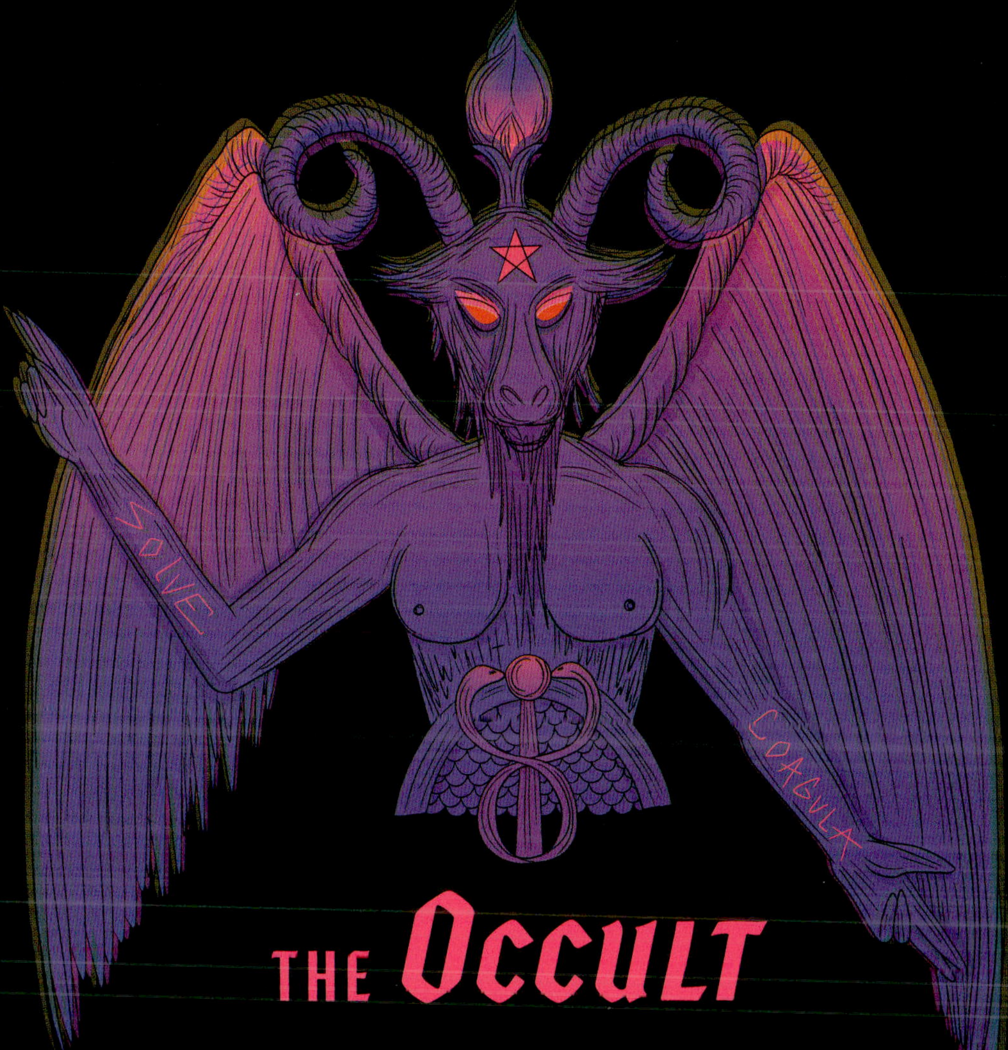

THE OCCULT

The occult, a term that encompasses a collection of esoteric practices and beliefs that center around arcane, taboo, and forbidden knowledge that fall outside the realm of science and organized religion, is one of the most drawn upon entities in the horror genre.

Occultism has waxed and waned from ancient Greece and Egypt, through the Renaissance, the Enlightenment, and up to today. Although its practices didn't exist to explicitly challenge the church, attributed answers of unknown forces to paranormal entities outside of science or the Christian God made its practices a threat to religious and societal order. This pursuit of knowledge outside of common religious and scientific understanding made it something that was feared, and those who practiced occultism were labeled devil worshippers.

THE ABCs OF THE OCCULT

ALCHEMY

BAPHOMET

CRYSTALS & ALEISTER CROWLEY

DIVINATION & DEMONOLOGY

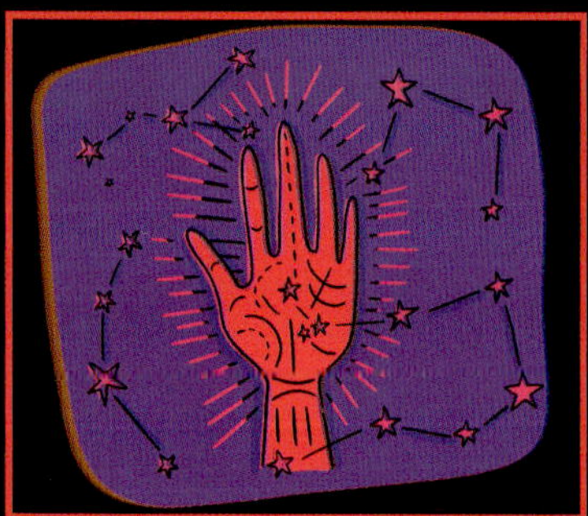

ÉLIPHAS LÉVI & THE ENLIGHTENMENT

FETISHES & FORTUNE TELLERS

GEOMANCY & GRIMOIRES

HARUSPICY & HERMETISM

ILLUMINATI & INVOCATION

JOHN DEE

KABBALAH & THE KNIGHTS TEMPLAR

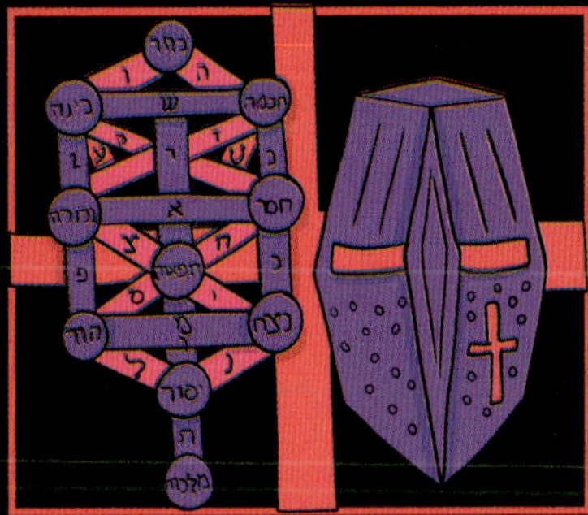

LEY LINES

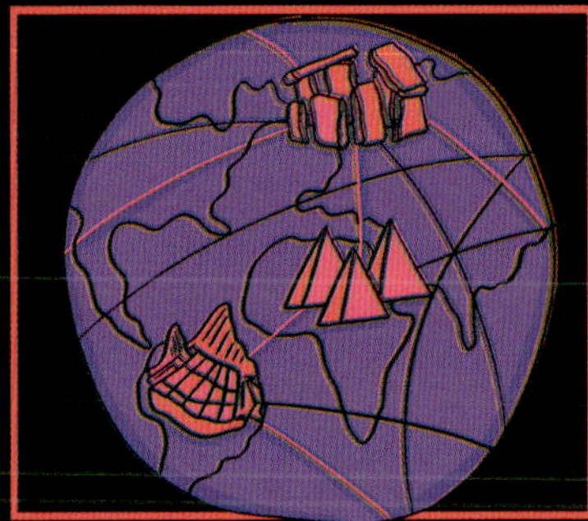

MAGIC, MAGICK & MESMERISM

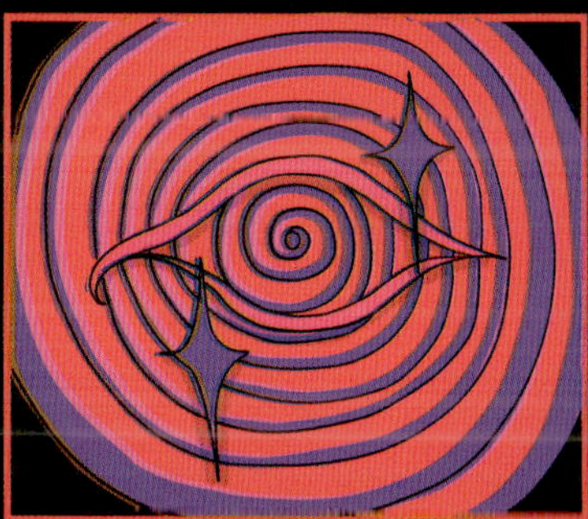

NECROMANCY & NOSTRADAMUS

OUIJA BOARDS & ORACLES

PENTAGRAMS & THE PHILOSOPHER'S STONE

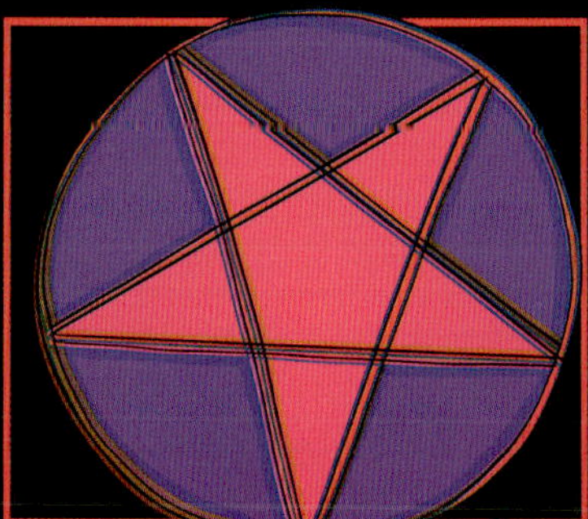

QUATERNITY

ROSICRUCIANISM & THE RENAISSANCE

SATAN & SEANCE

TAROT CARDS

UMBRA

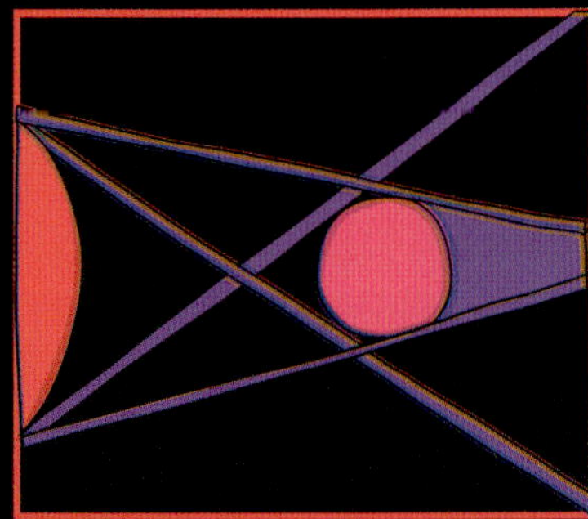

VOODOO

WICCA

XOANON

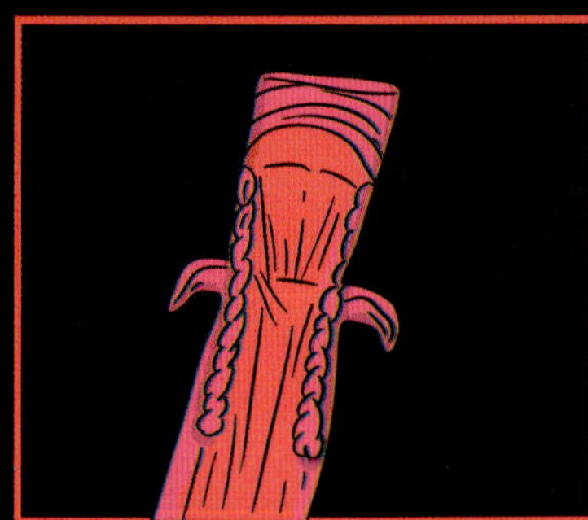

YULE

ZODIAC

Autopsy of

A SÉANCE

THE *SÉANCE*

Attempting to contact the spirit world is an ancient practice commonly used by Greeks and Romans who sought guidance from mediums and oracles, and Indigenous cultures who looked to shamans to be intermediaries between the living and the dead. Necromancy gained momentum in the Middle Ages as scholars and clerics, influenced by ancient texts, sought to summon spirits for knowledge, divination, and power. The church condemned it as demonic, but the exceptional amount of death due to wars, plagues, and societal unrest at the time fueled its secret practice.

But the modern images that flash into our heads when we hear the word *séance*, the images of groups of finely dressed men and women around a round table chanting, didn't evolve until the nineteenth century, with the birth of Spiritualism.

The Spiritualist movement was founded in 1848 by the Fox sisters who attributed the mysterious knocking they heard in their New York home to spirits of the dead trying to communicate with them.

Spiritualism continued to rage like wildfire through the Victorian era, an era fueled by the obsession with death and the afterlife. Even Mary Todd Lincoln held séances in the Red Room of the White House to contact her deceased son.

So grab one another's hands and close the circle, let's have a séance.

THE PARLOR

Enter the parlor, the most popular space for summoning spirits. In the Victorian era, they were typically furnished with one large round table for sitting, and easily dimmable gas lamps. Even though they were designed for social gatherings, they were also quite intimate in size, making them perfect for a private but shared experience among party guests.

STARTING THE SÉANCE

To begin, participants sit around a large round table and hold hands. Holding hands in this position closes the circle to outside energies and focuses the space. The participants are then asked to concentrate on one question or intention collectively, and with the help of the medium welcoming in any willing spirits, the séance commences. Are you here? Give us a sign.

PROPS AND TRICKS

In higher profile séances, props like spirit cabinets, sliding panels, and trap doors were installed prior to increase the drama of the show.

PARAPSYCHOLOGY

Although most séances were seen as a hoax, at the height of their popularity, researchers began to study them scientifically, giving life to the field of parapsychology.

OUIJA BOARDS

Also known as talking boards, witch boards, spirit boards, and Egyptian luck boards, Ouija boards traditionally have each letter of the alphabet, the numbers one through ten, along with the words *yes*, *no*, and *goodbye*. Don't forget to say goodbye once you're done talking with the dead—or they might take it as an invitation to stay.

PLANCHETTE OR GLASS

The planchette, "little plank" in French, is the small wooden tool with a glass insert and engravings that séance participants rest their fingers on to be guided across a Ouija board by a spirit.

SPIRIT BELLS AND TRUMPETS

Nineteenth-century séances weren't complete without spirit bells and trumpets. More tools to prove the unseen was present, spirit bells were tiny bells strung on a string or placed on a stand that could ring with no apparent physical touch. Spirit trumpets were used as a type of megaphone for the spirit world to amplify their faint voices.

DARKNESS

It is rumored that bright light makes communication with spirits more difficult, so séances are always held in darkness.

CANDLES

Their dim light makes for a focused, meditative space, and their flame acts as a beacon to draw spirits in. Candles provide the element of fire, associated with the soul, and they create a protective boundary for the space. Beware, when evil is present, candles will be the first to go out.

MEDIUMS AND ORACLES

Mediums stand on both sides of the veil; they are in the middle, or the "medium" space between the living and the dead, able to interpret the spirit's answers to the participants' questions. Mediums commonly enter a trancelike state so spirits can speak directly through them.

TABLE RAPPING

Invented by the Fox sisters, their form of communication with spirits became such a popular trend that it single-handedly started the Spiritualist practice of "rapping" or knocking on the table—one knock means *yes*, two knocks *no*, and a series of knocks indicated different letters.

TABLE TURNING, TIPPING, AND TILTING

Table tilting is when the participants of the séance speak the alphabet out loud with their palms flat on the table. When the table tilts or shifts in certain ways, it signifies which letter the spirit is using to spell out a word.

NOW, AS WE EMERGE FROM the cave of origins, we come to the first break of our horror tour.

So far, we've been blown by gods and storms, confronted our primal fears, picked flowers in a poison garden, walked the pages of epic poetry, Greek mythology, and the wooded trail to a cannibal grandmother's house. We've met creatures across all seven continents, celebrated Samhain, attended funerals, and were even buried alive with our coffin bells. We held a séance in our chic Victorian parlor, and traveled to hell and back.

Now that we've walked through these foundational elements of horror together, we can see that the origin of horror is simultaneous with the origin of mankind. Humans are born with fear; we have no ability to escape it. Whether we like it or not, fear is a part of us and always will be. The good news is that fear has been more beneficial than harmful to us. It's protected us, kept us alive, built community, educated us, and kept us from committing unspeakable acts upon each other, all of which have additionally provided a historical record of our evolution as human beings!

Through these examples, we can see that the origins of horror often stem from fictional narratives and misunderstandings. Horror is external and made-up, right? We now have science to explain the unexplainable: We know now it's just an eclipse, not the moon eating the sun, and that religions use it as a way to scare and control us. Horror is our tendency to pretend like we know what's going on. It's all hocus-pocus, and *definitely* all in our heads . . .

So, if it's all in our heads, dare to venture forward into them to examine the horrors that lie inside our minds?

You're not too scared to look inward, are you? Shouldn't be too bad . . . you're probably perfectly sane.

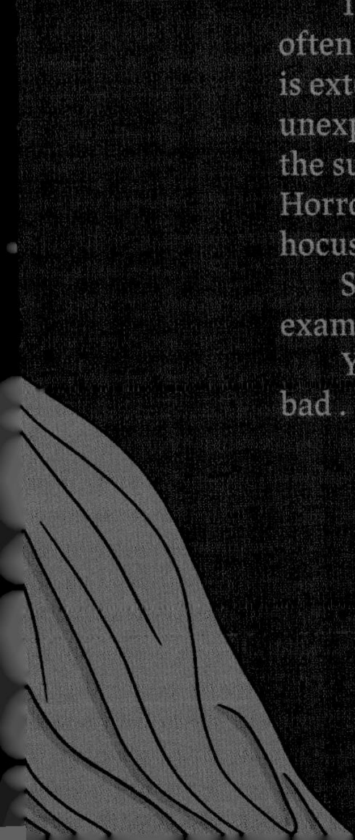

2 THE SCIENCE OF HORROR

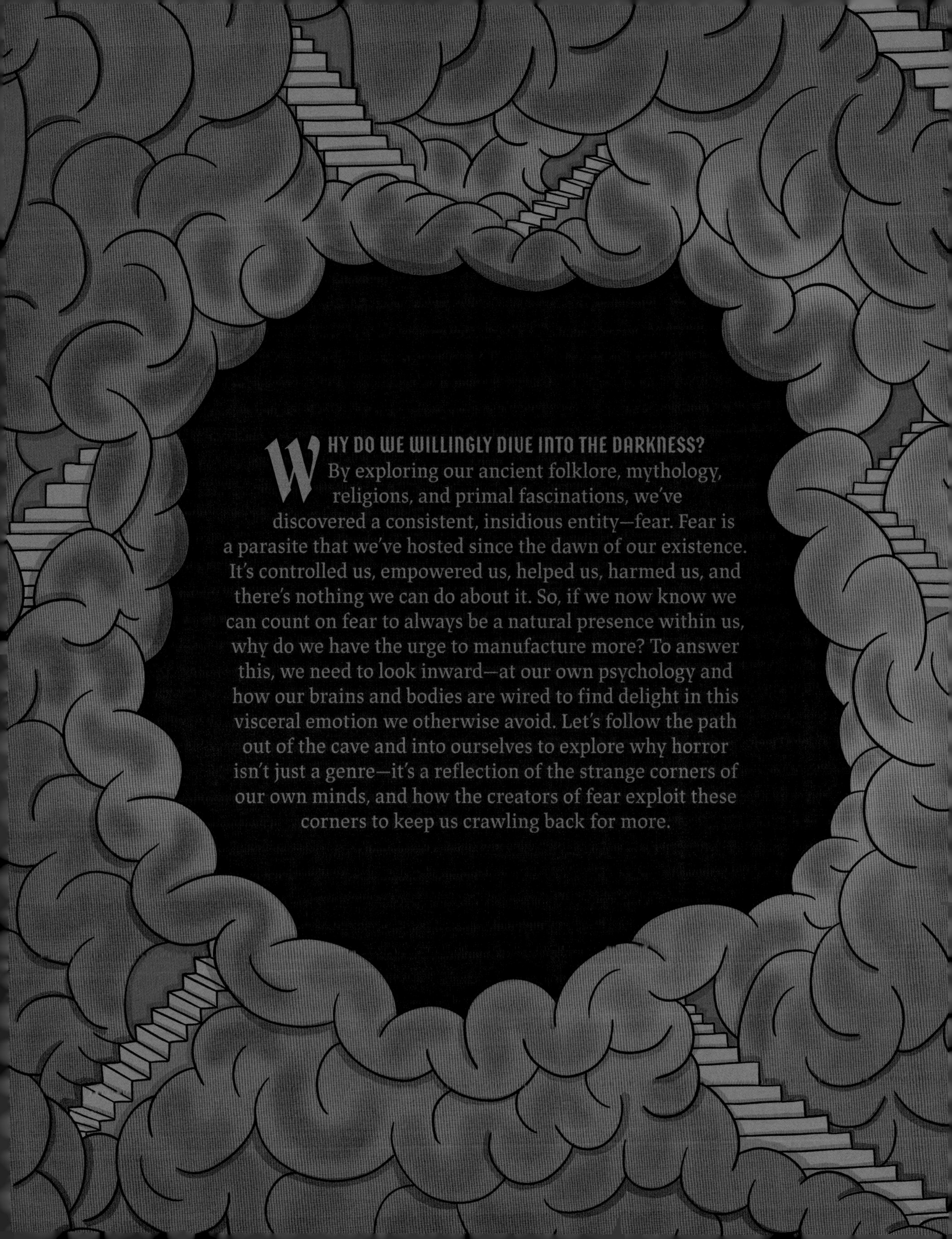

WHY DO WE WILLINGLY DIVE INTO THE DARKNESS? By exploring our ancient folklore, mythology, religions, and primal fascinations, we've discovered a consistent, insidious entity—fear. Fear is a parasite that we've hosted since the dawn of our existence. It's controlled us, empowered us, helped us, harmed us, and there's nothing we can do about it. So, if we now know we can count on fear to always be a natural presence within us, why do we have the urge to manufacture more? To answer this, we need to look inward—at our own psychology and how our brains and bodies are wired to find delight in this visceral emotion we otherwise avoid. Let's follow the path out of the cave and into ourselves to explore why horror isn't just a genre—it's a reflection of the strange corners of our own minds, and how the creators of fear exploit these corners to keep us crawling back for more.

PART ONE

THE PSYCHOLOGY OF FEAR

Historically, many of the mysteries that once scared us, and which laid the foundation for the horror genre, have now been solved. We don't need folktales to tell us not to cannibalize each other or to keep our children from wandering into the woods at night. We are relatively safe and aware of nature now; cougars don't typically rip into us while we sleep in our homes, and science has explained many reasons why illness can suddenly take lives. We observe religions but don't widely fear demonic possession, and we aren't constantly concerned with our dead rising like bread loaves every time we put them in the ground. Our original reasons for telling horror stories are, for the most part, obsolete. Now, we choose fear, create it, seek it out, crave it, perpetuate it, and even glean pleasure and euphoria from it. Why is this? Is it ego? Bravado? Pride? Thrill seeking? Perhaps there's something else within us looking to be fed. Why does horror scratch such a seemingly unnecessary itch? Let's dive in!

THE HORROR FLICK FIX

Doing something scary, like watching a horror movie at home, allows us to experience fear in a controlled environment without any real consequences. As we come down from a jump scare, dopamine and endorphins blast through our bodies, making us feel pleasure and bringing us closer to whoever we're with.

OTHERWORLDLY

Immersion into horror stories can provide an escape and distraction from real-life worries and fears.

FRIGHT-OR-FLIGHT

Fear sharpens our focus and makes the mind more alert, which can be an ultra-exhilarating experience.

OUIJA BE MINE?

Experiencing fear with others can create strong, even lifelong, social bonds. Laughing about and recounting our shared experiences together post scare is a shortcut to camaraderie.

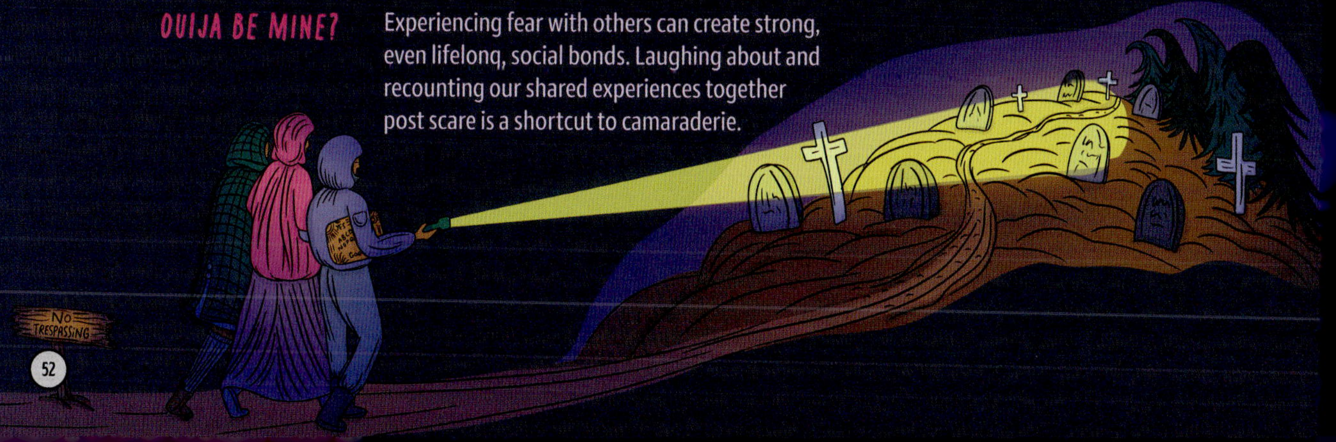

EXPL-HORROR-ATION

Horror is a portal that transports us across realms, through history, and into alternate realities.

TRUE CRIME

Horror allows us to dissect our darker selves and dive into our questions of nature, evil, and morality. It can also spark the imagination and allow us to come up with how we'd manage scenarios while in someone else's scary shoes.

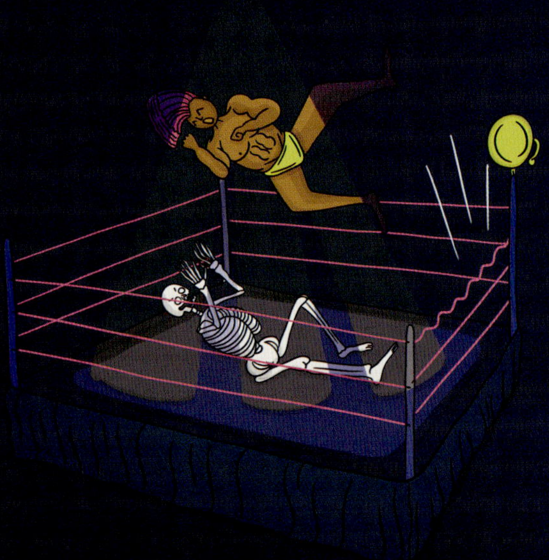

SCARE-APY

Horror provides a controlled way to face our everyday fears, making it a powerful tool for those with anxiety. By choosing to experience terror, whether through haunted houses or masked killers on the screen or in a book, we practice managing panic in a safe space. Over time, this exposure helps lessen anxiety's grip, proving to us that our fears can be confronted and survived.

SCARY SMACKDOWN

Experiencing horror tests our bravery and allows us to flex our ability to be resilient when faced with a challenge, even if that challenge is as far-fetched as surviving a zombie apocalypse.

THRILL RIDE

Experiencing fear triggers a thrill through the release of adrenaline. Strapping ourselves into cages and throwing ourselves out of planes is hilariously what a lot of us call fun! Keep your hands, arms, and legs inside the moving vehicle at all times . . .

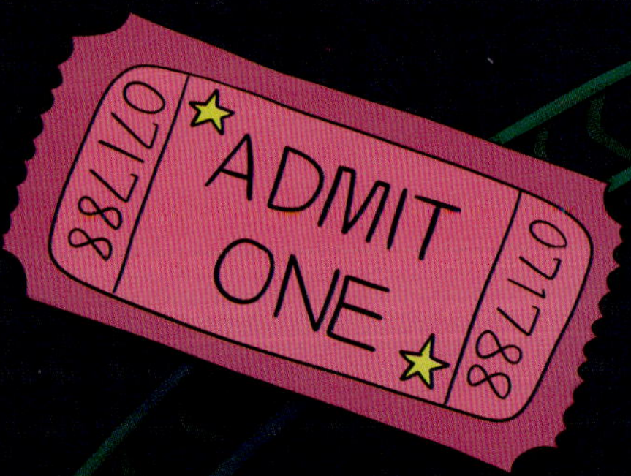

The Creepy Carnival

CAN YOU FIND?

- 6 scary clowns
- 2 ghosts
- 5 ride tickets
- 7 popcorn boxes
- 1 caramel apple
- 1 ice cream cone
- 1 toupee
- 3 fortune cards
- 1 loose ride bolt
- 4 flume-igator boats
- 1 skydiver
- 1 rat
- 3 tunnel-of-terror boats
- 1 broken pirate ship ride

Scaro-sel
WHEEL OF MIS-FORTUNE
THE FLUME-IGATOR
DEATH SPIN
FORTUNES
TUNNEL OF TERROR
NCE

ARE WE Good OR Evil?

HORROR CAN HELP US ANSWER THE QUESTION

The question whether our true nature is good or evil extends beyond the realm of curiosity—for us humans, it's an obsession. We now understand that humans are complex. No being is either light or dark, right or wrong, good or evil. There are no absolutes in the human condition, and every single one of us contains elements of both. This inability to place all humans in a strict binary is maddening to us. Like death, man's failure to reconcile the human condition has only fueled our obsessive desire to find meaning in it—propelling it to the front as a central theme of every art form, genre, and manner of human expression.

The horror genre, however, with its unapologetic willingness to confront our morality head-on, satiates our desire to find meaning in the chaos. For without dark, there is no light, and horror leads us further into the dark than any other genre, allowing us to more deeply explore, investigate, and examine the full, authentic, gradient of human nature.

It also allows us to investigate where we land among the spectrum ourselves. Horror makes us think about which character we relate to the most and what that says about our own morals, mind, and soul. When we see heinous acts carried out in horror stories, our natural tendency is to weigh ourselves against them. We all have darkness within us, but horror stories let us see what happens to those who act upon it. They make us question what we would have done in ethically ambiguous situations, where we would've drawn the line, and at what point our own white shade of morality starts to gray.

By embodying the spectrum of good and evil more literally than any other genre, horror gives us the opportunity to do what we desire most: Explore what it truly means to be human.

Carl Jung

Whether we like it or not, all minds contain darkness within them—and although we've explored this fascination for many moons, it wasn't until the early twentieth century when Carl Jung, a Swiss psychiatrist and psychoanalyst, gave this dark side of our psyche a name, the Shadow.

Jung's concept of the Shadow represents the unconscious aspects of our self, our darker half, or our evil twin, if you will. The Shadow is the part of us we possess but often repress or deny because of the nonsocial-conforming emotions and behaviors contained within it. The Shadow is where our aggression, selfishness, envy, resentment, and morbidity lie. It contains our undesirable thoughts, our darkest humor, desires, and doubts. It's where we hold all that we consider to be dirty and shameful.

Jung's philosophy was that by confronting and integrating the Shadow, we can achieve psychological growth and a higher self-awareness. He believed that by acknowledging the Shadow, individuals can better understand themselves and develop a more balanced and authentic personality. This is also exactly what the horror genre exists to do.

Horror is the only genre truly willing to fully confront the Shadow. It ventures into the corners of the mind other storytellers aren't willing to go. We hide the "negative" and "shameful" parts of ourselves because we're afraid to be judged or cast out, but horror screams our secrets out for everyone to hear. This radical act of exposing our human nature for all is one of the most beautiful and beneficial things horror does, for by taking the hit, and revealing our hidden secrets to each other, it transforms the human experience from an isolating one into a collective one. Horror demonstrates that by shining a spotlight on the Shadow, it dissipates, and we find relief from our own anxieties and gain empathy for others.

It is only through stories that are willing to face the darkness and the Shadow that we see the true, honest, and holistic representations of ourselves. This makes horror, and I'm sure Jung would agree, an art form of great value to our human growth, understanding, and development.

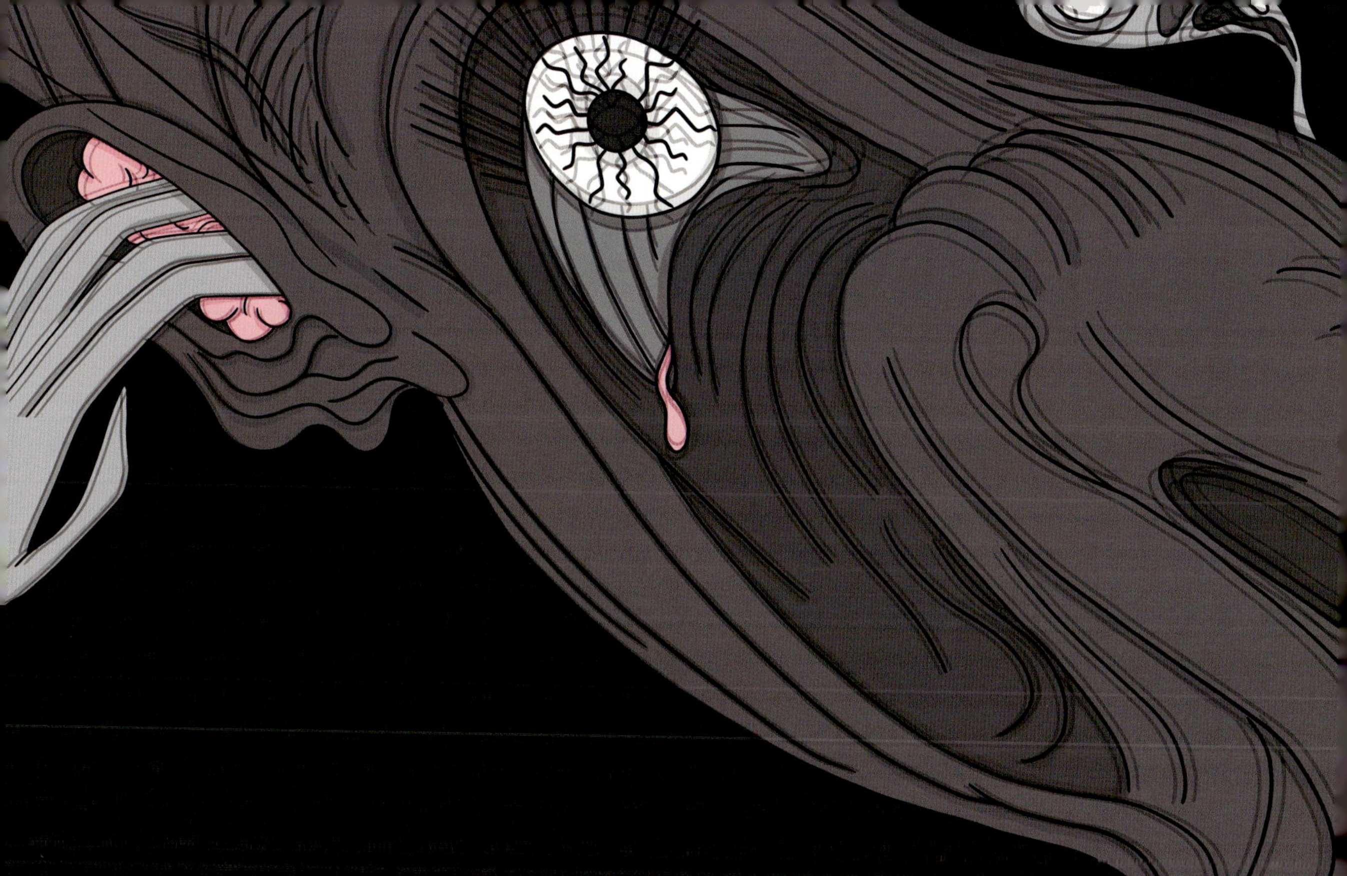

Psycho-Analysis

Madness, a fear both deeply personal and universal, rooted in the fragility of consciousness—the seat of our identity, reason, and reality—has long haunted the horror genre. Madness in horror serves as a powerful and horrific reminder that we rely on our minds to interpret the world, and how that process can easily falter.

Madness in horror reflects the terrifying possibility that our own minds could betray us at any moment, an experience that would plunge us into a living, uncontrollable nightmare. Madness questions reality and destabilizes what is real and what is imagined. Could everything we perceive to be true fracture in a mere moment? How quickly can time and reality warp? How easily can the control and agency of our self slip away? Will we be locked away to slowly, tortuously plunge into the abyss?

Madness is pervasive in horror because it portrays an unpredictable experience. Horror stories of madness reveal not just the fear of losing control, but the fear of becoming lost within our minds and having to face, arguably, the scariest monster within the genre, ourselves.

Turn the page, let's lose our minds . . .

Horror High's

Maddest of the Mad!

From psychosis to obsession, delusions, and paranoia, madness is ever present in horror. The following characters belong to some of the most famous horror stories of all time, and personify insanity's different forms best.

MOST MAD
Jack Torrance,
The Shining

MOST AMBITIOUS
Nina Sayers,
Black Swan

MOST FAMILY ORIENTED
Norman Bates, *Psycho*

MOST HUNGRY FOR KNOWLEDGE
Hannibal Lecter,
The Silence of the Lambs

MOST PSYCHOTIC
Patrick Bateman,
American Psycho

MOST LIKELY TO JOIN A CULT
Dani Ardor, *Midsommar*

MOST LIKELY TO BE VOTED PROM QUEEN
Carrie White, *Carrie*

MOST DELUSIONAL
Merricat Blackwood,
We Have Always Lived in the Castle

MOST COMPETITIVE (TIE)
Dr. Jekyll and Mr. Hyde,
The Strange Case of Dr. Jekyll and Mr. Hyde

MOST OBSESSIVE
Annie Wilkes, *Misery*

MOST GASLIT
Jane, "The Yellow Wallpaper"

MOST PARANOID
Narrator,
"The Tell-Tale Heart"

The Horrors of Mental Health

The relationship between mental health and horror has been a long, difficult, and complicated one. As humans, we instinctively fear and seek to distance ourselves from "the other." Madness, with its associations of unpredictability, loss of control, and danger, falls outside our societal framework of normalcy and is thus marginalized and perceived as other. This occurrence has led madness to be one of the most popular tropes used to induce fear in the horror genre and unfortunately led to countless misrepresentations, inaccurate depictions, stigmatizations, and villainizing of those who suffer from real-life trauma and legitimate, involuntary, mental disorders.

Incredibly, as horror has evolved, we've shifted away from using those who suffer from mental illness as a scare tactic and have instead reclaimed the genre as a space to more accurately depict the terror of living with a mental illness. Instead of portraying those with mental illness as the monsters, contemporary horror has masterfully begun to tell stories in which the monster is the mental illness itself. Grief, depression, and emotional pain all remain within our stories because they are some of the most powerful and terrifying universal human experiences, but horror's unique way of personifying these experiences allows us to confront them as external monsters, separate from ourselves, making those living with mental illness feel seen and validated.

This radical reclaiming of the genre to more accurately tell our story once again proves that, above all other genres, horror has the ability to most honestly and artistically represent the true human experience.

Regardless of this evolution, the asylum has remained a powerful symbol, setting, and antagonist within the genre. Mental institutions, especially abandoned ones, represent our innate fears of losing control, feeling trapped, and being isolated, alienated, and harmed—forever making them the perfect setting to showcase the horrors of our minds.

So tell me . . . what would you do if you were locked in the sanatorium? Could you make it out? Or would you lose your mind first? . . . Flip the page to see . . .

ENTER

EXIT

PART TWO

THE PHYSIOLOGY OF HORROR

As humans who all carry the same primal instincts, we've made ourselves vulnerable to be preyed upon. And I'm not talking about being preyed on by animals or monsters this time, but by other humans—humans that only need to look within their own minds, and use what scares them, to scare us. Writers, producers, and directors have mastered the art of taking what's under their own skin to get under ours. They read our bodies' heartbeats, brain waves, goose bumps, and each physical reaction we have while consuming horror to figure out how to further push the boundaries. We can't escape how our bodies work, and horror creators use our reactions (voluntary or not) to let them know whether what they've created is scary enough . . . or needs to be scarier.

Using effects like distortion, asymmetry, and upside-down camera angles, or sensory details like smeared lipstick, strange noises, and creepy insects, horror preys on all our senses to make us truly uncomfortable.

Let's explore the ways in which horror creators use our bodies to get the reaction they want by starting with the brain!

The Brain on Horror

When we experience horror, it can feel like we're at the mercy of our bodies; they tense, they jump, they contract when something disgusting crawls across the screen. Why is this? What actually happens inside the brain when we watch horror? How does horror use our brains against us?

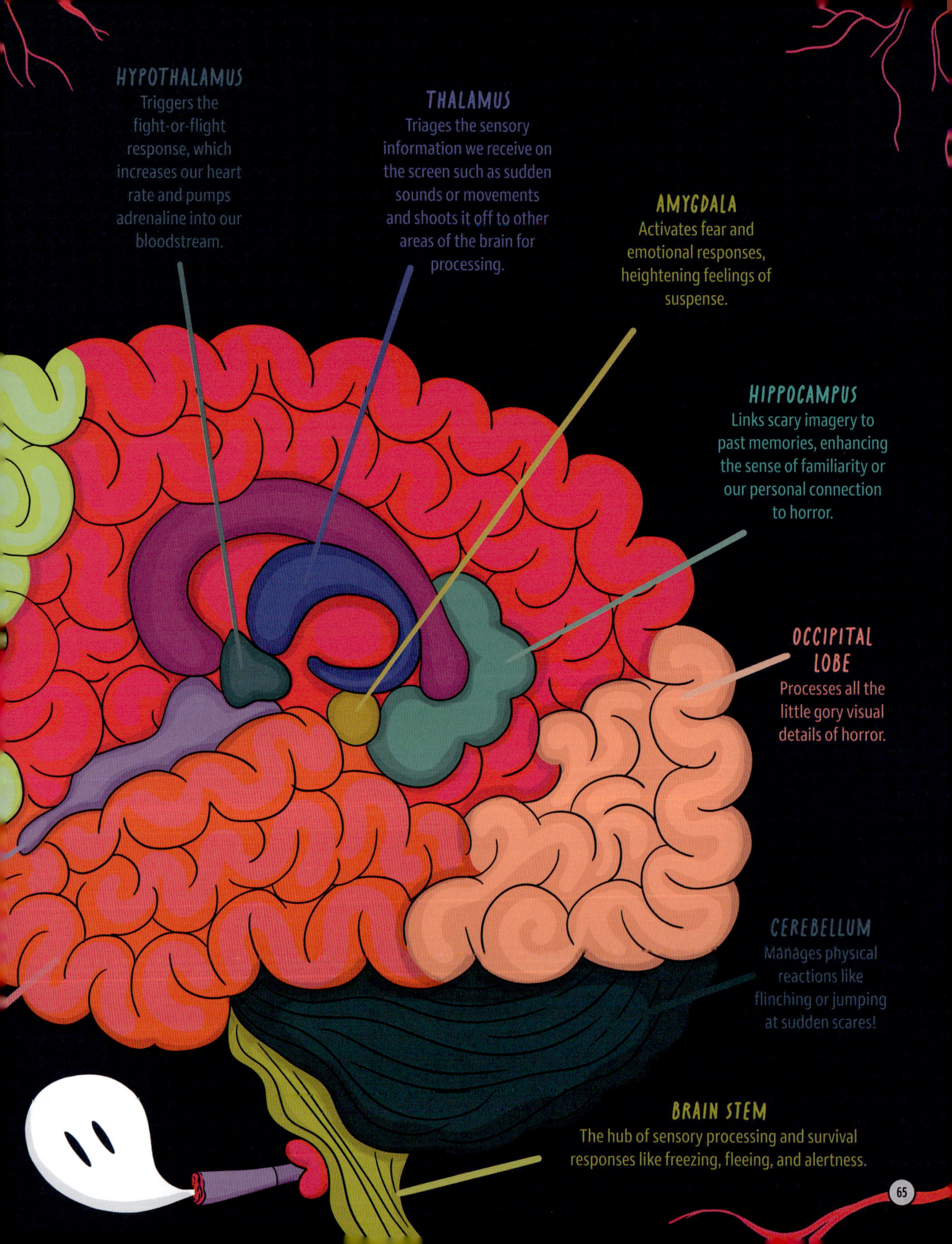
HYPOTHALAMUS
Triggers the fight-or-flight response, which increases our heart rate and pumps adrenaline into our bloodstream.
THALAMUS
Triages the sensory information we receive on the screen such as sudden sounds or movements and shoots it off to other areas of the brain for processing.
AMYGDALA
Activates fear and emotional responses, heightening feelings of suspense.
HIPPOCAMPUS
Links scary imagery to past memories, enhancing the sense of familiarity or our personal connection to horror.
OCCIPITAL LOBE
Processes all the little gory visual details of horror.
CEREBELLUM
Manages physical reactions like flinching or jumping at sudden scares!
BRAIN STEM
The hub of sensory processing and survival responses like freezing, fleeing, and alertness.

Autopsy of a Jump Scare

In the 1942 film *Cat People*, the character Alice Moore is being followed by Irena Dubrovna. The tension is building, the audience is nervous, and BAM! A bus bursts into the frame shocking everyone into oblivion. That moment, known as the "Lewton bus scare," is considered the first real jump scare, and has been a staple of horror films since. Now jump scares are to be expected; they're part of the thrill of watching a scary movie and creators are constantly leveling up the elements to get bigger reactions out of us. Filmmakers do this by using different tricks, all of which play on our body's physiological responses. They deliberately use our senses and systems to slowly wind, wind, wind us up as far as possible, before . . . POP! Hurling us screaming across the theater. This is the autopsy of a jump scare.

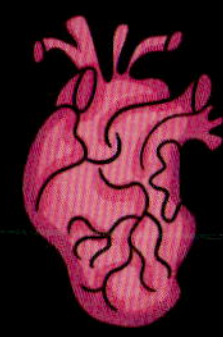

The scare always begins with a dimly lit or obscured environment; we can't see, our senses are compromised, and the tension in the darkness seems to last forever. The suspense starts to heighten our awareness, we want to get out but can't, and just like that our heart rate starts to climb . . .

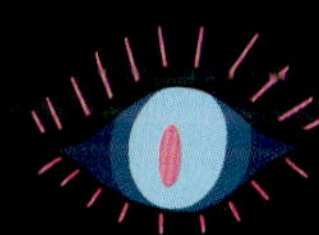

Now that our hearts are pumping, our adrenaline is too, and with it comes heightened visual sensitivity. We're alert, focused, and scanning the screen for movement. Cue something small moving in the shadows or the periphery . . . Wait, what was that? Did someone just walk past the doorway behind our scream queen? Why is the camera shot leaving that huge amount of negative space? What's going to fill it? AND WHEN?

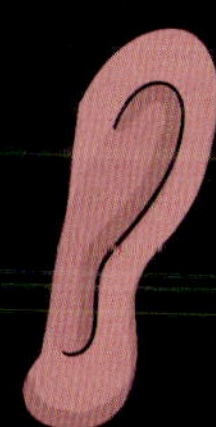

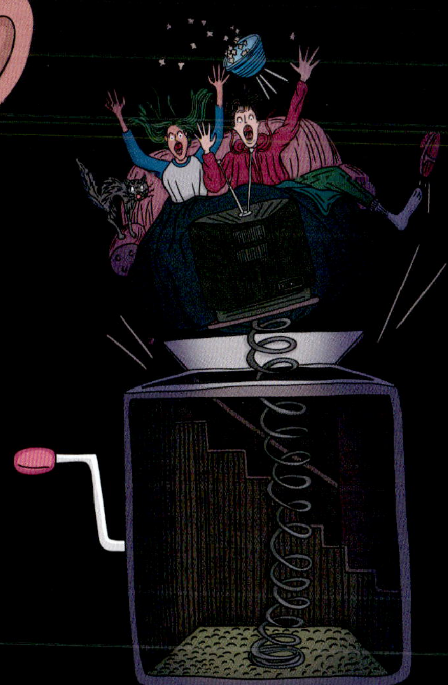

Knowing, but not seeing, makes our muscles tense, and we're aware we're at the mercy of the movie. It's trapped our hearts, our eyes, and now it goes for the ears. The music starts to swell, and a floorboard creaks, making us flinch because we're already wound so tight, but we know it's not the big one, we're just being toyed with now.

With everything ripped away, we're left on the edge of the cliff. We're in total silence, total darkness, we're braced and holding our breath, our bodies have received every signal that we need to be prepared and have made all the necessary arrangements. All we can do now is wait.

BAM! We're smacked with a perfectly timed sensory assault. The shock activates our fight-or-flight response, adrenaline surges through us, and we're done for.

The aftermath is good news. The bigger the scare you get, the more endorphins and dopamine rush through your body, and the greater the relief will be.

The Scariest Stories of All Time

(According to Our Hearts)

Because of unique experiences, tastes, beliefs, kinks, et cetera, what scares someone is deeply subjective. That being said, several heart rate studies have illuminated the fact that no matter what you think scares you the most, your heart may say otherwise. According to our hearts, and the beats per minute they reach during jump scares, these are the current scariest movies of all time.

INSIDIOUS
133 BPM

SINISTER
131 BPM

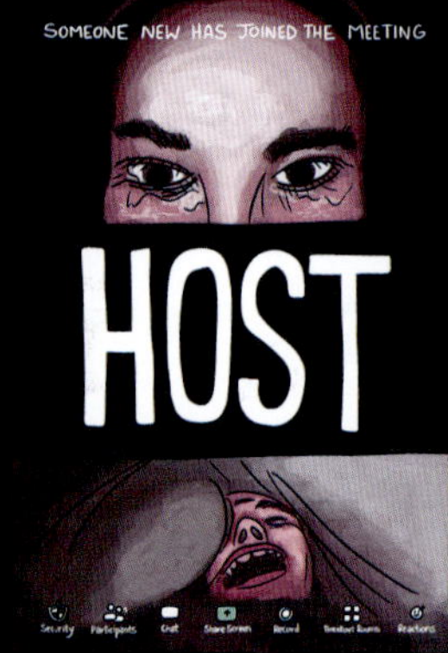

THE HOST
130 BPM

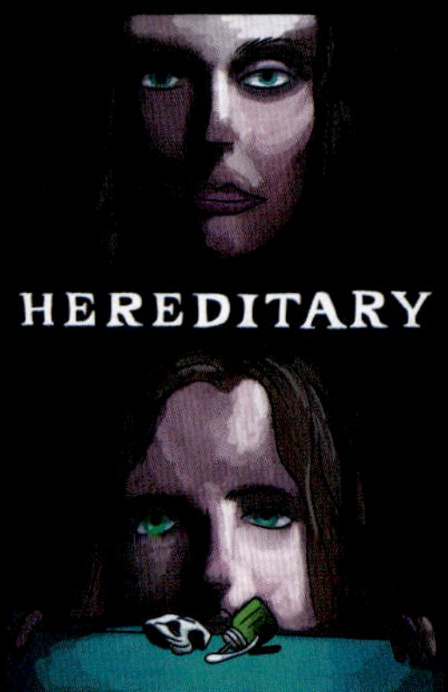

HEREDITARY
115 BPM

SKINAMARINK
114 BPM

THE BABADOOK
110 BPM

Welcome to UNCANNY LAND

The game that takes you through the ways chill crafters exploit the natural reactions of our minds and bodies to get under our skin. Head to start.

The Swamp of Contagion

Contamination, illness, and grotesque imagery are ever oozing in horror because of our natural discomfort around death and disease.

The Uncanny Valley

When you see something that looks almost human but just isn't quite right, you're deep in the discomfort of the Uncanny Valley. Horror lures us here with creepy lifelike dolls and humanoid robots.

The Desert of Distortion

Filmmakers love to destabilize and disorient us because when our senses are compromised, we become confused, vulnerable, and perfectly primed for a scare.

The Subliminal Sea

Horror often hides small, unsettling details in plain sight to trigger our subconscious unease, causing us to feel a vague sense of dread while watching.

The Canyon of Cognitive Dissonance

Melting faces and twisted trees . . . Are you going mad? Seeing things? No, you're just being subjected to imagery that just doesn't quite make sense. Scary, huh?

The Cave of Instinctual Fears

Horror never misses the opportunity to heighten our senses by exploiting the fears hardwired into our brains like darkness, predators, and loud noises.

The Fountain of Phobias

Horror is jam-packed with common phobias like spiders, tight spaces, and heights to make you viscerally uncomfortable (and more easily scared).

Finish

Creepy Critters

How do you feel when you see this image? A little squeamish? A little unsettled? Is your throat a little tight? Did you just feel something crawl down your neck? What you're experiencing is the human biological mechanism of visceral disgust, and it's exactly how and why the masters of horror infest their stories with the creepiest-crawlies imaginable.

Even though a lot of insects are beneficial, others are dirty, slimy, carry disease, feast on feces and rot, and are inherently dangerous. Their bodies look different from our bodies, which makes them "the other," something we naturally fear. To keep us safe from the potential threats and otherness of creepy-crawlies, our bodies automatically react to their presence with a physical repulsion that makes our skin crawl. So, the next time you see a spider crawl out of someone's mouth, or a rat run across your screen, know that your full-body goose bumps can't be helped, and that bugs are just another tool horror creators use to get under our skin.

THE COLORS

RED - VIOLENCE, PASSION, DANGER, AGGRESSION, SEDUCTION, SIN

GREEN - TOXICITY, CORRUPTION, POISON, POSSESSION, DISEASE

BLUE - SADNESS, DESPAIR, SUPERNATURAL, ISOLATION, GRIEF

WHITE - DECEPTION, SUBVERSION, TAINTED PURITY AND INNOCENCE, DEATH

BLACK - POWER, MOURNING, MYSTERY, THE VOID, EVIL

of Horror

WHEW! WHAT AN *INSANE* CHAPTER. As we come to our second break on our tour of horror, I'd like to welcome you back to reality. At least I think that's where we are . . .

It's nice to see that some of you made it through the dark passages of your minds. We'll mourn the ones who didn't.

From this cerebral expedition, we now know that many horrors come from within ourselves, and that we don't need to look much further than our minds to find great fear. We know that our bodies are read, studied, and preyed upon, that we are at the mercy of those who want to scare us . . . and that we actually like it?

Don't worry though, we may be monsters, but we're not alone. There are so many more living creatures within the genre we have yet to encounter, learn about, and study . . . In fact, I've just been notified that they're ready for us now . . . Would you care to meet them?

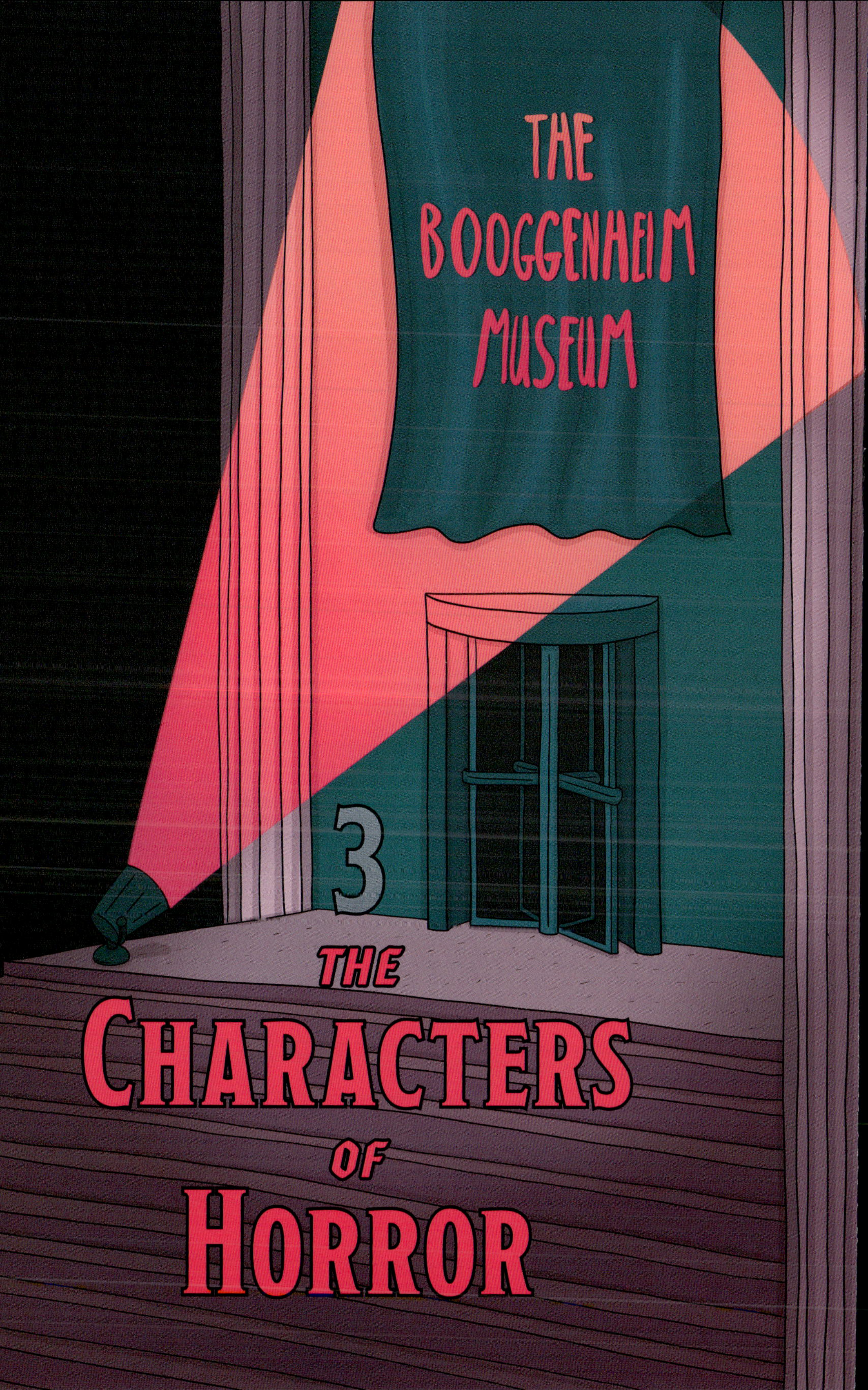
THE
BOOGGENHEIM
MUSEUM
3
THE
CHARACTERS
OF
HORROR

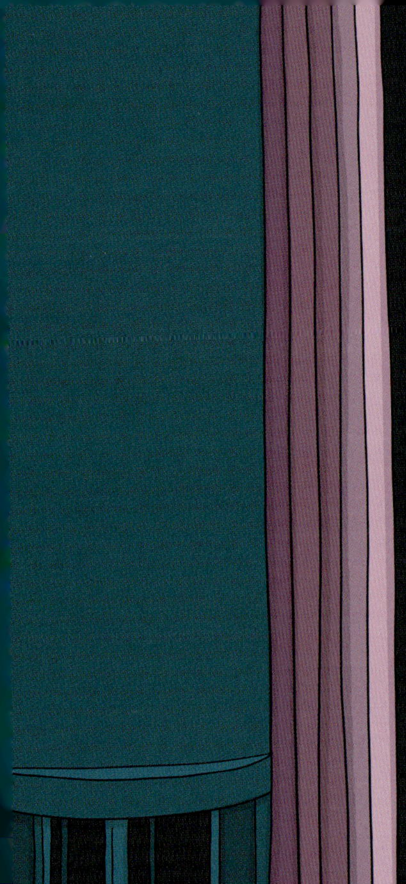

WELCOME, VISITORS. OUR LATEST EXHIBITION is eagerly awaiting you. For the past hundred years, the Boogenheim has dedicated its efforts to sending anthropologists, historians, documentarians, and explorers not only across the globe but through time and space to source something very special for you.

You'll be the first to witness a one-of-a-kind immersive experience showcasing the results of our voracious expedition. Now, you may have wondered why our doors have been closed and windows shuttered during installation, and I can finally reveal the truth. Our researchers came back with not only information *about* their findings, but their findings themselves.

That's correct, the exhibit you are about to enter is *alive*.

Those you are about to witness have traveled great distances to be here, and they're all so excited that you've finally arrived. So as to not keep them waiting any longer, please proceed to the lower level and enter the doors you see positioned around the museum. And finally, for your own safety, please keep your hands to yourselves; some have agreed to be here but didn't agree not to bite.

We are pleased to present *The Characters of Horror*.

Vampires

Vampires are arguably the most iconic creature of the horror genre. Whether they've seduced us through glamours or preyed on our primal fears of death, these immortals have had us wrapped around their claws for centuries.

We are most familiar with the vampires who have stalked the pages of great literary works like Bram Stoker's *Dracula*, and Anne Rice's *Interview with the Vampire*, but evidence from ancient burial rituals suggests that belief in these creatures predates even our most beloved fictional creations, demonstrating that the vampire has more to do with the fascination with our own mortality than the fascination with a scary story.

Transformation, superstrength, and superspeed with otherworldly abilities that vampires possess are only part of what makes them so alluring. Their real power, despite having no reflection of their own, is the ability to reflect the darkest and most curious parts of human nature.

Through vampires, we get to live through the undead.

AUTOPSY OF A BITE The most common route to reanimation is the bite of an existing vampire, but legends reveal that one can also be "turned" by illness, suicide, or even a cat jumping over your grave.

Autopsy of a Vampire

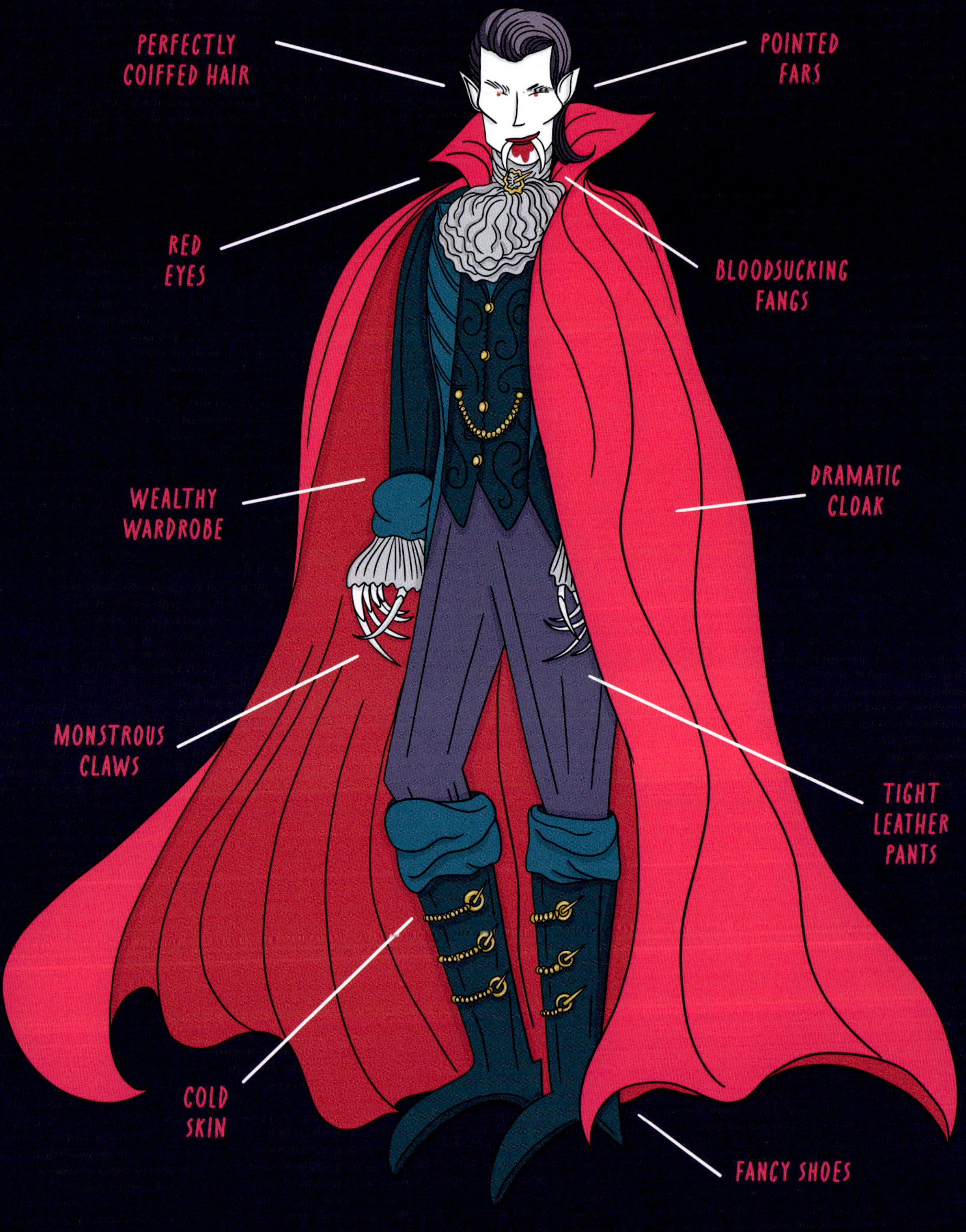

THE *EVOLUTION* OF THE Vampire

The vampire, while most commonly depicted as originating in Eastern Europe, is actually part of a broad, cross-cultural folklore tradition stretching back thousands of years and across wider geography.

ANCIENT MESOPOTAMIA (CA. 4000 BCE)

LILITH

The myth of Lilith began in ancient Mesopotamia—the earliest urban civilization. Lilith, also known as Lamashtu or Lilitu, was said to be Adam's first wife, but because she refused to submit to his authority, she was cast out of paradise. Because of her obstinacy, she was given the name Lilith, derived from the Mesopotamian word *lilu*, meaning "night creature." This name associates her with a demon who preys on children and pregnant women. She is among the earliest recorded tales of bloodsucking demons.

ANCIENT BABYLONIA (CA. 2000–3000 BCE)

Ekimmu

Found in Assyria, Babylonia, and ancient Egypt, the ekimmu, or "evil gust of wind," were believed to be incorporeal vampire spirits. People with any indication of otherness or evil surrounding their death, like being left-handed or dying in childbirth, were thought to have been possessed by an ekimmu. It was also believed that an improper burial would lead the dead to rise again as one.

ANCIENT ROME (CA. 750 BCE–476 CE)

Strix

The ancient Romans' most feared vampiric creature was not one that came back to life after death, but a mythological birdlike woman who drank the blood of children. The strix was seen as an ill omen and originated from the fear of metamorphosis.

ANCIENT GREECE
(CA. 1200–500 BCE)

Lamia

Lamia was born from Greek mythology. With the head of a woman and the body of a serpent, Greeks believed she was transformed from a beautiful queen into a bloodsucking monster as a curse from Hera for having an affair with her husband, Zeus. Lamia is the first vampire myth based on a woman being a seductress.

ANCIENT GREECE
(CA. 1200–500 BCE)

Vrykolakas

The vrykolakas was not a bloodsucking vampire but a flesh-eating one with doglike teeth and a particular penchant for livers, created by the death of a person who lived a sinful or sacrilegious life. Unlike the gaunt vampire figures we see in later legends, vrykolakas were large, swollen, and bloated creatures.

MIDDLE AGES (CA. 500–1000 CE)

Upir

Demons in Slavic, Baltic, and Turkic folklore, the upir, also known as upior and upyr, were some of the most dangerous of the vampiric creatures, for sunlight didn't harm them and their thirst for blood was insatiable. Upir were souls of the dead who hadn't been baptized, had taken their own life, or had sinned greatly during life. Instead of the neck, the upir bit the chests of their victims.

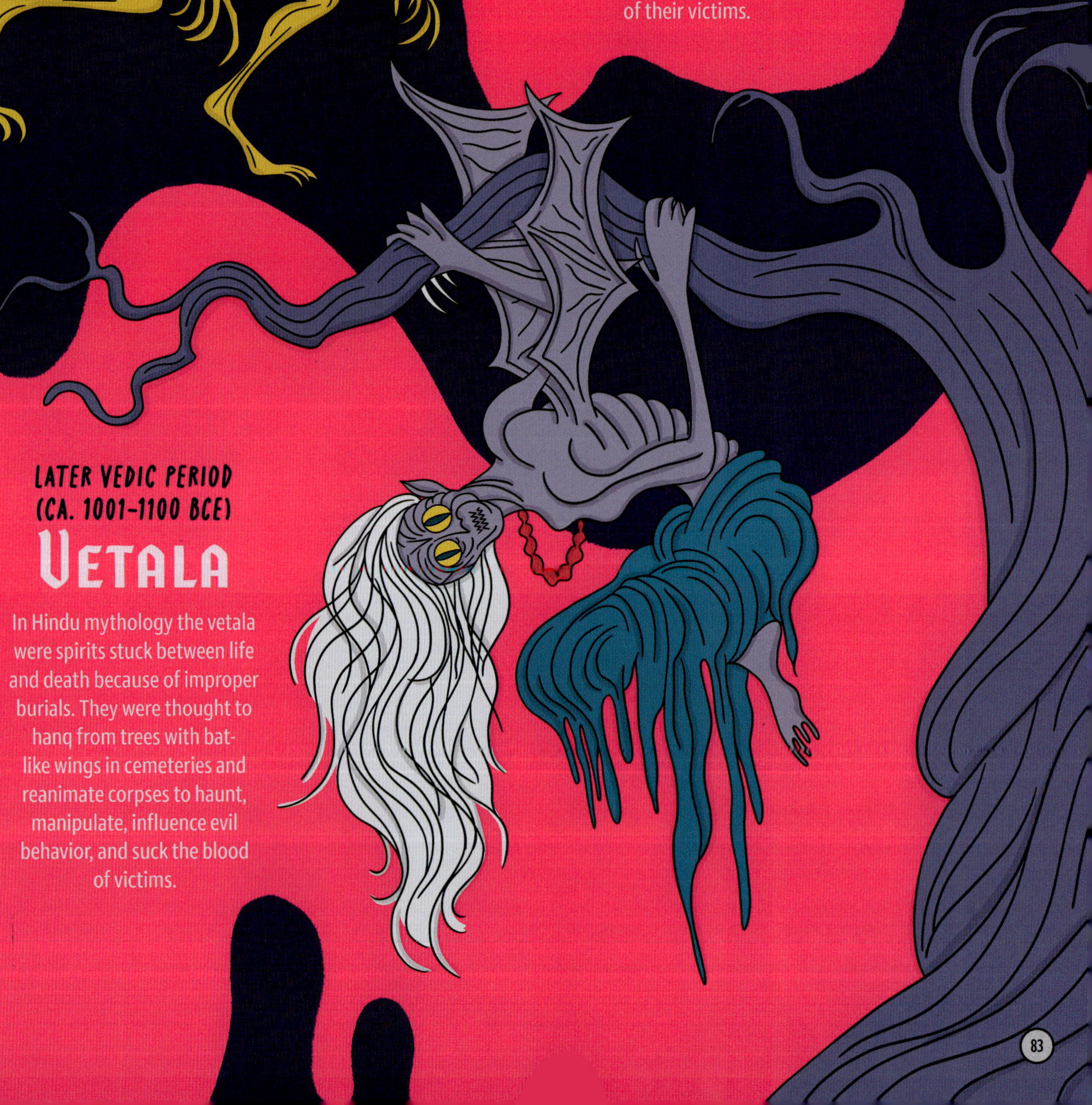

LATER VEDIC PERIOD (CA. 1001–1100 BCE)

Vetala

In Hindu mythology the vetala were spirits stuck between life and death because of improper burials. They were thought to hang from trees with bat-like wings in cemeteries and reanimate corpses to haunt, manipulate, influence evil behavior, and suck the blood of victims.

Vampire Abilities

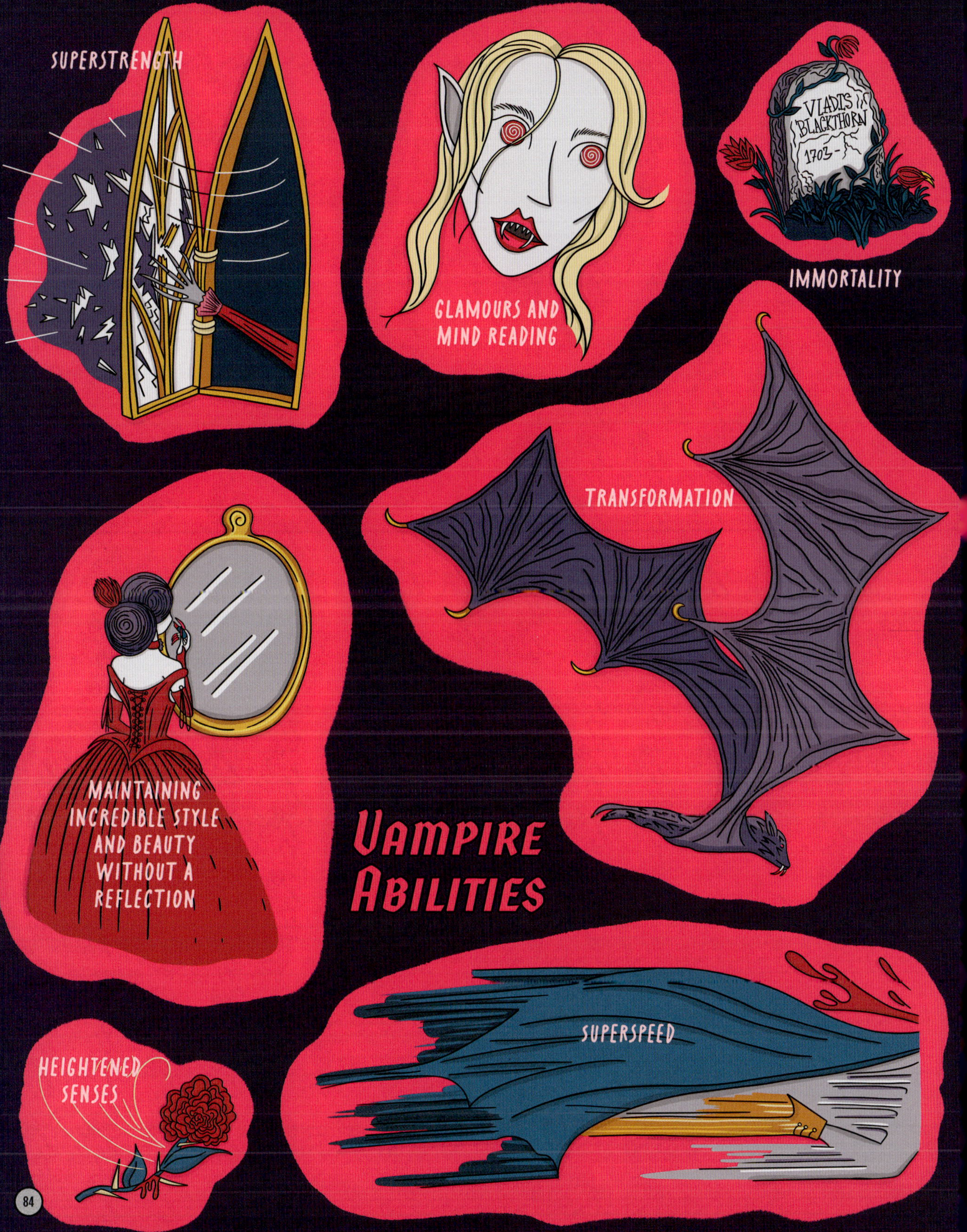

Vampire Weaknesses

Blood-Sworn Slayers and Famous Fangs

Where there are vampires, there's Van Helsing. The doctor, philosopher, professor, metaphysician, lawyer, and slayer of all slayers.

Buffy Summers, the high school cheerleader who wants to live a normal life but is destined to fight evil.

Blade, a superhero and vampire himself, chooses to use his powers to fight his kind instead of joining them.

Preceding Bram Stoker's Dracula by twenty-five years, Carmilla is not only one of the first gothic literary vampires but also a queer icon.

The most infamous vampire of all time and the prototype for all great vampire stories we know and love today.

Lestat de Lioncourt, Anne Rice's brooding antihero of *Interview with the Vampire*, is known for being a literary icon with legendary blond locks.

As the smoldering yet sparkling one-hundred-year-old teen heartthrob of *Twilight*, Edward Cullen showed the world what the skin of a killer looked like.

Fresh Blood
1000s
1100s
1200s
1300s
1400s
1500s
1600s
1700s
1800s
1900s
2000s
THE SUN ALSO RISES
THE CARE AND KEEPING OF BATS
DRACULA
WHAT'S YOUR BLOOD TYPE? - DATING FOR VAMPIRES
ESSENTIAL NIGHT LIFE
TWILIGHT
NEW MOON
ECLIPSE
DIY BATHOUSES
STAKE MY HEART
FANGS AND FASHION
FANG-SHUI
MEMOIRS OF AN IMMORTAL
BLOOD MEAL
FLIES
I'll SLEEP when I'm DEAD
VITAMIN E
SANGUI-SHINE
SLAYS EVEN THE TOUGHEST STAINS!
VITAMIN D
Journal 2387488
100 THINGS TO DO BEFORE YOU GET STAKED

MVT's Crypts:

Modern Vampire Television's *Inside the Lair*

CAN YOU FIND:

- 1 bottle of sunscreen
- Bat food
- 8 coffins
- 1 bulb of garlic
- Blood meal
- 1 pair of contact lenses
- 1 pair of sunglasses
- 6 flies
- 1 scented candle

Witches

Whether she's luring men and children into candy traps to feed on, making blood pacts under the full moon, possessing animals to do her bidding, selling her soul to Satan, or hexing an entire village because they wronged or inconvenienced her, the witch remains one of horror's most iconic and enduring figures. The witch's superficial appearance within horror—a gnarled, grotesque, and visually caustic hag—is only half the reason she is used to scare in horror. The true horror of the witch, and why she is an everlasting character in the genre, is more about what she represents, something most monstrous, most unsettling, and most disturbing—a woman that cannot be controlled!

The character of the witch (as with most characters within the horror genre) doesn't solely originate from folklore fears and myths, but it is rooted in, and shaped from, the darkest corners of human history.

Through the Salem witch trials of 1692, where paranoia led to executions, and the European witch hunts, where thousands were burned at the stake, the real-life accounts of women being murdered for exercising their free will and independence bled into fiction, solidifying the witch as a sinister archetype within the horror genre, because truly, what's scarier than a woman who holds knowledge and power over the patriarchy?

Autopsy of a Witch

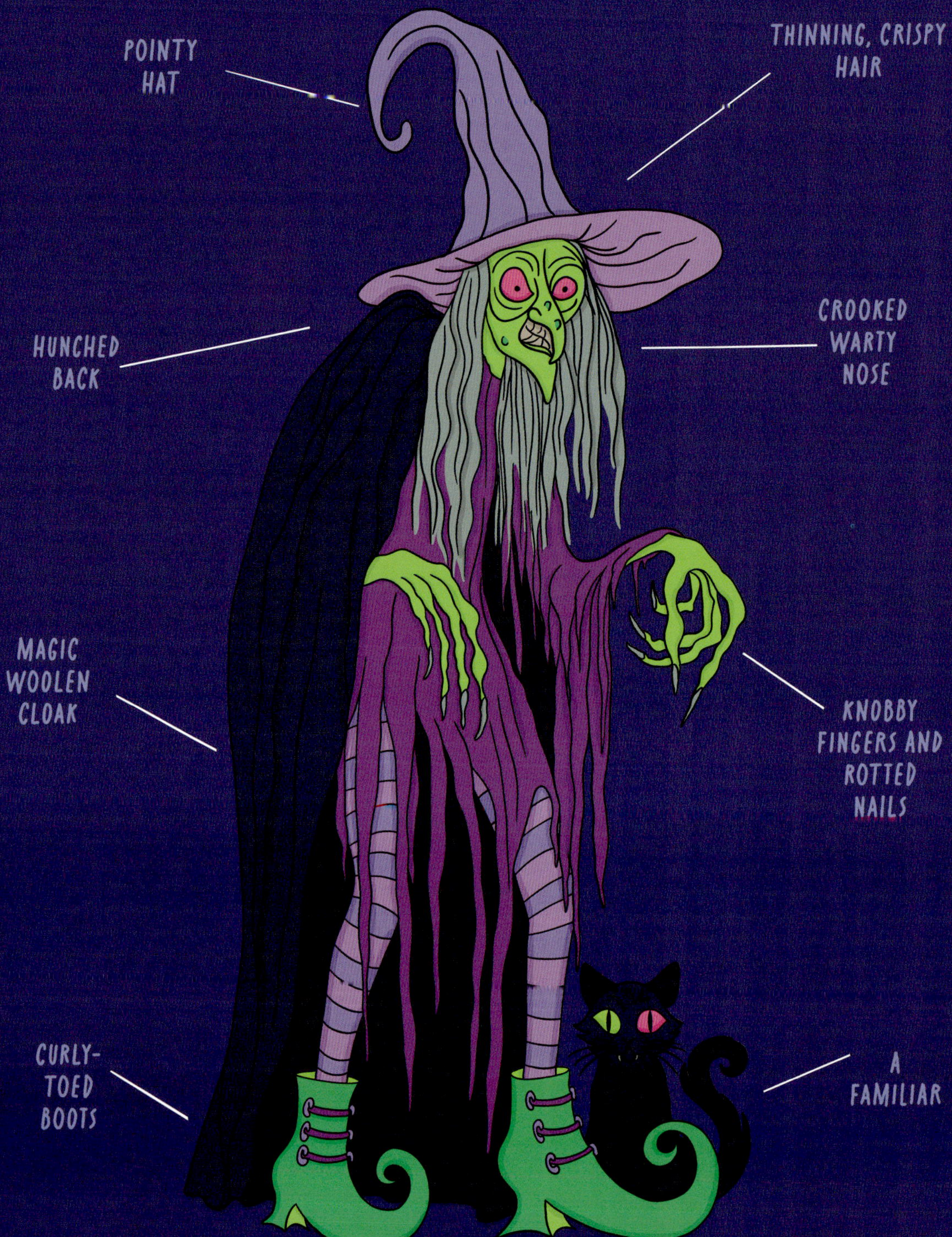

THE ORIGINS OF THE Witch

The witch we encounter most often in contemporary horror has primarily evolved out of ancient Greek mythology and Indo-European folklore. The following women, their stories, and their powers form the basis for the witch we recognize today.

THE MORRÍGAN

The Celtic goddess of war deemed a witch for her gift of prophecy used to foretell fate, doom, victory, and death on the battlefield. The lore of the Morrígan tells of her ability to shape-shift into many forms but most commonly Badb—a warrior crow that aids, protects, and washes the bloodstained clothes of those fated to die.

HECATE

The Greek goddess of witchcraft and mother of all witches. She was worshipped as a deity of magic, spells, necromancy, the night, the moon, dogs, and ghosts. She was often depicted as three figures that represent the three realms her power transcends—the living, the dead, and the divine.

MEDEA

The Greek goddess of sorcery, a priestess to the goddess Hecate, and enchantress most known for her gift of prophecy (and being a bit unhinged). Medea used her witchcraft to aid Jason—leader of the Argonauts—on his quest for the Golden Fleece, the magical wool of a celestial ram with healing powers. Medea succeeded but not without murdering her own brother and children. She then flew away in a chariot driven by dragons.

CIRCE

Perhaps the most famous witch in Greek mythology. She lived on the island of Aeaea, best known for its appearance in Homer's *Odyssey*. When Odysseus and his men arrived in her home, she used her potions and incantations to transform the intruding men into swine as an act of self-defense after they attempted to force themselves on her. Despite just wanting to protect herself, history has continued to regard Circe as an "evil witch" and a "beguiling temptress," labels commonly given to women who dared to not succumb to men's desire.

BABA YAGA

The original "wicked witch of the woods" from Slavic folklore, who lives in a cottage that walks through the forest supported on long chicken legs, has a ferocious appetite for children, and occasionally flies around in a mortar and pestle. Baba Yaga walked so every evil hag in the horror genre could run.

THE Basic Witch Archetypes

THE DEMON WORSHIPPER

Usually convinced they're in some kind of romantic relationship with Satan. Willing to make sacrifices.

THE EVIL HAG

Lives in the woods, eats children, grinds up bones, cottage core meets crone core.

THE SEDUCTIVE SORCERESS

Often just the evil hag who's fed on enough men to preserve her glass skin for a spell.

THE TEEN WICCAN OUTCAST

Uses magic to sort out high school jocks and hair color.

THE HISTORICAL HUSSY

Actually just a woman.

THE COVEN

You've been invited to step into the circle of salt as an initiate. How far will you rise among the ranks?

HIGH PRIESTESS

Ruling from the top of the coven's hierarchy, the High Priestess is the embodiment of the divine feminine force aka the goddess's power—keeper of dark secrets, master of rituals, and the wise, often terrifying force that leads the coven's dealings.

PRIESTESS, MAIDEN, PROTECTOR

The one who stands beside the High Priestess as an apprentice and a rising force within the coven. Her path is to learn the sacred rituals and rites of the witches, for she is destined to claim her place as their future leader.

INITIATES

There are three degrees of initiates within a coven.

FIRST DEGREE

The lowest rank. One who is learning, watching, and practicing.

SECOND DEGREE

One who's learned enough to begin initiating others into the coven. They may also start to lean into their own specialty within the craft.

THIRD DEGREE

A master of practice and understanding of the craft. Can start their own coven if they wish.

COVEN SPECIALTIES

- Cursing & hexing
- Necromancy
- Divining
- Scrying
- Shadow magic
- Poison craft
- Blood magic
- Demonolatry

"SHE'S A *WITCH!*"

The association of witches with women in horror stems from deep-rooted cultural biases. In horror, witches frequently embody anxieties about female autonomy, sexuality, and knowledge. They challenge traditional gender roles, often living outside the confines of marriage and motherhood, which *of course* makes them a threat. This is why many horror stories depict witches as women who, by embracing their power, are persecuted for it. Witch trials, which overwhelmingly targeted women, reinforced the idea that female independence was dangerous, subversive, and linked to evil!

Traditionally, the witch has been a symbol of female power, rebellion, and social transgression, qualities that have of course been feared and demonized in patriarchal societies. The perfect example of this is the stereotypical "evil crone" who first appeared among folklore and fairy tales told with the intention of exemplifying the "wrong way" of life to children, for a childless woman who lives alone must be evil, right?! Horror further villainizes women who don't have children by including the specific trait within their personality of having an appetite for them.

Witches stand in stark contrast to another horror archetype: the sorcerer! While a sorcerer is often a man portrayed as a powerful scholar who seeks power through knowledge, the witch gleans her power and intuition through external supernatural forces.

That said, modern horror has started to shake up these tropes reclaiming the witch as a feminist symbol and shifting the narrative away from the traditional gender binary. Let's celebrate them. Here are some of the best, most powerful, fearless, and uncontrollable WOMEN of the horror genre!

THE BLAIR WITCH
The Blair Witch Project

NANCY DOWNS
The Craft

THE WEIRD SISTERS
Macbeth

HELENA "MOTHER" MARKOS
Suspiria

THE GRAND HIGH WITCH
The Witches

THE VVITCH
The VVitch

THE SANDERSON SISTERS
Hocus Pocus

BATHSHEBA SHERMAN
The Conjuring

ROWAN MAYFAIR
The Witching Hour

HAGGIS
Pumpkinhead

THE GINGERBREAD WITCH
"Hansel and Gretel"

SALLY AND GILLIAN OWENS
Practical Magic

Autopsy of the Craft

Welcome to the witch's hut, where magic is brewed and evil is granted, curses are conjured, and spells are chanted. Levitation is nigh as grimoires soar cross the ink night sky. Slimy toads hop, five-legged rats skitter, the snake hisses venomous breath, and the black candles' flames aflicker. Take hold of your broom for you can't turn back, let me take you through the witch's craft!

The Cauldron

At the center of every witch's arsenal is the cauldron, the foundational tool and most dangerous accessory used to participate in the craft. When set upon flame, its rounded iron body turns oddly paired ingredients into complex deadly potions and poisonous brews. Some say they represent the womb as they can nurture and create, but in horror stories, they're more often used to cook a child or two.

THE Grimoire

The witch's grimoire isn't just a spell book, it's a living, ink-stained relic of forbidden knowledge. Bound in cracked leather (or skin), its pages hum with centuries of spells, curses, potion recipes, hexes, incantations, and evil enchantments, all sentient and waiting, eager to be recalled, all probably best left in the dark. The ink? Maybe just ink . . . maybe blood of the witch herself . . . maybe her victims . . . best not break the spine of the witch's book of shadows and find out.

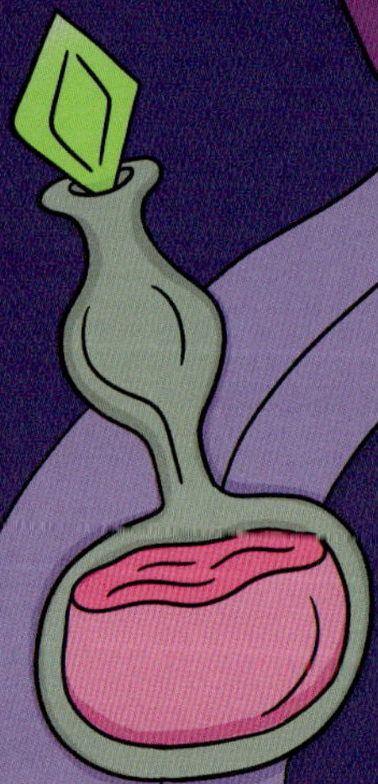

So you cracked the spine anyway . . . too late to turn back now! Here's a spell to curse your enemies. Use it, or you'll be the one to reap the consequences!

To Summon Fear in the Heart of an Enemy

Prick your finger and let three drops of blood fall into the nearest pool of water at midnight on the next full moon. Bind the intended cursed by writing their name on parchment and floating it face down in the bloodstained water. Light one candle and immediately extinguish it in the pool as you repeat the following . . . "By the shadow, by the night, let the cursed heart beat with fright."

THE Potion Pantry

Familiars

Magical animal companions thought to have been sent by the devil to assist with spells, guidance, and protection.

THE Altar

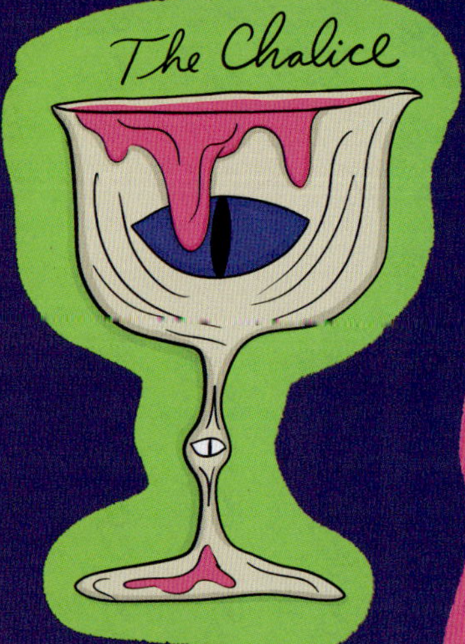
The Chalice

The Candle

The Effigy

The Broom

The Stones + Bones for scrying

The Herbs

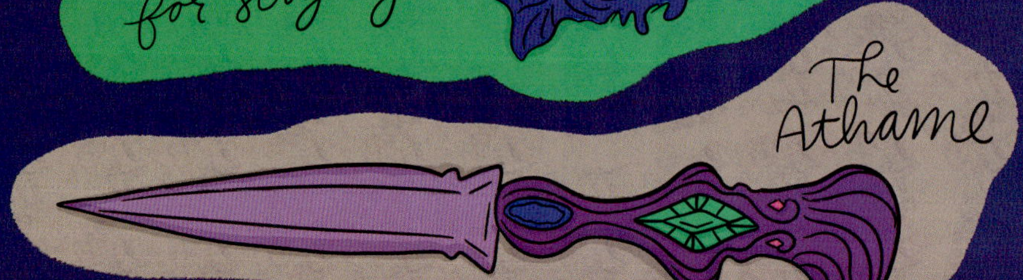
The Athame

THE Witch's Garden

WELCOME TO THE WITCH'S GARDEN. FIND THE ITEMS BEFORE SHE RETURNS.

- 1 black flame candle
- 2 hatched moths
- 5 toads
- 1 Book of Shadows
- 4 mandrake roots
- 2 broomsticks
- 12 fairies
- 3 eyeball bottle stoppers
- 9 grimoires
- 1 athame

Zombies

When zombies first lurched their way into horror stories, it became clear that there may never be a more metaphorically rich monster in the genre.

At their core, zombies embody one of humanity's deepest and most enduring battles, the struggle to maintain one's individuality in the face of conformity. They force us to confront the question of what happens when we give our minds over. When we actively let something eat away at our brains, our ability to think, question, and resist. These walking corpses aren't just terrifying because they want to eat you, they're terrifying because they used to be you.

From their origins in Haitian Vodou folklore as reanimated bodies controlled by sorcery to their modern depiction as virus-spreading, rabid creatures, zombies may seem like they're stumbling toward you for a simple scare. And yes, there's something uniquely unsettling about a creature that was once human, someone that could have been your friend, neighbor, or even mother, that's now a mindless husk, driven by an insatiable hunger for your flesh and brains . . . but zombies have layers! Rotten layers, but layers nonetheless. Underneath their decayed skin lies the grim reflection of some of our most severe societal anxieties we harbor, such as fears of government control, environmental destruction, unchecked consumerism, addiction to social media, and complete societal collapse.

Zombies brilliantly represent us, serving as an ever-moaning warning of what happens when we succumb to the masses, unquestioning, mindlessly consuming, scrolling, letting others think for us, and abandoning our greatest gift: our individuality.

Zombies exemplify what horror does best—they remind us that the monster who could devour us at any moment when we aren't paying attention, is us.

Autopsy of a Zombie

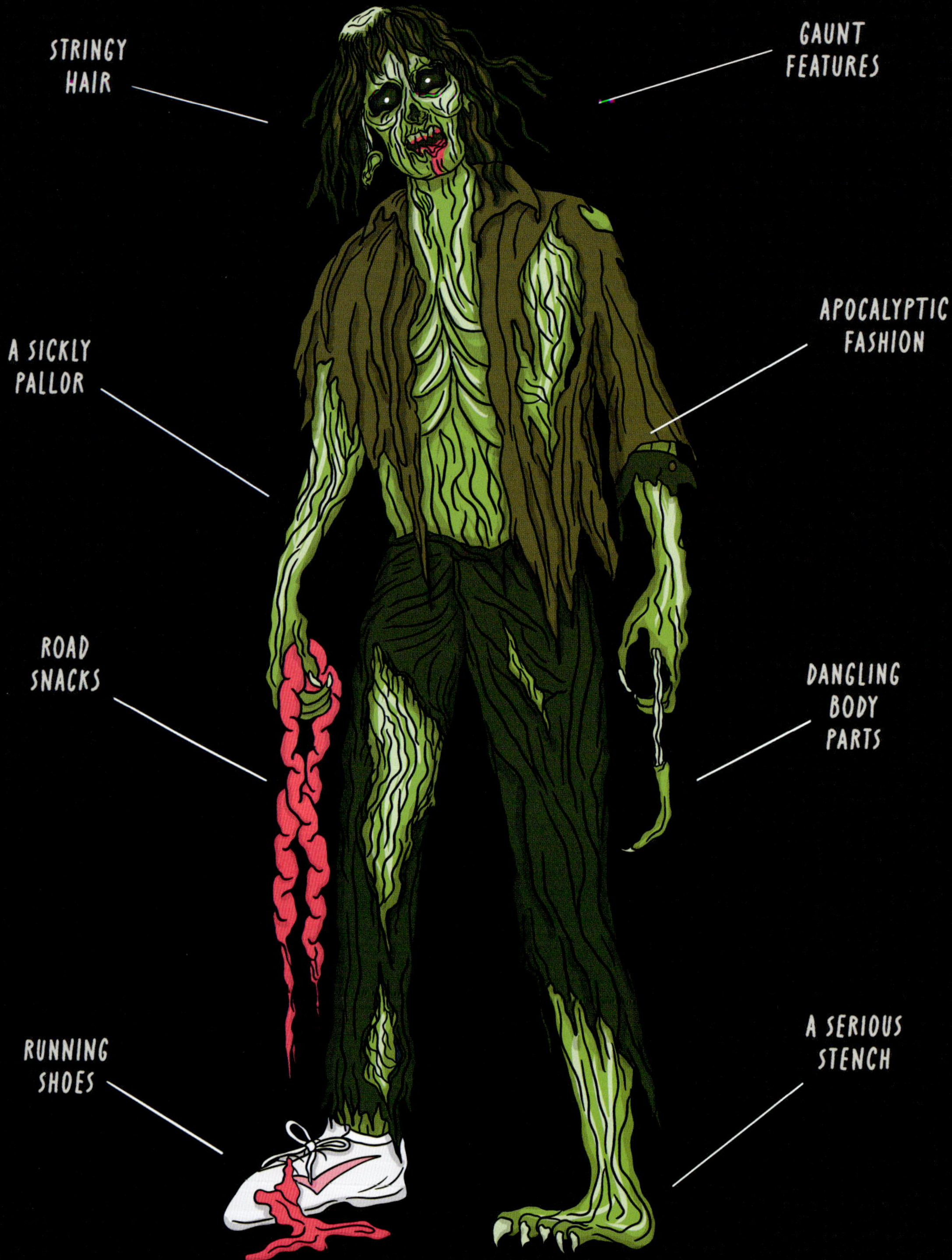

Autopsy of a Zombie Apocalypse

Leading Causes

VIRAL OUTBREAK

CHEMICAL EXPOSURE

NECROMANCY

WITCHCRAFT

MIND CONTROL

PARASITIC INFECTION

SOCIAL MEDIA

How It Spreads

1. 2. 3.

BITES

AIRBORNE PATHOGENS

BLOOD

INCUBATION PERIOD

The Horde

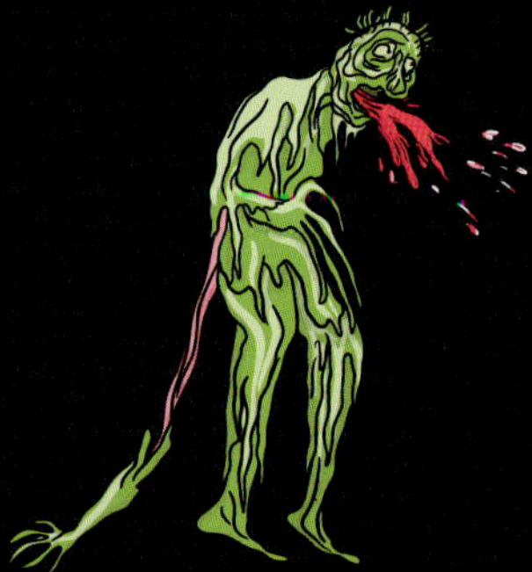

SPITTER

SPEED
INTELLIGENCE
STRENGTH

BONEY

SPEED
INTELLIGENCE
STRENGTH

RUNNER

SPEED
INTELLIGENCE
STRENGTH

SCREAMER

SPEED
INTELLIGENCE
STRENGTH

BLOATER

SPEED
INTELLIGENCE
STRENGTH

The Zombie Food Pyramid

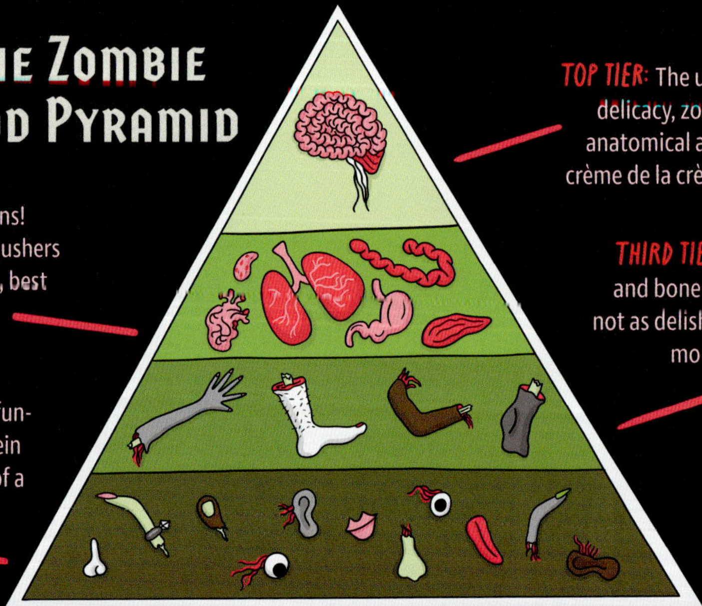

TOP TIER: The ultimate undead delicacy, zombie caviar, anatomical ambrosia, the crème de la crème—the brain!

SECOND TIER: Organs! Meaty, rich little iron gushers and bubblegum guts, best served warm!

THIRD TIER: Limbs, gristle, and bone—substantial but not as delish. Think less fat cap, more kneecap.

BOTTOM TIER: Grab 'n' go fun-sized Ring Pops and protein bites. Best when in need of a quick fix on the run.

The Zombie Survival Kit

Unliving LEGENDS

THE GREATEST ZOMBIE STORIES OF ALL TIME

NIGHT OF THE LIVING DEAD (1968) With hordes of hungry flesh-eating corpses spilling out of graves and onto our screen, George A. Romero gave us this cult classic.

DAWN OF THE DEAD (1978) Romero's reanimation of *Night of the Living Dead* ten years later, set in a shopping mall—a brilliant metaphorical stage for our zombielike tendency to overconsume.

28 DAYS LATER (2002) The British film directed by Danny Boyle that popularized the concept of fast-moving zombies (or "infected"). It seared one-thousand-body pileups into our brains.

THE WALKING DEAD (2010–2022) One of the most popular zombie TV series based on the comic book series, by Robert Kirkman, which follows survivors navigating a postapocalyptic world overrun by the undead.

TRAIN TO BUSAN (2016) This South Korean film follows passengers on a train attempting to survive a typical zombie outbreak, but Yeon Sang-ho's storytelling, emotional depth, and beloved characters are what really bring it to life.

THE LAST OF US (2023–2027) Based on the iconic video game, the series follows the unlikely pair of Joel and Ellie through a brutal, decayed world contaminated by cordyceps-hosting zombies.

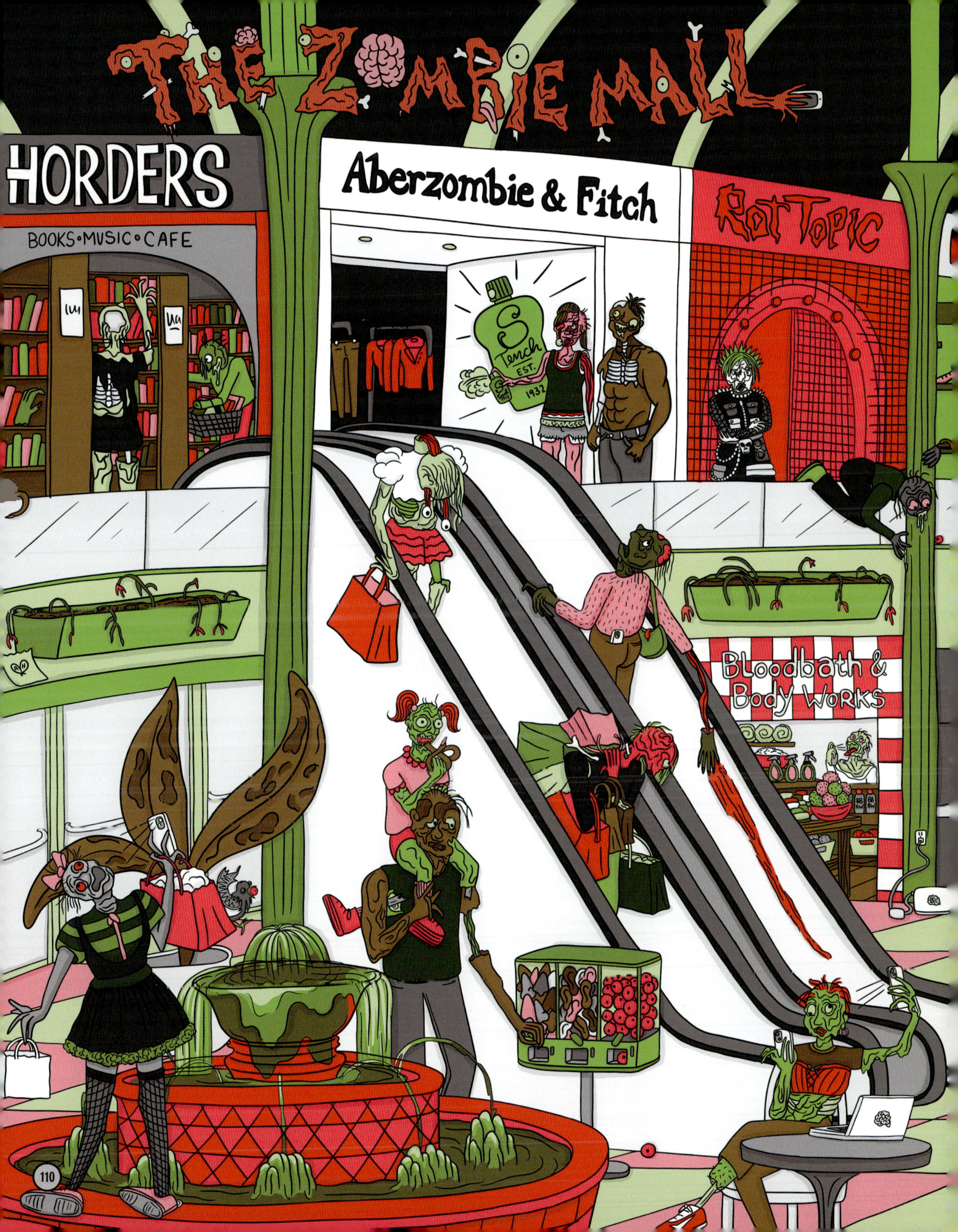
THE ZOMBIE MALL
HORDERS
BOOKS•MUSIC•CAFE
Aberzombie & Fitch
Rot Topic
Stench
EST.
1932
Bloodbath & Body Works

WELCOME TO THE ZOMBIE MALL WHERE YOU CAN CONSUME, SCROLL, AND GLEEFULLY ROT AWAY! CAN YOU FIND:

- 4 loose gum *eye* balls
- 6 Auntie's Hands "pretzels"
- 3 left-behind limbs
- 9 Brain Store purchases
- 3 bottles of S. Tench
- Carnage the zombie dog
- 1 zombinfluencer
- Some hand-pressed juice
- 2 zombie pigeons
- 3 cups of Drip and Clots

Werewolves

Shhhh! Did you hear a howl when you turned the page? We've just entered the beast's domain, the deadly creature at the mercy of the moon, one that can pick up our scent from miles away, and one that with a simple bite can turn you into its furry kin. We're now in the domain of the werewolf! You must be-WERE!

The classic character of the werewolf, ever present in horror, evolved from ancient folklore rooted in our basic human fear of losing control. Stories that tap into our deeply human terror that, beneath our carefully constructed civility, we are still just animals waiting for the right trigger to set us off.

Always bending to the moon's will, these towering, razor-clawed creatures of the forest embody our fear of being powerless to nature, of having no say, no control over the animalistic mind, basic instincts, darkest urges, compulsions, desires, rage, violence, bloodlust, and hunger. Whether controlled by a celestial body or an inescapable internal pull, werewolves beg the evergreen question: Are we more man than monster, or more monster than man?

Another one of horror's most metaphorical creatures, the werewolf (interestingly most commonly portrayed as male) is so much more. With its uncontrollable transformation and loss of autonomy every thirty days or so, the werewolf brilliantly symbolizes the violent, terrifying, and often isolating human experiences of puberty, menstruation, gender identity, queer identity, emotional turmoil, hypermasculinity, and physical "otherness."

Shall we proceed into the den of one of horror's most transformative monsters? AWWWWOOOOOOOOO!

Autopsy of a Werewolf

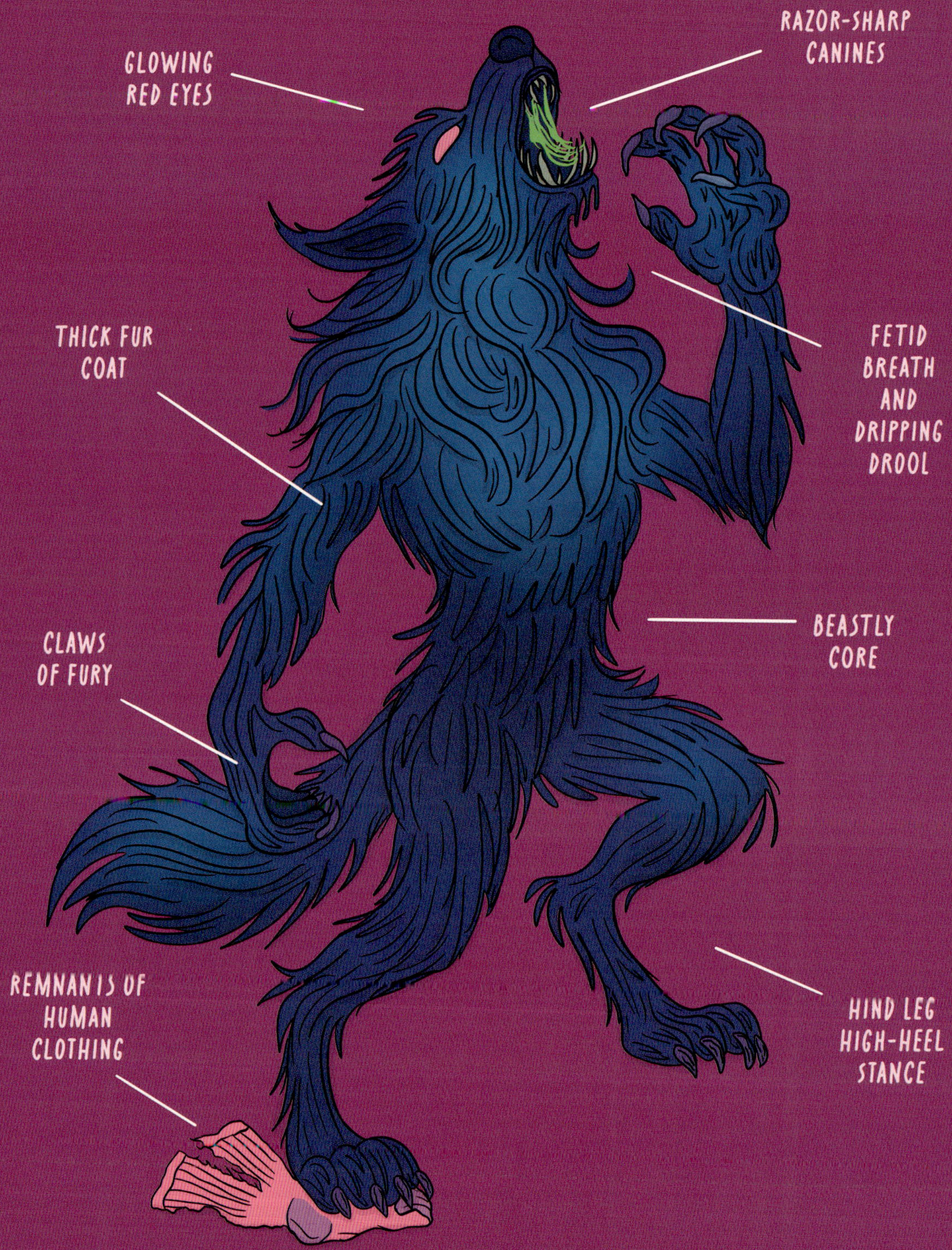

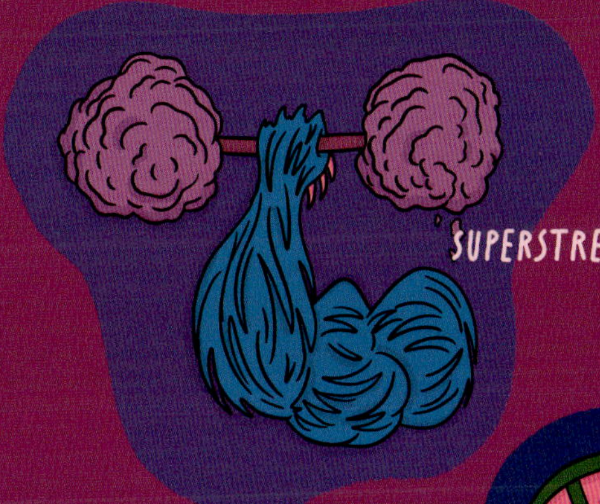

WEREWOLF Abilities

Werewolf Weaknesses

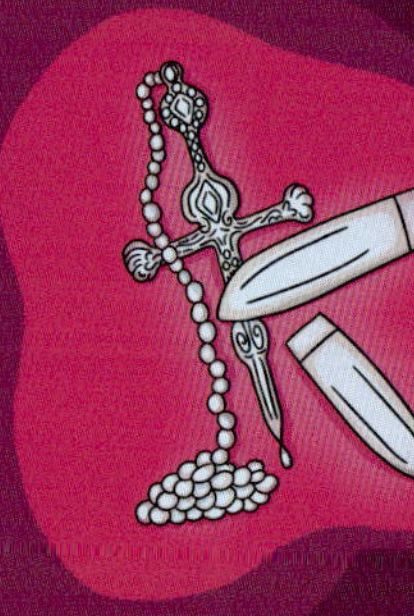

SILVER

FIRE

WOLFSBANE

THE IN-BETWEEN PHASES

MAGIC

The Pack

The Alpha 180HP

ALPHA LEADER - LEGENDARY WEREWOLF
TYPE: Dark/Moon
ABILITY: The Crimson Fang (120 Power) - A devastating bite with a 50% chance to inflict Lycaon's Curse weakening the opponent's attack for 3 turns.

100 90 120 95 98

The Beta 160HP

ELITE - SECOND-IN-COMMAND
TYPE: Moon/Shadow
ABILITY: The Tactile Mind (80 Power) - Selene can analyze enemy movements, reducing the effectiveness of opponent attacks by 20%.

80 75 100 90 95

The Delta 150HP

ELITE - WARRIOR
TYPE: Shadow/Dark
ABILITY: The Umbra's Cloak (75 Power) - Korr can blend into darkness, making him untargetable for one turn. If used in moonlight attack +30%.

95 80 110 85 70

The Omega 130HP

LOW RANK - SURVIVOR
TYPE: Shadow/Moon
ABILITY: The Survivor's Instinct (Utility) - Allows Rook to avoid any single attack once per turn. Can be used to switch him out of battle without penalty.

70 65 105 90 95

The Pup 100HP

YOUNGLING - FUTURE PACK MEMBER
TYPE: Moon/Spirit
ABILITY: The Preying Pounce (60 Power) - A surprise leap attack that has a 50% chance to lower the opponent's defense by 10%.

60 55 95 100 80

THE Evolution OF THE WEREWOLF

The werewolf archetype didn't magically appear over the last full moonlit night, it slowly evolved out of a long and transformative journey through history.

HOW ARE YOU LYCAON-ING YOUR FOOD?

The first recorded account of a man transforming into a wolf appears in *The Epic of Gilgamesh*, but the Greek myth of Lycaon established the werewolf as the lasting horror figure we know today. Appearing in both Plato's *Republic* and Ovid's *Metamorphoses*, the myth recounts how King Lycaon was skeptical of Zeus's power, so he served him a meal made from human meat to test his divine power of discernment. In response to being tested, Zeus struck Lycaon with lightning, which transformed him into a wolf. The myth of King Lycaon is where we get the term *lycanthropy*, which we now use to describe the supernatural condition of human-to-wolf shape-shifting.

WEREWOLF IN LONDON . . . PARIS

Just like the witch trials, Europe saw werewolf hunts and executions from the sixteenth to the seventeenth century. Accused werewolves, or loup garous in France, were often peasants, outcasts, or people with mental illnesses that were blamed for murders, disappearances, and livestock killings. The two most famous being Gilles Garnier, a hermit accused of being a werewolf and eating children, and Peter Stumpp, known as the Werewolf of Bedburg, who was tortured until he "confessed" to being a werewolf under the influence of the devil.

RENAISSANCE WOLF

During the medieval and Renaissance periods, as Christianity spread rapidly, people wanted to distance themselves from their prior pagan beliefs, which regarded shape-shifting wolves as deities, for the Bible classified wolves as evil, and no one wanted to be associated with evil.

READER, BE-WERE, YOU'RE IN FOR A SCARE!

In the eighteenth and nineteenth century, the werewolf most commonly appeared in literature. Three notable works that featured the werewolf include the 1865 deep-dive nonfiction work of Sabine Baring-Gould entitled *The Book of Were-Wolves*, the serial penny dreadful *Wagner, the Wehr-Wolf* by George W. M. Reynolds, and *The Were-Wolf*, an allegorical erotic short story by the brilliant suffragette Clemence Housman written in 1896, which used the werewolf to represent the woman's struggle between domestic and working roles.

SILVER BULLETS ON THE SILVER SCREEN

Even though werewolves are notoriously wounded by silver, it's never stopped them from appearing on the silver screen—starting with their debut in 1931 with the mysteriously lost silent film *The Werewolf*. And most notably during Hollywood's Universal Monsters' era in films like *The Wolf Man* starring Lon Chaney Jr., which defined the modern werewolf, introducing the full moon transformation, silver bullets, and the werewolf's curse. In the 1970s and '80s we saw a boom in horror flicks featuring werewolves, one of them being the infamous 1981 werewolf horror comedy *An American Werewolf in London*.

THE TEEN WOLF

In the late twentieth century, werewolves traded their forest fits for letterman jackets. With shows like *Silver Bullet* and *Teen Wolf*, suddenly the werewolf, although still an icon of the horror genre, became accessible to younger audiences, and oh, they were hot. Stephenie Meyer's fantasy horror series, *Twilight*, used Jacob Black to rocket werewolves through the genre barrier even further solidifying them within pop culture's hall of fame. In contemporary horror, we're seeing the werewolf return to a dark and violent figure in films like *Ginger Snaps* with depictions of the creature rooted back in its most terrifying folklore beginnings. With werewolves, it's all a cycle.

THE Transformation

Witnessing the transformation of a werewolf can be very dangerous, and rarely do people make it through the experience alive. Lucky for you . . . I've secured the exclusive opportunity to witness one tonight.

Look now . . . it's starting to happen . . . that cloud just caught the night wind and has slowly revealed the swollen glowing moon. The lunar menace has once again reached the last stage in its monthly growth. Its bioluminescent light is piercing the dark sky and signaling that the cycle of transformation is to once again begin, and the werewolf, the creature most at the mercy of its power, will now begin to change before our eyes. Now gather around and watch closely. I'm certain you'll make it out alive . . . However, I can't promise you'll make it out unbitten.

STAGE 1

The "uh-oh, I forgot to check my moon calendar" moment.

STAGE 2

The heart races, nails elongate, fever and a cold sweat break out, muscles twitch, and senses explode with awareness.

STAGE 3

The human bones start to bend and grow, causing gut-wrenching agony, ribs crack, skin stretches, fur starts to spread, teeth start to grow.

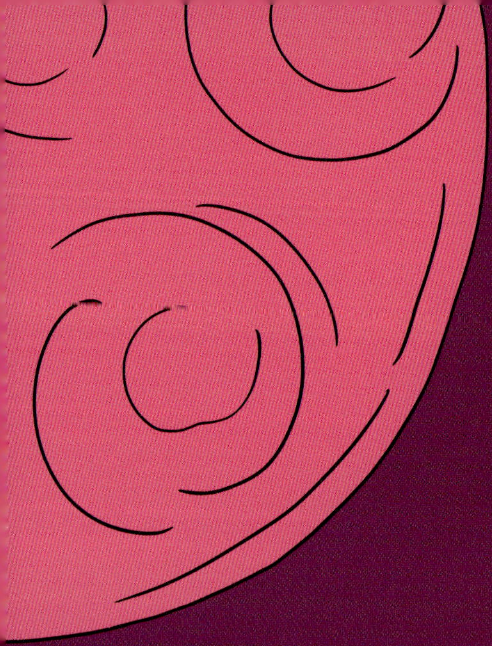

Horror Fact

Lunacy is derived from the Latin word *luna*, meaning "moon," because of the beliefs from ancient folklore and medieval superstition that when the full moon bled its eerie silver light across the earth, it stirred something unconsciously wild, unhinged, and mad within the human mind.

STAGE 4

The werewolf is now more beast than man. His eyes glow red, he stands over eight feet tall, and his claws can shred metal like butter.

STAGE 5

The moon has done its work, and the transformation is complete. Saliva drips from razor-blade teeth, thick gnarled fur covers the body of the wolf, all human identity has vanished, and the haunted werewolf howl signals the beginning of the hunt. Watch out!

Ghosts

There is nothing more classically horror than the ghost story.

Ghosts are staples of the horror genre, unmatched in their ability to symbolize one universal human truth—that we all have something to hide. Whether it's a mistake, an ill-fated choice, a transgression, or a secret you swore to take to your grave, we're all haunted by something, we all have ghosts we cannot escape.

Ghosts' methods of attack are deeply personal. Ghosts don't just haunt for pleasure; they haunt with a unique targeted intention. They don't haunt arbitrarily—they haunt you, your past, your unique experiences, and your guilts. Ghosts torture you with your own secrets. They are your conscience in form, they are you.

Unlike other famous characters within the genre, ghosts do not succumb to measly methods of defeat. Silver bullets, stakes through the heart, fire, so on and so forth are all useless on their incorporeal bodies. Ghosts are spiritual inhabitants of the mind more than physical inhabitants of the earth, and the only way to vanquish a manifestation of the mind is to vanquish the mind itself. Because their haunts are personal, ghosts have the power to destroy you from the inside out, to drive you to madness through hallucinations, all while going unseen and unheard by anyone else. We cannot escape what personally haunts us, it is our unfinished business to face alone.

Because ghosts are internal threats, our external methods of protection are virtually nullified. With their ability to haunt both our waking hours and deepest dreams, they breach the boundaries of our consciousness. With their ability to glide through walls, doors, and locks, they sidestep the physical boundaries we foolishly build to keep us in and evil out.

Ghosts terrify us most because they render us powerless.

So . . . what are you hiding?

Autopsy of a Ghost

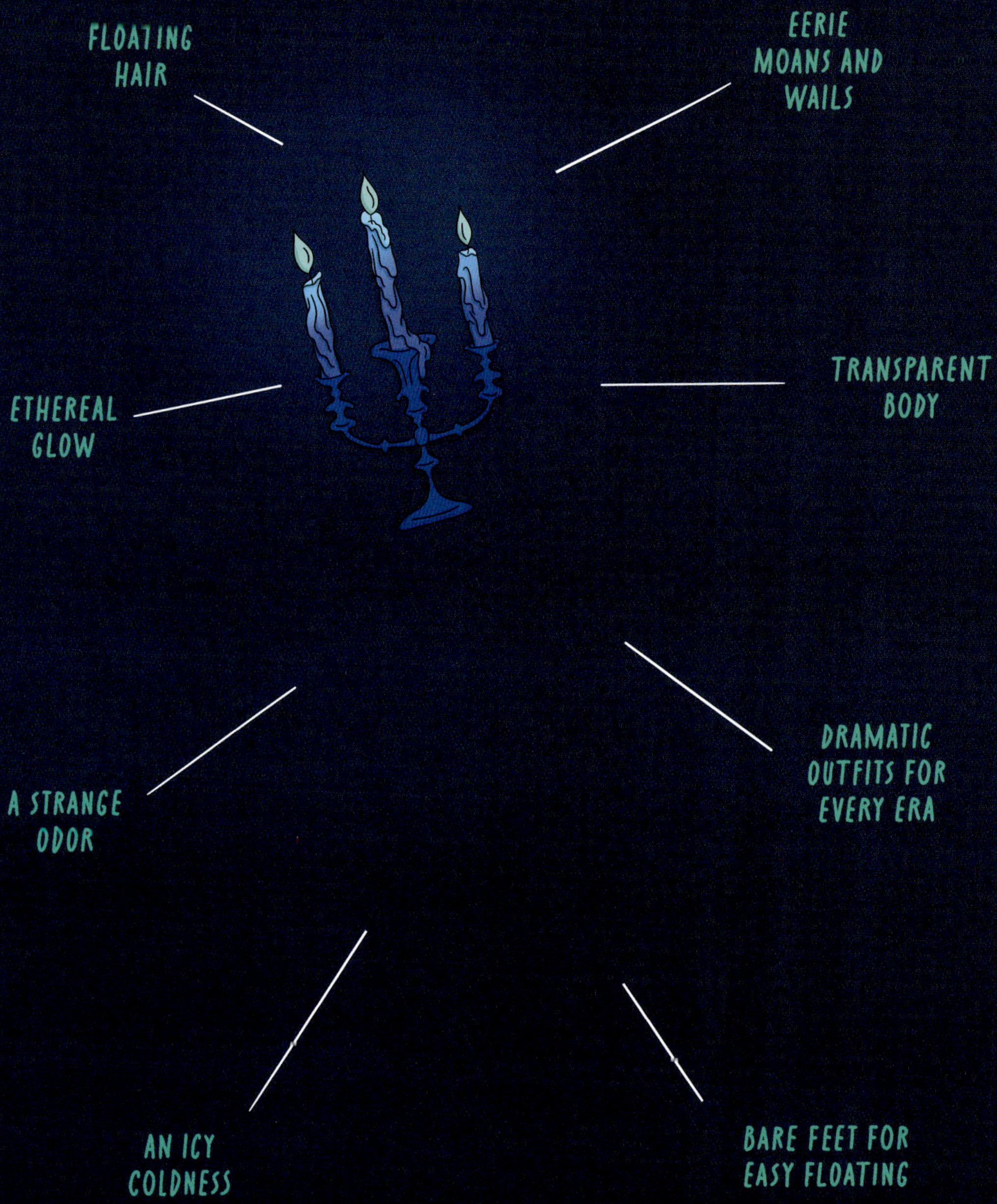

TRUE LIFE: I'm A Ghost

We regret to inform you that you have died—RIP, babe. Now comes the fun part, your afterlife. What would you like it to look like?

CHOOSE 1

POLTERGEIST
Noisy and unhinged

SHADE
XOXO Gossip Ghost

FRIENDLY
Just here to hang

PHANTOM
Loves opera

SLIMER
Messy

SPECTER
A sophisticated sort

BANSHEE
Great scream

WRAITH
Pale and emo

VENGEFUL
Holds grudges

REVENANT
Can't let go

SPIRIT
Loves an open bar

PHANTASM
Phantom with flair

APPARITION
Great at ghosting

SHADOW
A follower

FETCH
Copycat

WHAT WILL YOU Haunt?

CHOOSE 1

THE CEMETERY

THE ATTIC

THE LAKE

THE LONESOME HIGHWAY

THE BATHROOM

THE FOOT OF THE BED

THE ORPHANAGE

HAUNT FACT:
Theaters are never truly dark, for there is always a "ghost light" kept on—even when performances aren't running.

THE THEATER

Ghost Outfit

CHOOSE 1

VICTORIAN GOWN

NIGHTGOWN

MILITARY UNIFORM

CLASSIC SHEET

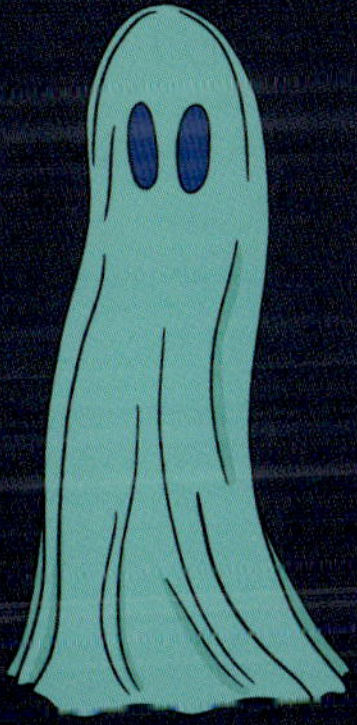

TATTERED RAGS

NUDE

PRISON UNIFORM

HOSPITAL GOWN

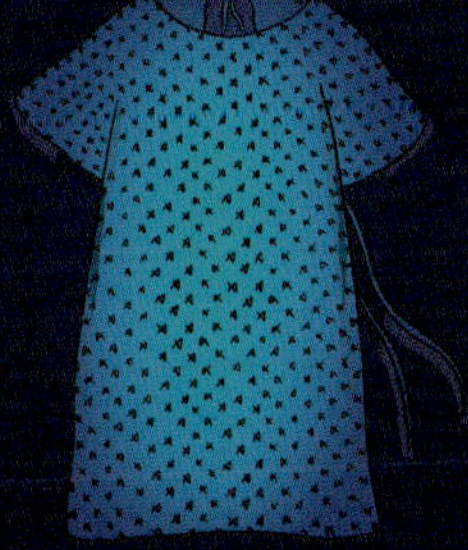

CHILDREN'S SAILOR DRESS

Ghost Accessories

CHOOSE AS MANY AS YOU WANT, IT'S YOUR AFTERLIFE.

CHAINS

LANTERN

VEIL

FOG MACHINE

CURSED LOCKET

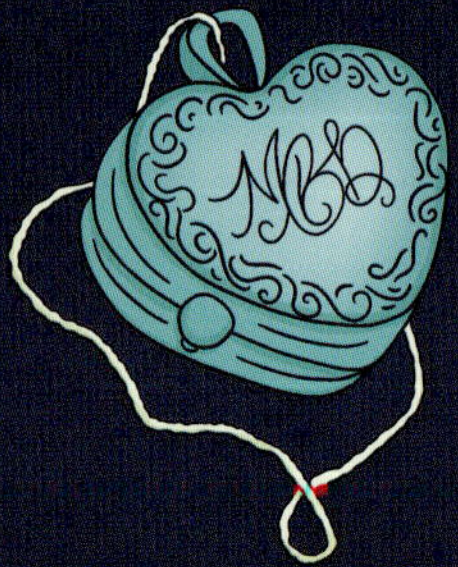

DRAMATIC CANDELABRA

MUSIC BOX

ROCKING HORSE

TEMPERATURE CONTROL

Popular Poltergeists

The Woman in Black

The Victorian-era funeral-crasher who loves long walks along the salt marsh in chic black attire.

Poltergeist

"It's hereeeeeeee."

Lorraine Massey

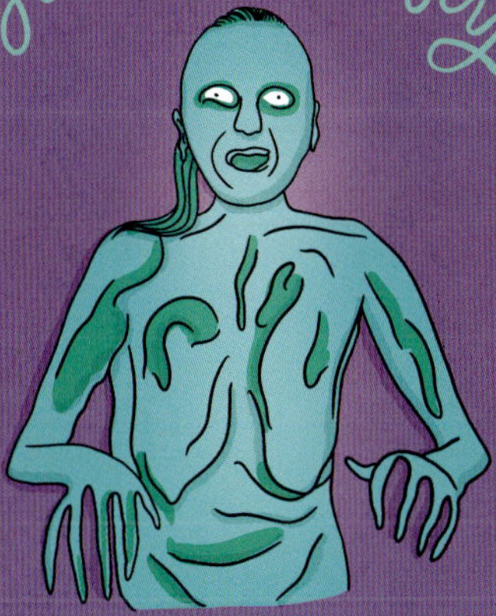

The Overlook Hotel's permanent resident of room 217 who just wants to stay in the bath until her skin is clean and Shining.

Casper

The littlest ghost of the horror genre, here to remind us that some ghosts are friendly.

Peter Quint & Miss Jessel

Henry James's *The Turn of the Screw* toxic caretakers with a terrible track record with children.

Dr. Malcom Crowe

The psychiatrist who only sees one patient because that patient is the only one who sees him.

Ghost Hunters

ED AND LORRAINE WARREN

In supernatural sightings, there are ghost hunters, and then there's Ed and Lorraine Warren—the king and queen of paranormal activity. From 1952 through the 1980s, Ed, a self-taught demonologist, and Lorraine, a trance medium, were your 311 for "my [fill in the blank] is haunted." During their career, they investigated more than ten thousand cases of paranormal phenomena, the most famous being the Amityville Horror House in Long Island, New York. Together they founded the New England Society for Psychic Research and built a museum entirely devoted to occult items they collected throughout the course of their career, one of which was the original Annabelle, the real-life doll made famous in the *Conjuring* movies and one of the most haunted artifacts known to man.

ANNABELLE

The Ghost Hunter's Starter Pack

AUDIO RECORDER

HEADSET

BOOM

NIGHT-VISION GOGGLES

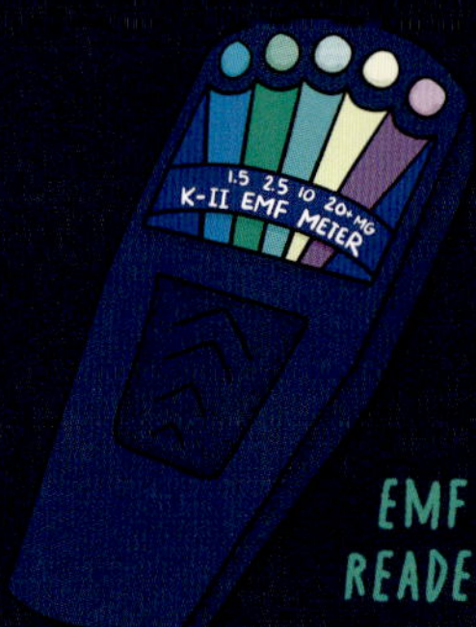

EMF READER

CAMCORDER

DIGITAL THERMOMETER

HONORABLE MENTIONS

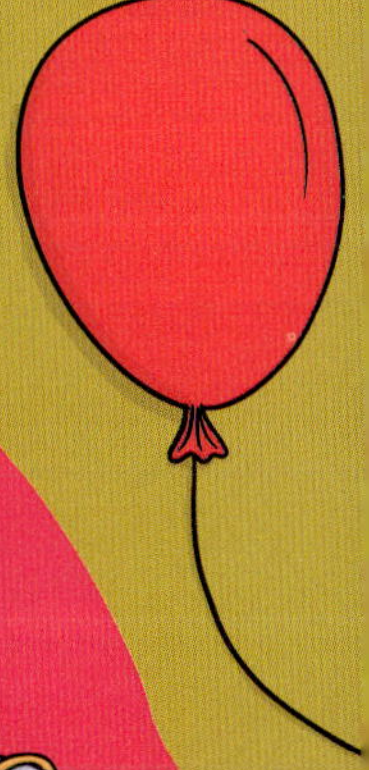

SATAN

THE BLIND CREATURE WITH HEIGHTENED HEARING

THE MAD SCIENTIST

THE MUMMY

THE ALIEN

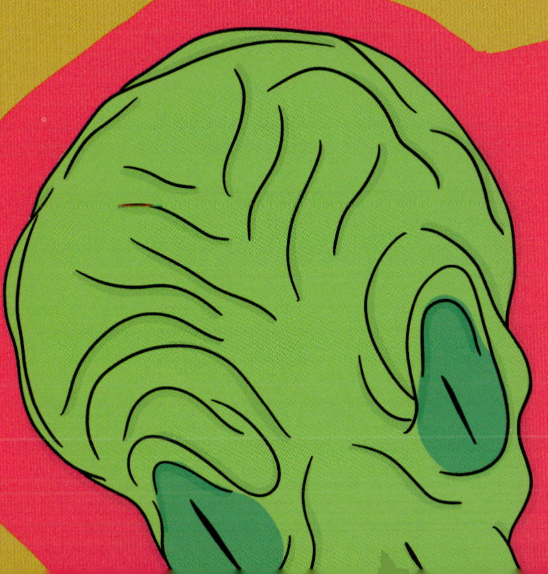

THE
CLOWN

THE
SCARY
FAIRY

THE
MONSTER

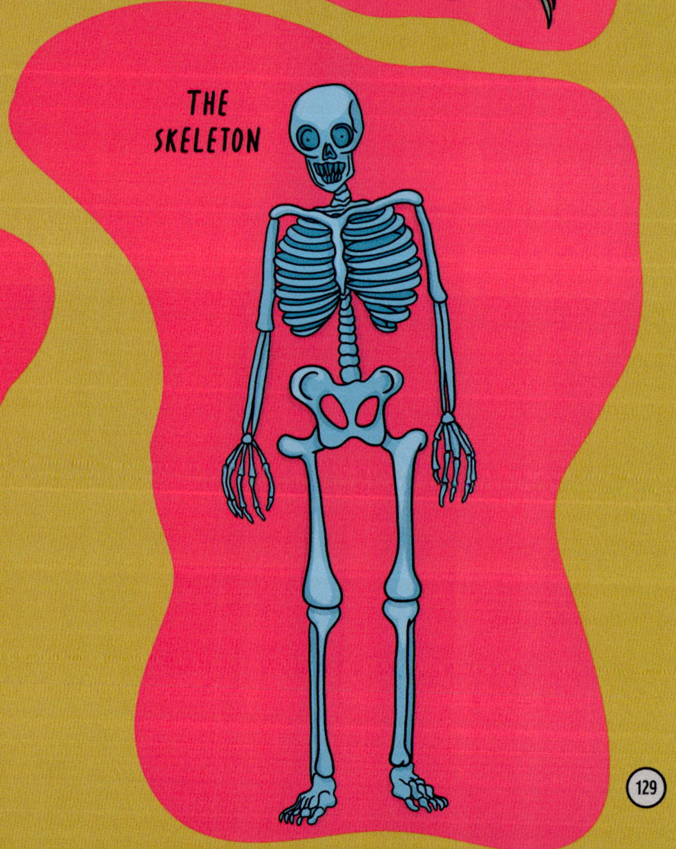
THE
SKELETON

The Monster Bash

CAN YOU FIND?
• 23 Solo cups of moon juice
• 8 cans of Witches Brew
• 5 brew pong balls
• A VHS tape
• The class clown
• 1 Bloody Mary
• 7 ghosts
• 1 ex getting hexed
• 2 missing Pizza Gut slices
• 1 high (school) priestess
• 2 skeletons in the closet
• 4 Horror High letterman jackets
• 1 emo werewolf
• 1 finger joint
PIZZA GUT

EXIT
Giftshop
WOODEN STAKES

AS YOU EXIT THROUGH THE gift shop with your fangs, stakes, and cauldrons, please gather around. I so hope you enjoyed the exhibit and meeting each of horror's iconic characters! I see we may have lost a few more tour members to bites and transformations, but it's for a good cause. No, truly! Without each of those characters we just met, the horror genre and its ability to serve as, in my opinion, the most metaphorical genre of them all, would be quite empty.

Those characters are the flesh, meat, *and* bone of horror. Their ability to reflect the human experiences of emotion, fear, growth and transformation, death, identity, and our own prejudices, is what makes the horror genre the delicious, illuminating, personal, and deeply meaningful feast it is.

And if none of that lands, you must admit that a dark, dank castle without an opulently clad man with some kind of wasting disease feasting on pale women is really just a . . . dark, dank castle and not very fun.

Speaking of those dark, dank castles though . . . Wow, we are getting quite cultured on this tour. Shall we travel a bit? If you'd like to continue on and explore horror around the world, swap your museum ticket for a transit ticket here. That is, unless you'd prefer to fly in your mortar and pestle à la Baba Yaga. Either way is fine. Let's go!

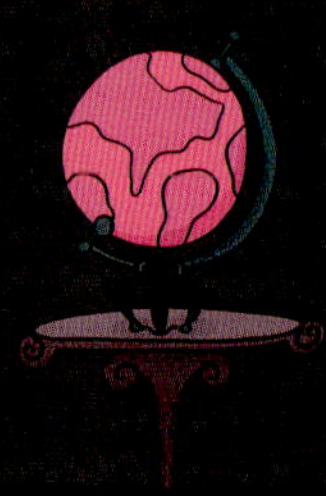

4

Horror Around the World

THERE'S ENOUGH HORROR IN OUR everyday lives that some shy away from consuming it for pleasure. And fair enough—life can be so terrifying, why voluntarily endure more? But what's true and quite beautiful about human nature is that we desire ways to process our experiences and emotions, and to do so we often turn to art. And what better form of art is there to process our real-life horrors, than the queen of metaphor herself, the horror genre?

Enduring life's horrors is a universal experience. It's also what's developed each region's unique horror brand. But what are the local ingredients that make up a country's contribution to the recipe of global horror? The individual combination of events, environmental influences, and cultural practices that have shaped each, thus giving us some of the most impactful contributions to the genre? What occurred in Japan that resulted in J-horror? What about Italy's *giallo*? And what the hell happened in France to make their horror so bloody extreme? Well, what else than the particular histories, beliefs, traumas, legends, rituals, religions, traditions, landscapes—even the food, games, colors, and smells of each? This is what we'll be dissecting next.

Oh! And who's the scariest you ask? That's a never-ending debate I refuse to answer for you. I can through this chapter, however, help you make your own choice . . .

So grab your luggage and sharpen your instruments, we'll now begin our autopsy of global horror—discovering what's under each country's skin by carving them open one at a time. As you board the train please note that between countries, we'll also be stopping by the world's most haunted sites, digging into legends, hunting some very elusive creatures, and diving into deep waters to really capture the full global picture of horror.

Tickets, please!

THE
Screamer

ASIA

you cant go anywhere without feet, can you?
ンリ4世(ブルボン家
ナントの王令
근금지 접근
POLAROID

South Korea

Looking for an evening of being emotionally barbecued while wondering what you did to deserve it?

I recommend taking a trip to South Korea. Korean horror was bred from their history of war, dictatorship, and the mix of a spiritually myth-rich culture that faced rapid modernization. Forget timid ghosts floating around haunted mansions, in Korean horror, the dead are pissed, and the families are violently cursed. Movies like *A Tale of Two Sisters*, *The Wailing*, and *Train to Busan* showed us that Korean horror films aren't about a cheap quick thrill—they're all about social commentary and slow character-driven journeys of survival to confront shame, pain, guilt, and grief. Korean horror . . . the go-to if you want to scream and cry at the same time.

Key Themes

- Fatalism
- Family trauma and curses
- Buried guilt and revenge
- Shame and societal pressure
- Class struggle and inequality
- Female rage and ghost girlies
- Historical trauma

Defining Works

- *Train to Busan*
- *I Saw the Devil*
- *The Wailing*
- *A Tale of Two Sisters*
- *Kingdom*
- *The Call*
- *Hellbound*
- *The Housemaid*
- *Parasite*
- *Squid Games*
- *The Host*

Autopsy of Korean Horror

K-HORROR: K-horror is known for its psychological and emotional depth, stories as social commentary, and gorgeous cinematography—the spoonful of sugar we need to swallow the grotesque bitter pill.

HAN: As we dissect our way through the body of Korean horror, we must examine a morsel found in the heart—han, a concept unique to Korean culture that describes a collective emotional pain felt from injustice and oppression. Han isn't a monster one sees, it's a feeling, and a force that haunts characters in nearly every Korean horror story.

PUJOK: Traditional yellow (the color that repels evil spirits) paper talismans inked in red used in Korean culture to bring good fortune and ward off evil spirits.

GUMIHO: The-nine tailed fox spirit of Korean folktales. Often appears as a demonic seductress who feeds on human flesh, representing vilified and repressed female power and sexuality.

MUDANG: Mudang (shamans, often women) and gut rituals (the ceremonies they perform) are a significant part of Korea's ancient spiritual practice of shamanism. As intermediaries between the mortal and spirit world, mudang use gut rituals to remove curses or exorcise evil.

GWISIN: The ghost who won't ghost . . . waiting to meet you in just a few short pages.

Japan

Japan is the QUEEN of horror. Long before its global explosion in the late 1990s and early 2000s when *Ringu* and *Ju-On* had us scared of VHS tapes, Japan was telling horror stories in all media forms. From kaidan, to kabuki, from manga to video games, few countries have done more to shape the genre into what it has become today.

In Japan, we get less gore and more soul reckoning. Godzilla aside, the monsters aren't green and carnivorous for the sake of a snack, but ghosts of those you've wronged, back for revenge. Fear is less about death and more about shame, guilt, and loneliness. And blood-boiling feminine rage is sharper and scarier than any creature's bloody teeth; just watch *Audition* to see for yourself.

Japan is also a big producer of techno-horror; not horror in the club, unfortunately, but horror exploring the fear of technology—think haunted Nokia bricks and chat rooms. Featuring atmospheric and otherworldly cinematography, Japanese horror sinks you into environments that feel both cold and hot sticky humid.

Defining Works

Film

- *Ringu*
- *Ju-On*
- *Audition*
- *Pulse*
- *Tetsuo: The Iron Man*
- *Onibaba*
- *Kwaidan*
- *One Missed Call*
- *Cure*
- *Dark Water*

Manga

- Uzumaki series: Junji Ito
- Tomie series: Junji Ito
- The Drifting Classroom series: Kazuo Umezu
- *Hell Baby*: Hideshi Hino

Video Games

- *Kuon*
- *Siren*
- *Resident Evil*
- *Silent Hill*

Key Themes

- Shame and regret
- Cursed objects
- Urban isolation
- Haunted technology
- Ghosts with grudges

Autopsy of Japanese Horror

KAIDAN: Traditional Japanese ghost stories with supernatural elements most commonly passed down orally.

KABUKI: Traditional Japanese theater scaring people before movies and manga. Starting in the 1600s, kabuki theater was full of ghosts, revenge stories, eerie makeup, and betrayed women.

YUREI: Japanese term for your basic ghost, can be any gender, with any lingering emotion.

ONYRO: More on the angry side of the spectrum, she's waiting to tell you all about it on the next page . . . proceed with caution.

YOKAI: Japanese folklore creatures like the kappa, kitsune, or oni.

J-HORROR: The modern style of Japanese horror that exploded in the late 1990s, early 2000s defined by vengeful spirits, emotional trauma, and cursed objects. Gore < Mood.

MANGA: Japanese comics and graphic novels are Japan's other horror powerhouse. Many of the countries scariest, most absurd, and most brutal stories came from manga horror masters like Junji Ito, Hideshi Hino, and Kazuo Umezu.

THE *RING* AND THE *GRUDGE*: *Ringu* and *Ju-On*'s Western adaptations placed people in two strict camps—invigorated horror fan or scarred viewer. *The Ring* was produced by Gore Verbinski while *The Grudge* was produced by Takashi Shimizu, the creator of the original Japanese *Ju-On*.

VIDEO GAMES: The horror games from Japan are some of the scariest, most gorgeous, and genre-influencing works of art among the entire genre.

Autopsy of the Vengeful Ghost

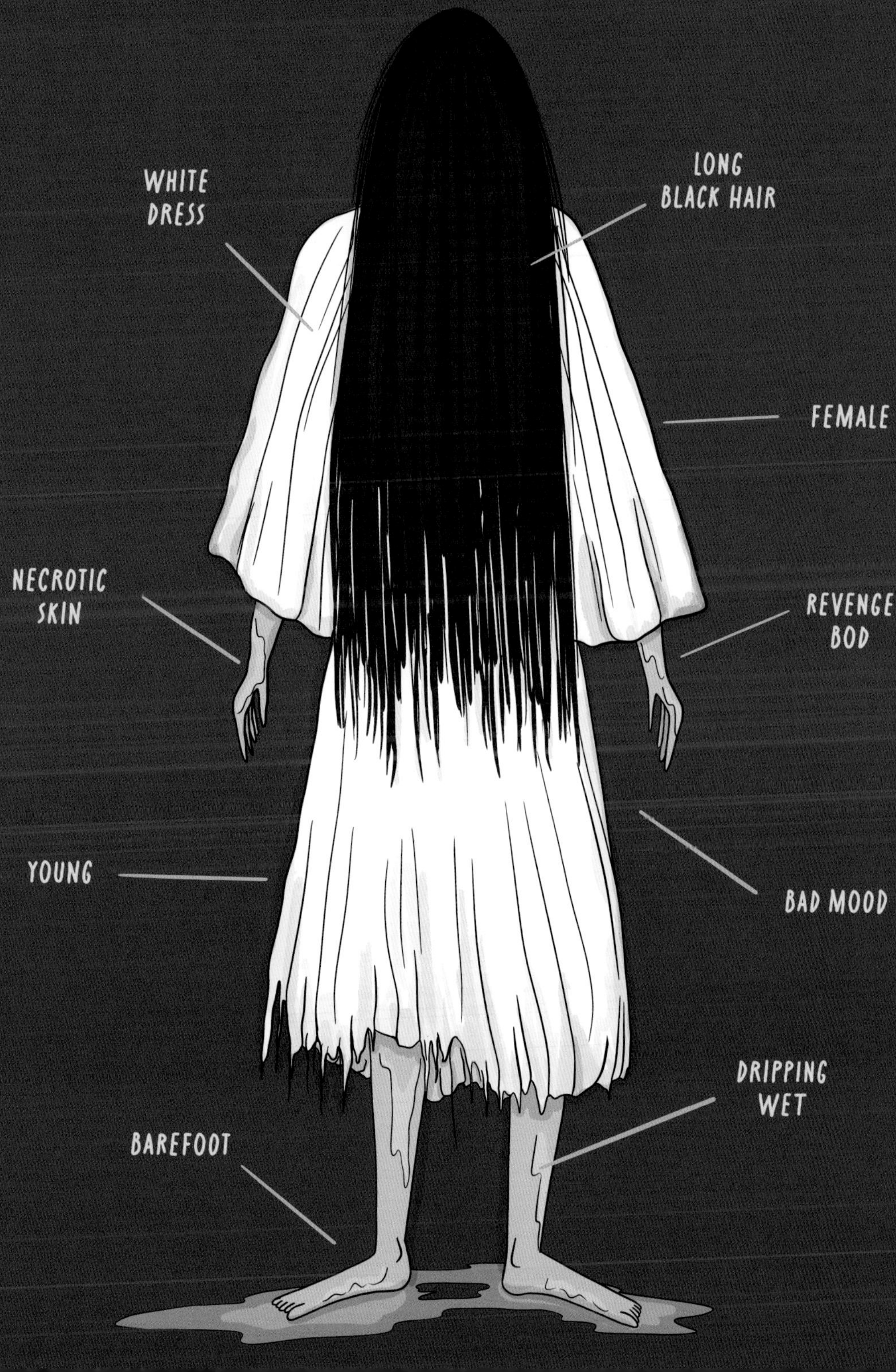

In the US, she crawled out of our TV sets dripping wet as Samara Morgan in 2002. But before her adapted Western appearance, and long before the dawn of cinema even, the vengeful female ghost, dressed in white with long black hair was already a mainstay in Asian lore.

Although each country's version of her has its own nuances and variations, there are many similarities beyond her OOTD. So let's dissect this iconic horror figure. Why does she haunt countries across Asia? Where did she come from? What does she represent? Why is she, always a she? And why is she always so pissed?

The long-haired female ghost in a white dress appears across Asian horror—from Japan's onyro to Indonesia's Pontianak—because she embodies painful unresolved trauma, and gendered injustice experienced during life personally and cross-culturally. Many of these women are portrayed as ghosts because they've died unmarried, pregnant, or in childbirth, a fate seen in Confucian, Buddhist, and other regional beliefs as an incomplete life that traps their souls forever in unrest . . . Whoa, not fair.

She's almost always a woman because she represents fear of the feminine uncontained—rage, grief, and power that was suppressed in life now returning with brutal unforgivable force. She was betrayed, cheated on, murdered, or abandoned in life. Her long, black, unbound hair reflects death rituals where a woman's hair is left loose, and her white dress mirrors the funeral shrouds and color of mourning in Japan, China, Korea, and Thailand.

These ghosts are terrifying but so justified. They died silenced, wronged, single, pregnant, and with unfinished business. If I were to go in this way, you bet I'd be climbing out of a dank well filled with stagnant inky water to serve justice too.

The following ghosts are born from Asian horror, but their rage transcends boundaries and represents the silent fury of women everywhere.

JAPAN - ONYRO

Vengeful spirits who died in rage or sorrow and return to seek revenge.

KOREA - GWISIN

Spirits of unmarried women who died unjustly or before fulfilling their societal roles of marriage and motherhood.

CHINA - NU GUI

Female ghosts who were betrayed or wronged, often returning for vengeance or justice. Sometimes wear red instead of white to symbolize their rage.

PHILIPPINES - WHITE LADIES

Spirits of women wronged by lovers or victims of violent deaths back for revenge.

INDONESIA AND MALAYSIA - KUNTILANAK AND PONTIANAK

Vengeful spirit of a woman who died during pregnancy or childbirth who hunts men by seducing them and killing them and steals infants to kill.

THAILAND - MAE NAK

A woman who died in childbirth returns donning the long black hair but dressed in traditional Thai garments of varying colors.

Aokigahara

At the base of Mount Fuji lies Aokigahara, known as the Sea of Trees—a dense, otherworldly moss-covered forest, woven across ancient lava beds. Its winding roots and haunting stillness have made it both a place of heartbreaking beauty and heartbreaking sorrow. For decades, the Aokigahara forest, also now known as the Suicide Forest, has drawn thousands in despair into its quiet labyrinthine depths to take their own lives. The forest's tragic history, spiritual weight, traditional beliefs in the restless spirits of Japanese folklore, yurei, and dark lore, have made it a recurring setting in horror films, poetry, video games, music, and urban legends. Warning signs at its entrance compassionately plea for reconsideration, yet horror continues to return and reinforce its global reputation as one of the most haunted places on earth.

Polaroid
Impulse

Thailand

Thai horror is infused with religion, folklore, and local traditions, but although these typical origins do shape the country's horror, they're not the primary trait that make it the unique and powerful art form that it is.

Buddhism, Thai Shamanism, ghost tales, and rituals gone wrong are the limbs of Thailand's scary stories, but what gives it its reputation for being so globally impactful, touching, and absolutely horrifying—what's really the *heart* of Thai horror—is our own complex experience as human beings, and how absolutely terrifying that truly can be. In Thailand, horror is personal. It's grief-stricken. It's not gore leaning, it's psychological. The stories center around the supernatural, but the ghosts are rarely "evil" and more often personify the most violent emotional pain that lives within us all. Heartbreak becomes the haunt, guilt becomes the ghost. In Thailand, the spirits seek resolution over retribution. The country is also known for incorporating contrasting genres into their horror, like comedy and romance. One may think this would dilute the fear factor, but in actuality, by sending us on a holistic and complex emotional journey akin to our authentic experience, it only makes the horror hit harder, and certainly more devastatingly than its Western counterparts. Thai horror goes back centuries with origins in oral storytelling; its modern era began in the 1950s. But in the early 2000s with films like *Shutter* and *Art of the Devil*, it exploded onto the scene and became a powerhouse of the genre.

Defining Works

Pee Mak

Laddaland

The Medium

Dorm

Body sob 19

Alone

The Promise

Key Themes

Ghosts as moral reckoning

Buddhism and reincarnation

Ritual and taboo

Love and loss

Karmic retribution

Autopsy Of Thai Horror

MAE NAK: Thailand's most iconic ghost, Mae Nak, is a woman who died during childbirth but is so deeply devoted and in love with her husband, she is unable to move on and returns for him. Her tragic tale has been retold countless times in Thai horror (like *Nang Nak* and *Pee Mak*), and her legend lives on—literally—at a real shrine in Bangkok where locals still leave offerings to honor her spirit.

SPIRIT HOUSES: Nearly all homes in Thailand have a san phra phum, a shrine for protective spirits. These structures often show up in Thai horror narratives as a location corrupted by a malevolent force or as a symbol of the supernatural.

SHUTTER: Banjong Pisanthanakun and Parkpoom Wongpoom's 2004 film, *Shutter*, is praised as one of the most iconic Asian horror films of all time and put Thailand on the global horror map. The story, involving a photographer, was so influential that camera-related ghost horror became its own trend in Asia. The film was remade in the US in 2008.

Europe

THE United Kingdom

The United Kingdom, made up of England, Scotland, Wales, and Northern Ireland, is one of the most foundational horror cultures in the world, with its distinct visuals of damp-to-the-bone foggy landscapes, cloaks, ghosts floating around manors with perfectly trimmed hedges, decaying class systems, small pubs in rocky coastal villages, tight-laced corsets, and prim manners contrasted with back-alley murder à la Jack the Ripper. It's where gothic horror was born (giving us Frankenstein and Dracula), Hammer horror was founded, and pagan traditions birthed folk horror like *The Wicker Man*. UK horror is where the ghosts still wear wool, the moors have eyes, and the pretty little tea cakes are laced with poison.

Key Themes

- Madness
- Obsession over social hierarchy and reputation
- Crumbling class systems
- Moral repression
- Folk rituals and paganism
- Mood as monster
- House as character

Defining Works

FILM

- *The Wicker Man*
- *Horror of Dracula*
- *The Curse of Frankenstein*
- *Kill List*
- *Saint Maud*
- *The Descent*
- *Hellraiser*
- *28 Days Later*
- *Shaun of the Dead*
- *The Devils*
- *An American Werewolf in London*
- *The Innocents*
- *Witchfinder General*
- *The Ritual*
- *Ghostwatch*

LITERATURE

- Mary Shelley – *Frankenstein*
- Bram Stoker – *Dracula*
- Susan Hill – *The Woman in Black*
- Clive Barker – *The Hellbound Heart*
- Daphne du Maurier – *Rebecca*

Autopsy of UK Horror

HAMMER HORROR: With enough fake blood to drown a vampire, Hammer horror is the gothic-meets-Technicolor style of the over 160 films made by small UK film studio—Hammer Film Productions—from the 1950s to the 1970s.

THE PENNY DREADFUL: Serialized stories published in pamphlets in the UK during the mid-nineteenth century, sold for one penny per issue. Filled with crime, pulpy horror, creatures, and gory gothic melodrama, they always ended on a cliff-hanger. At the time, horror was only in elite, high literature format, and the penny dreadful brought it to the working class. Illustrated with lurid woodcuts and quickly hacked together, they were the original zine!

SPAIN

A country so deeply influenced by its artists—Picasso, Goya, Velazquez, Dali, Miro, Gaudi—that it created its own unique visual language of horror: gritty, cracked, faded, and dry. You can feel the heat radiating off the crumbling orphanage walls, or bear witness to an atmosphere that's rich, gothic, and damp. Different, but both equally evocative, beautiful, and distinctly Spanish. In the wake of Franco's dictatorship and authoritarian control, filmmakers like Alejandro Amenábar and Paco Plaza use every bit of the country's experience as fodder for their twisted and painful but gorgeous horror stories.

Defining Works

The Devil's Backbone
Pan's Labyrinth
[•REC]
The Orphanage
Verónica
Who Can Kill a Child?
The Day of the Beast
Sleep Tight
The Nameless
The Spirit of the Beehive
The Platform
Witching & Bitching
Shrew's Nest
30 Coins
The Grandmother
The Skin I Live In

Key Themes

The Spanish Civil War and Franco's dictatorship are integral to Spanish horror. Filmmakers often set stories in orphanages, ruined towns, or homes under strict control to reflect trauma, repression, and fear. During Franco's regime, explicit political critique was banned, so filmmakers were compelled to use metaphor, symbolism, and allegory to tell their stories.

We experience a lot of Spanish horror through the eyes of children. Mexico's legendary filmmaker Guillermo del Toro's Spanish-produced films like *The Devil's Backbone* and *Pan's Labyrinth* (both set during the Spanish Civil War and told through children) are cornerstones of horror.

Italy

Welcome to the grand opera house of horror. It's crying, it's dying, it's bleeding, it's screaming. It's deeply shaped by the country's Catholic heritage, fine art traditions, dark political chaos of the Years of Lead, and flair for aesthetic transgression. It's horror as art and high fashion, where the mere act of bleeding is beautiful. Italian horror changed the genre forever by reframing horror as art, demonstrating that death—even murder—can be beautiful.

Key Themes

- Dreams and hallucinations
- Paranoia and power
- The Catholic Church
- Political terror
- The body as canvas
- Madness

Autopsy of Italian Horror

Cultural Influences

- Venetian Carnival and masquerade festivals
- Opera and theater
- The Years of Lead
- The malocchio (evil eye)
- High fashion

Italian Horror Style

Bloody. Baroque. Chiaroscuro. Neon on marble. Blood as paint. Gliding cameras. Long takes. Vivid, rich palettes. Noir. Eyes. Masks. Mirrors. Espresso. Red lipstick. Fast cars. Cigarettes. Operatic opulence. Black velvet. Carnal sin.

GIALLO: Before it was a film genre, giallo was the name for Italy's cheap, sensational crime novels—think penny dreadfuls but with more sex, murder, and mystery in vintage Prada smoking a cigarette. These paperbacks with bright yellow covers (*giallo* is "yellow" in Italian), drove the people wild, shaping a national obsession that eventually made its way onto the screen.

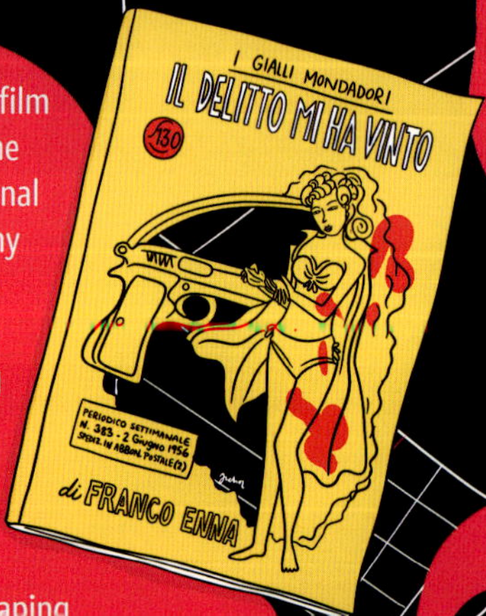

DARIO ARGENTO: Giallo god Dario Argento's work, most notably *Suspiria* (1977), with its crazy bold colors, atmosphere, fever dream Expressionistic sets, and music (he hired the prog rock band Goblin to score it) changed horror forever.

Defining Works

- *Suspiria*
- *Black Sabbath*
- *Deep Red*
- *Don't Torture a Duckling*
- *The Beyond*
- *Blood and Black Lace*
- *Black Sunday*
- *Bay of Blood*
- *Tenebrae*
- *Inferno*
- *Opera*
- *Cannibal Holocaust*

Germany

From the country that gave us psychology—the scientific study of the human mind—comes the most cerebral contribution to the horror genre yet.

Through jagged nightmarish dreamscapes, exaggerated vampiric shadows, brutalist architecture, harsh lighting, and twisted angles, German horror, specifically the horror created during the German Expressionist movement of the 1920s, manifested the darkest, most distorted corners of our psyche, and essentially invented the visual language of horror. Unlike other countries that rely on external entities like ghosts and monsters (although Germany's famous film *The Golem* is seen as one of horror's earliest man-made monster movies), German horror tends to look more inward, finding terror in psychology, and philosophy.

Key Themes

- Madness, duality, and identity
- Authority and obedience
- Existential and philosophical dread
- Isolation and paganism

Defining Works

Nosferatu: A Symphony of Horror (dir. F. W. Murnau, 1922)
The unauthorized adaptation of Bram Stoker's *Dracula*, known for being an influential masterpiece and the most iconic vampire film of all time. Stoker's widow, Florence Stoker, sued the makers of the film, demanding that all negatives be destroyed. Even though she won the suit, negatives resurfaced, and the film was out by 1929. *Nosferatu* was remade by Werner Herzog in 1979 and Robert Eggers in 2024.

- *The Cabinet of Dr. Caligari*
- *The Golem*
- *Funny Games*
- *The White Ribbon*
- *The Samurai*
- *Goodnight Mommy*
- *Hagazussa*
- *Luz*

Autopsy of German Horror

German Expressionism

German Expressionism emerged in the silent film era of the 1920s, marked by a distorted, exaggerated visual style that reflected the fractured psyche of post–World War I society. The films became psychological landscapes—like M. C. Escher drawings (although he was Dutch, not German), full of geometric harshness that bred intentional unease. Because that unease was both effective and gorgeously striking, it laid the groundwork for global visual horror, influencing everything from Universal's classic monsters to Tim Burton, David Lynch, and every college indie kid with a film degree.

German horror evolved out of folklore, through the gruesome Grimms' fairy tales, and into early silent films like *Nosferatu* and *The Cabinet of Dr. Caligari*. It survived the Weimar Republic and Nazi rule effectively banning it and came back with vengeance and depth during the postwar era of Germany's attempt to redefine its identity. It skyrocketed with a shock wave of underground filmmakers like Jörg Buttgereit, who explored taboos with films like *Nekromantik* in the 1980s, and is thriving today in contemporary horror where a new wave of filmmakers are using the art form to discuss feminist and gender themes in unnervingly scary and poignant ways.

France

In 1896, Georges Méliès rolled hand-colored film on *The House of the Devil,* a silent short now regarded as the first horror film ever made.

The House of the Devil was tame, your classic silent film with elements that were more silly than scary. It wasn't until a year later, in 1897, that France galvanized its position in the genre with the establishment of the Grand-Guignol—a radical horror theater focusing on sensational macabre scenes full of violence and shock. Out of the Grand-Guignol grew mid-century French cult classics like *Diabolique* and *Eyes Without a Face*, films that can't go unmentioned but still paled in comparison to the bloodbath to come—the New French Extremity. In the early 2000s, the New French Extremity hit like a knife in the chest as the most graphic, violent, vulgar, and confrontational horror style to ever exist. It not only redefined French horror as one of the most intellectually disturbing genres in global cinema, but it massacred and reshaped the entire genre itself, leaving a lasting legacy that is as radical, raw, and as bloody as beef tartare.

Defining Works

- *The House of the Devil*
- *Diabolique*
- *Eyes Without a Face*
- *La rose de fer* (*The Iron Rose*)
- *Trouble Every Day*
- *High Tension*
- *Inside*
- *Frontier(s)*
- *Martyrs*
- *Raw*
- *Climax*
- *Titane*

Key Themes

- Transgression
- Body horror
- Existential dread
- Alienation
- Sadism and suffering
- Sexuality
- Moral ambiguity
- Societal collapse
- Taboo confrontation

Autopsy Of French Horror

GRAND-GUIGNOL

The Grand-Guignol was the birthplace of live horror theater and known for its grisly short plays that blended graphic gore with psychological torment, always about the horrors of human nature. Audiences flooded to the smallest theater in Paris and sat in confessional-like boxes. The effects were so intense that audience members regularly fainted, screamed, or burst into applause—it was all very dramatic.

NEW FRENCH EXTREMITY

Nothing is off-limits when it comes to the defining style of New French Extremity. Yes, this wave of artful, boundary-pushing films contains cannibalism, incest, sadism, self-harm, maternal violence, rape, mutilation, and a whole lot of screaming. They are shocking, but it's not for shock's sake. Though occasionally hyperbolic, they're honest, unhindered critiques of repression, purity, and control. French Extremity steps around horror's typical format of lesson through suggestive metaphor and makes us face the horrors of ourselves and our world straight on. It's existential. It's brutal. And it's brilliant.

Europe's Most Haunted

Moosham Castle

As the site of both the seventeenth-century Zaubererjackl witch trials (Austria's grisliest, killing 139 people including children, most of whom were poor and homeless, in slow torturous deaths) and "werewolf hunts" (more killing of innocent people), this castle is vibrating with restless spirits.

Poveglia Island

This plague pit holding a hundred thousand of those who died from the Black Death in fourteenth-century Italy is considered one of the most haunted places on earth. Wear a mask when you visit.

York, England

Following centuries of Roman, Viking, and medieval carnage, more than the pubs are filled with spirits in York, England. With over five hundred ghost sightings, the city of York claims the title of the most haunted city in Europe.

The Tower of London

On the top of every "Most Haunted Places in the World" list lies the Tower of London. Built by William the Conqueror in 1066, the tower is the best place to visit if you're looking to run into the ghosts of the murdered, imprisoned, trapped, or executed there over the last one thousand years. You may even bump into Anne Boleyn carrying her own head around like a purse.

Leap Castle

Ireland's most-haunted, not-so-basic, spooky castle. Home to an extra special treat, the "elemental," a grotesque ghost said to reek of death and sulfur. Lore says it was conjured during occult rituals being performed in the castle's hidden oubliette. But what did they expect?

The Edinburgh Vaults

With its violent history saturated with vampires, witches, cannibalism, murder, haunted castles, graveyards, and ghosts, Edinburgh, Scotland, is one of the most well-rounded haunted cities. The real haunt actually lies beneath the seventeenth century streets, though, in the Edinburgh Vaults, the series of tunnels where body snatchers used to stash their stolen corpses.

The Ten Bells Pub

Located in London's East End, the Ten Bells is gin soaked in Victorian grime and murder. Infamous for its connection to Jack the Ripper, two of his victims were last seen drinking here and have now appropriately made it their local haunt.

Chateau De Brissac

The tallest castle in France and home to Charlotte de Brézé, who, after being caught cheating on her husband in the fifteenth century, was murdered in a fit of rage while wearing her signature green dress. After the murder-divorce she changed her name to La Dame Verte, or the "green lady," and can be found moaning around the castle halls to this day.

Bran Castle

Perched high in the Carpathian Mountains, Romania's Bran Castle is forever linked to the legend of Dracula. While its ties to Vlad the Impaler (Dracula's inspo) are loose, it's the iconic gothic style of stone halls, secret passageways, and turrets piercing a full blood-moon sky that keep the vampire lore alive here.

The Paris Catacombs

Beneath the streets of Paris lies a labyrinth of tunnels holding the bones of over six million people. Originally created to replace the city's overflowing cemeteries, the catacombs are now overflowing with ghosts, and to be honest, I wouldn't mind having my bones arranged after death in a decorative manner for viewing. So chic!

THE HAUNTED Castle

The castle is barren, yet the torches are lit. A ghost of a king on a throne he doth sit, with his headless wife roaming the halls, can you find your way along the walls? Begin in the boat launch then choose your route, heed green fire to the dungeon, and you'll surely get out.

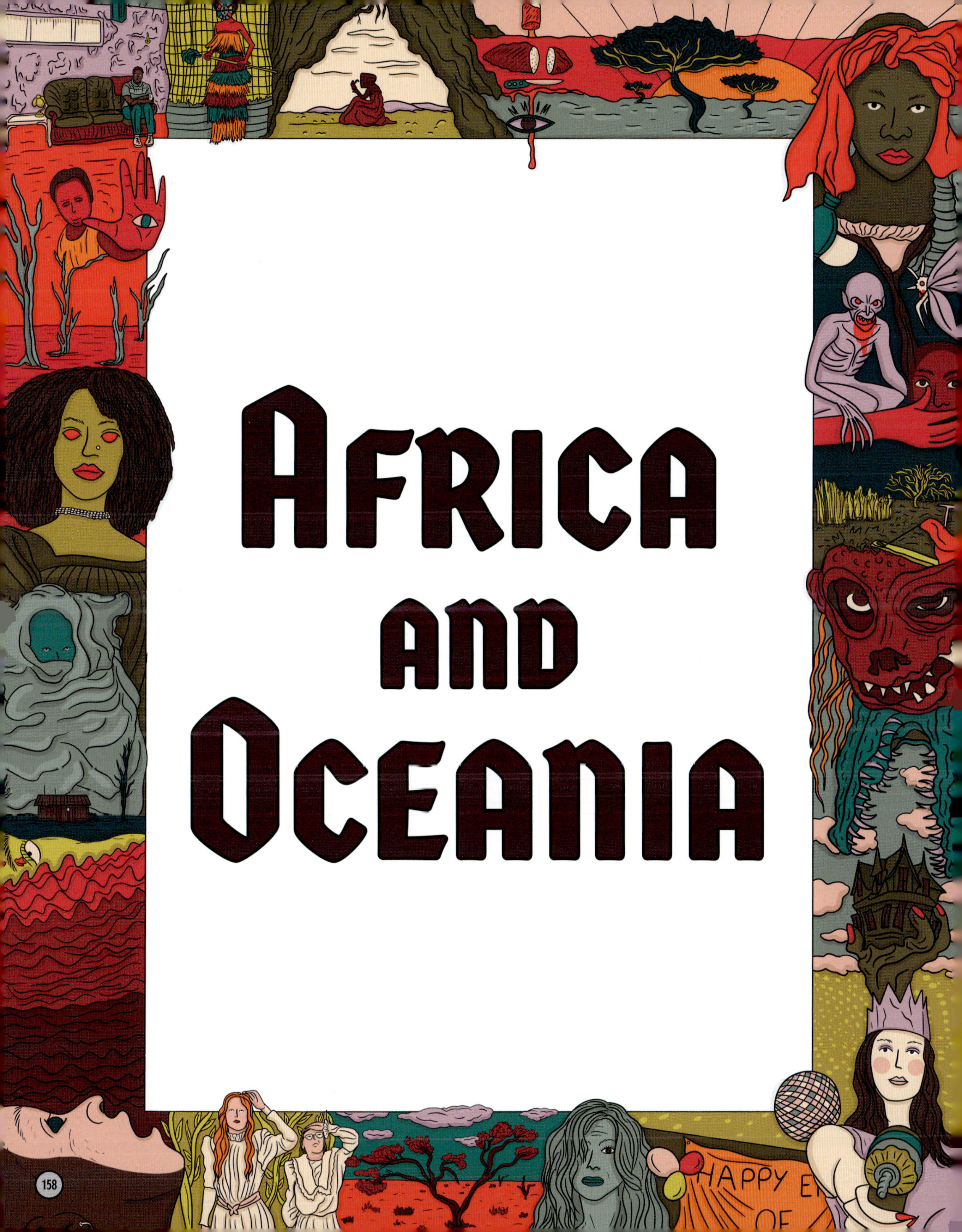

Africa and Oceania

Australia

Like a fly swarming around sun-bleached animal bones, Australia is buzzing with horror. Australia's stories have been shaped over 65,000 years on vast brutal landscapes, unforgiving sun, drought, endless highways, and bloodred earth. The Australian film boom hit in the 1970s and 1980s during the Ozploitation era, when films like *Long Weekend*, *Roadgames*, and *Razorback* mixed eco-horror, slashers, and grindhouse gore with unique Aussie nihilism. Then came the 2000s resurgence, led by *Wolf Creek*—a feral, landmark film that redefined Outback terror and introduced the world to the sadistic charm of Mick Taylor. Modern Aussie horror continues to thrive but is leaning away from external fear forces and into internal ones with revolutionary films like *The Babadook*, *Relic*, and *Talk to Me*, which explore psychological themes like depression, grief, and family trauma. First Nations horror voices are also rising and emerging creators are using horror to retell Dreamtime stories, challenge settler narratives, and confront the true ghosts of their history.

Key Themes

- Colonial horror, Indigenous silence, an erasure
- Emotional repression
- The land as antagonist
- Madness and isolation
- Gender violence and power struggle

Defining Works

- *Wake in Fright*
- *Picnic at Hanging Rock*
- *The Last Wave*
- *Long Weekend*
- *Roadgames*
- *Razorback*
- *Rogue*
- *Lake Mungo*
- *Wolf Creek*
- *Snowtown*
- *The Loved Ones*
- *The Tunnel*
- *The Babadook*
- *Hounds of Love*
- *Relic*
- *Sissy*
- *Late Night with the Devil*
- *Talk to Me*

Autopsy of Aussie Horror

***WAKE IN FRIGHT*:** This movie was lost for years but when resurrected it was deemed "the scariest Australian film ever made."

THE YOWIE: Australia's Bigfoot is a popular cryptid appearing in oral stories, schoolyard legend, and indie horror.

THE LANDSCAPE: Stories of vanished campers, haunted mine shafts, and cursed stretches of highway are all part of Australia's regional folklore.

***LAKE MUNGO*:** This film is so convincing it's often mistaken for a real documentary.

***WOLF CREEK*:** This film inspired a massive tourism drop in Outback hostels. Oops.

DREAMTIME STORYTELLING: First Nations creation stories that tell of how the land and life began—ancient, spiritual tales that still influence Aussie horror today.

OZPLOITATION: A genre of cinema, particularly in vogue in Australia during the seventies and eighties. These films were low-budget, raw, exploitative, and featured elements of horror, action, sex, and gore.

Nigeria

Nigeria is one of the most underexplored yet rapidly emerging forces in global horror. In the 1990s, as Nollywood exploded with straight to VHS films shot on shoestring budgets, horror began to permeate living rooms across the country. With little government funding, strict religious censorship, and a deeply spiritual public, filmmakers didn't turn to vampires and aliens for fear factor but instead real-life fears that spoke directly to faith, community, survival, morality, crime, and traditional practices and belief systems.

Living in Bondage kicked it off in 1992, telling the story of a man who sacrifices his wife for wealth and is haunted by her ghost. *Karishika* followed in 1998, which unleashed a seductive demon from hell to drag the sinful down with her. These films became iconic immediate cult classics and had a huge impact on Nigerian pop culture. While we were trying to avoid the "seven days" phone call after watching *The Ring*, Nigerians were avoiding the allegedly cursed VHS tapes being circulated.

Today, innovative contemporary film studios like Surreal16 Collective are disrupting the scene by blending the roots of folklore and urban legends with an Afrofuturist edge and beautiful cinematography, keeping Nigerian horror fresh, rich, and really scary.

Key Themes

- The church
- Conflicting spiritual and religious beliefs
- Witchcraft, spirits, and possession
- Ancestral curses and supernatural
- Generational sin and family legacy
- Community vs. the individual
- Unfinished business
- Morality
- Jealousy

Autopsy of Nigerian Horror

OGBANJE: Evil spirits believed to be within children who die young and return to torment.

JUJU AND RITUAL MAGIC: In horror, rituals often reflect real practices or exaggerated fears of traditional religions to show the consequences of seeking power, wealth, revenge, or anything nefarious.

DREAMS: Spending time in dreams is a signature of Nigerian horror. Dreams aren't metaphorical, they're active battlegrounds that can affect characters who wake up marked, cursed, or changed.

MADAM KOI KOI: The African urban legend of a beautiful ghost who in her signature red heels haunts school hallways.

Nollywood

Nollywood is Nigeria's prolific film industry based in Lagos known for its fast-paced, low-budget productions that go straight to the people. The decades of Nollywood's horror films are raw and full of shaky handheld camera shots and fast-paced editing (classic Nollywood style) and have massively influenced global horror.

Defining Works

Karishika	*Raging Storm*
Oracle	*Ijogbon* (*The Chaos*)
Sakobi	*Blood Money*
Living in Bondage	*Witches*
End of the Wicked	*The Last Burial*
Juju Stories	*Willie Willie*

South Africa

South Africa's stories are shaped by its history—the unhealed wounds of apartheid, land theft, political and domestic violence, and cultural division all bleed into its horror. By using horror to confront its past, it's become one of the most politically overt horror scenes in the world. South African horror also leans hard on metaphor. Films like *District 9* (a South Africa and New Zealand coproduction) reframe xenophobia through alien segregation, while intentional settings, architecture, and landscapes like asylums and cursed rural land represent being trapped in environments shaped by racial violence, psychological trauma, and national denial. Traditional practices, beliefs, myths, and African folklore often appear in horror as well. Today, with its blend of Indigenous cosmology, politically charged voices, and a genre-savvy generation of new creators, we get a bold, visceral, brutal, and authentically African contribution to the genre.

Autopsy of South African Horror

APARTHEID: The system of legalized racial segregation enforced in South Africa from 1948 to the early 1990s. Under apartheid, the white minority government controlled nearly every aspect of life, stripping Black South Africans of land, rights, and freedom. Its legacy still haunts the country, and infiltrates the majority of South African artistic expression.

MUTI/MUTHI: Horror films about South Africa sometimes feature references to muti—a traditional African spiritual and medicinal practice—that are often exaggerated or misrepresented for dramatic effect. While muti itself is a respected part of many Indigenous belief systems, horror unfortunately leans into one of its cheapest ways of soliciting a scare by focusing on its darker, more sensationalized and outsider interpretations of rituals.

THE TOKOLOSHE: The most famous figure of South African folklore (catch him in chapter 1). This impish water sprite plays tricks and wreaks havoc on the unfortunate to a tortuous and sometimes fatal extent.

SOUTH AFRICAN HORROR FEST: Starting in 2005, it's Africa's biggest horror event! The annual horror fest doesn't exclusively show South African films but instead celebrates all mediums of horror from around the world.

Defining Works

The Demon	*Good Madam*	*Fried Barry*
Dust Devil	*The Tokoloshe*	*Glasshouse*
The Soul Collector	*District 9*	*Rage*
Gaia	*Breathing In*	

New Zealand (Aotearoa)

When you think of New Zealand you might be thrown into a serene vision of lush blue-green fields, hobbits, country living, and garden patches . . . But I'm sorry to tell you it's about to be splattered in sheep's blood (good thing red and green are complementary colors). New Zealand might be small in size, but it punches way above its weight in horror. This island nation's horror style is absurdist, gorgeous, campy, and with its national sense of dark and dry humor . . . funny? Kiwi horror thrives on genre-bending contrast, and it all started with Peter Jackson. Yes, that Peter Jackson, and his unhinged early work that splashed gore across the screen with wild abandon and punk glee. As the genre matured, it began to fold in deeper, older voices of the Māori, their legends, and their postcolonial experience. Together, New Zealand has carved out a genre space that's wild, weird, and full of mana.

Key Themes

- Isolation in nature
- Historical haunting
- Dark humor and gore
- Māori spiritual influence
- Monsters as metaphors

NZ Adjacent

- *X*
- *Pearl*
- *M3GAN*
- *Evil Dead Rise*

Defining Works

- *Dead Alive (Braindead)*
- *Bad Taste*
- *Meet the Feebles*
- *Black Sheep*
- *The Frighteners*
- *Housebound*
- *What We Do in the Shadows*
- *The Dead Lands*
- *Deathgasm*

Autopsy Of Kiwi Horror

MĀORI: The Māori people give New Zealand horror its spine, grounding it in a spiritual worldview where land (whenua), spirit (wairua), and sacredness (tapu) are inseparable. Contemporary Māori voices are reshaping the genre—using horror to confront colonial violence and reclaim stories through myth and terror.

COLLAB-HORROR-ATION: Some of the most famous American-produced horror films in the past decade, like Ti West's *X* and *Pearl* and New Zealand's own Gerard Johnstone's *M3GAN*, were filmed in New Zealand with large amounts of Kiwi cast and crew members.

***WHAT WE DO IN THE SHADOWS*:** (NZ film preceding the TV series) is the perfect example of how Kiwis love to genre mix and serve their scary with a side of silly.

PETER JACKSON: Before he ruled Middle-earth, Peter Jackson was the Lord of the Gore. Armed with household tools, a twisted sense of humor, and buckets of fake blood, he launched his career with low-budget splatterfests like *Bad Taste*, *Meet the Feebles*, and *Dead Alive* (still hailed as the goriest horror film of all time). His production company, WingNut Films, now known for *The Lord of the Rings* films, originally carved its name into horror history—helping shape New Zealand's proudly DIY bloody film scene.

THE Haunted High Seas

Our world's vast landscapes host horrors of all sorts: They creep in caves, crawl among jungles, plains, and rainforests, they live in our minds, our houses, our basements, the structures we build, and the soil we build them on. But what about the vast expanse that connects our lands? And what's to say it's not the largest horror host of them all?

The horror genre has an ancient love affair with the sea. With its endless monotonous expanse that so easily drives us to madness, its unpredictability, and its stillness—just as threatening as its tempests. Its sentient nature and merciless power, one we foolishly believe we can conquer and appease. Its mystique and lore that fuels our superstitious minds, and the vengeful controlling forces that make us turn on each other, commit mutiny, and cannibalism. We are transfixed by the horrors of the sea, at the mercy of it, and forever falling prey to its hypnotic pull. Only through the horror genre can we fully explore this sublime body that swallows us whole, never to return our souls. The ship is now boarding, find your lantern-lit cabin, we embark at nightfall.

A Descent into the Depths

The watery elements that make up the horror stories of the sea.

The *Flying Dutchman*

Maritime myth royalty, this ghost ship eternally sails the seas, cursed to never come ashore.

The *Mary Celeste*

A true ghost ship—the *Mary Celeste* was found drifting in perfect condition, with dinner still set, without a soul on board.

Octavius

The ghostly vessel found in the Arctic's Northwest Passage completely frozen for thirteen years . . . the captain was found mid-log entry, pen in hand, frozen solid.

Ghost Ships

SS *Ourang Medan*

Legend says that after making a distress call saying "I die," the crew of the phantom freighter was found dead with looks of terror frozen on their faces.

SS *Baychimo*

The longest surviving ghost ship, this Arctic trading steamer appeared drifting on and off over a span of forty years. Its last sighting was in 1969.

El Caleuche

A luminescent, music-filled ghost ship from Chilean folklore said to be crewed by demons and witches. The ship can shape-shift to camouflage itself or disappear in a flash.

Those Who Haunt the Decks

JACKIE

One of the lingering ghosts upon another famous ship, the *Queen Mary*, this young girl dressed in white is said to haunt the swimming pool. Makes sense since her last act was drowning in it.

DAVY JONES

The legendary nautical grim reaper who presides over all evil entities of the deep (not someone you want to share a locker with).

CAPTAIN VAN DER DECKEN

The eternally damned captain of the *Flying Dutchman*, cursed never to make landfall again.

CAPTAIN BLAKE

The captain who returned one hundred years later to avenge himself and his crew for their murder in the 1980 film *The Fog*.

Lighthouses

Perched on the edge of the world, their beacons barely permeating the darkness that shrouds the ancient hungry sea, lighthouses stand as the barrier between the living and the dead. These crumbling forts trap their keepers in isolated spirals of routine, driving fragile human minds to obsession, decay, and madness. If you ever find yourself in the liminal space of a lighthouse you may want to follow the protection ritual of burying a dead black cat or rooster near the foundation.

Creatures of the Deep

Mermaids with serrated teeth, sirens, selkies, sea witches, and giant tentacled monsters swim among our stories, ready to drag you to your watery grave. These mythical creatures woven from sailor superstitions and coastal folklore act as warnings—don't stray too far from home, don't take what's not yours, and never be foolish enough to think you're more powerful than the force that is the ocean; after all, it's not you who can breathe under water.

Fisherman Lore Superstition and Myth

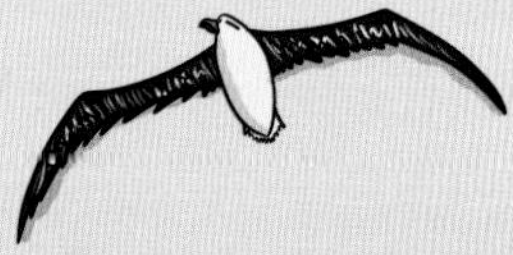

Killing an **ALBATROSS** brings doom, for they are believed to carry the souls of dead sailors.

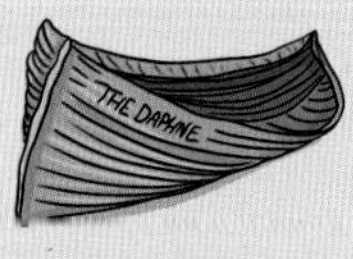

It's said the sea gods keep a ledger of all **SHIP NAMES**. Changing them without permission is tempting fate.

WHISTLING is said to summon the wind, potentially bringing storms and angering the spirits of the drowned.

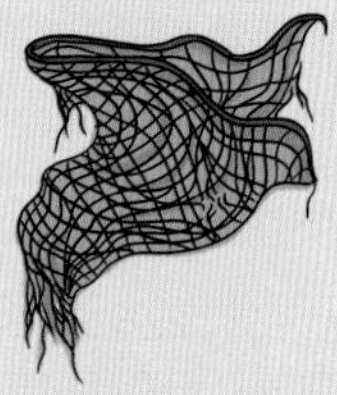

FISHING NETS lost at sea (ghost nets) are cursed traps that catch souls or lead boats into dangerous waters.

Speaking **CERTAIN WORDS** like *pig*, *priest*, or *rabbit* at sea is taboo and will bring bad luck to those who whisper them.

After the drowning of coastal villages, sometimes their **CHURCH BELLS** continue to toll. Hearing them is considered a bad omen.

Symbols of the Sea

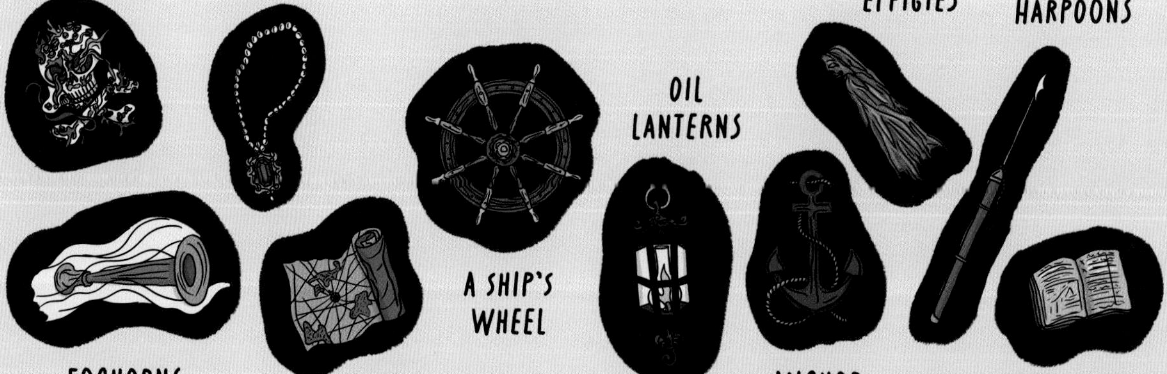

AUTOPSY OF A

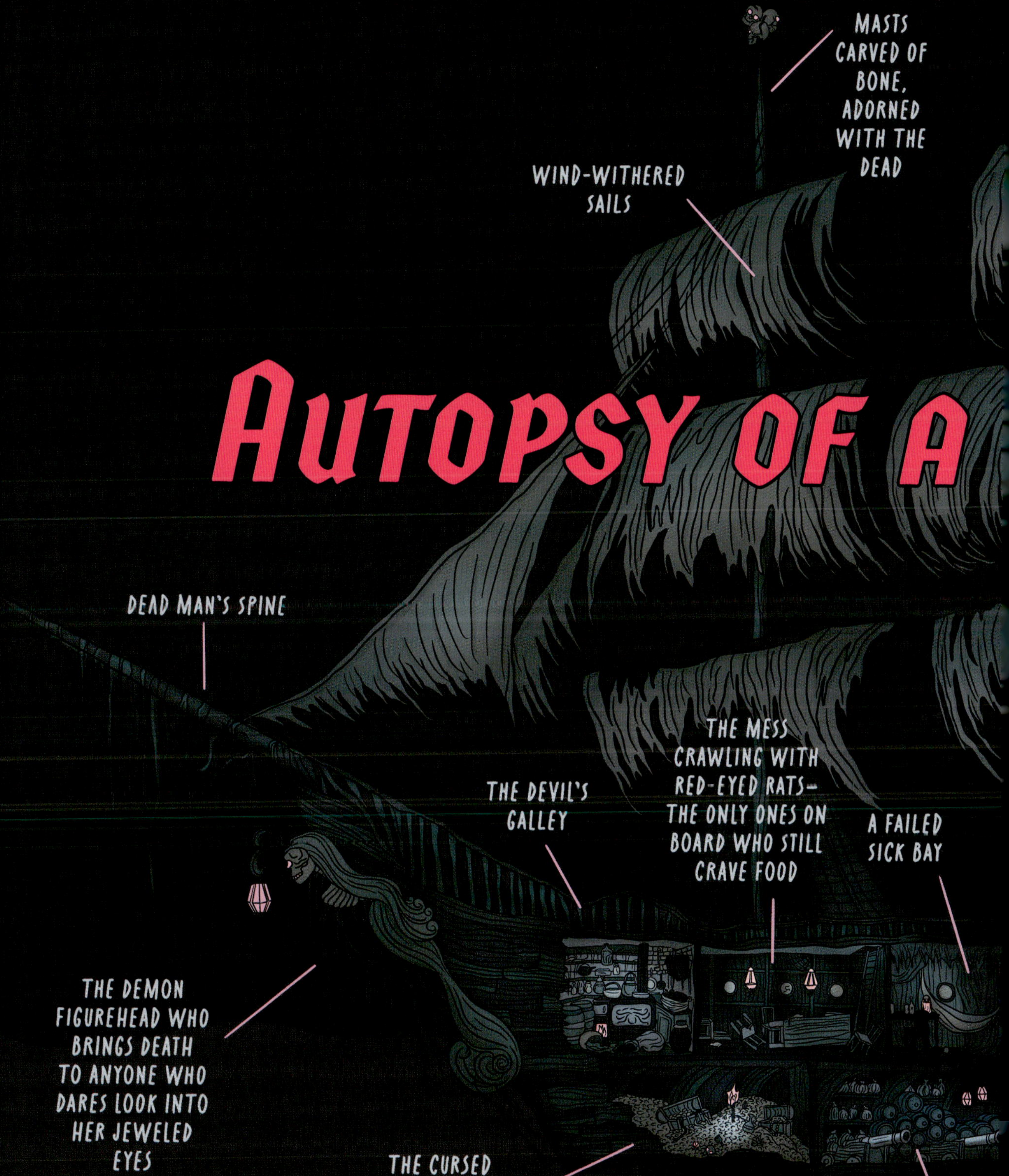
MASTS CARVED OF BONE, ADORNED WITH THE DEAD
WIND-WITHERED SAILS
DEAD MAN'S SPINE
THE DEVIL'S GALLEY
THE MESS CRAWLING WITH RED-EYED RATS— THE ONLY ONES ON BOARD WHO STILL CRAVE FOOD
A FAILED SICK BAY
THE DEMON FIGUREHEAD WHO BRINGS DEATH TO ANYONE WHO DARES LOOK INTO HER JEWELED EYES
THE CURSED TREASURE TROVE
THE MURDERER'S MAGAZINE

Ghost Ship

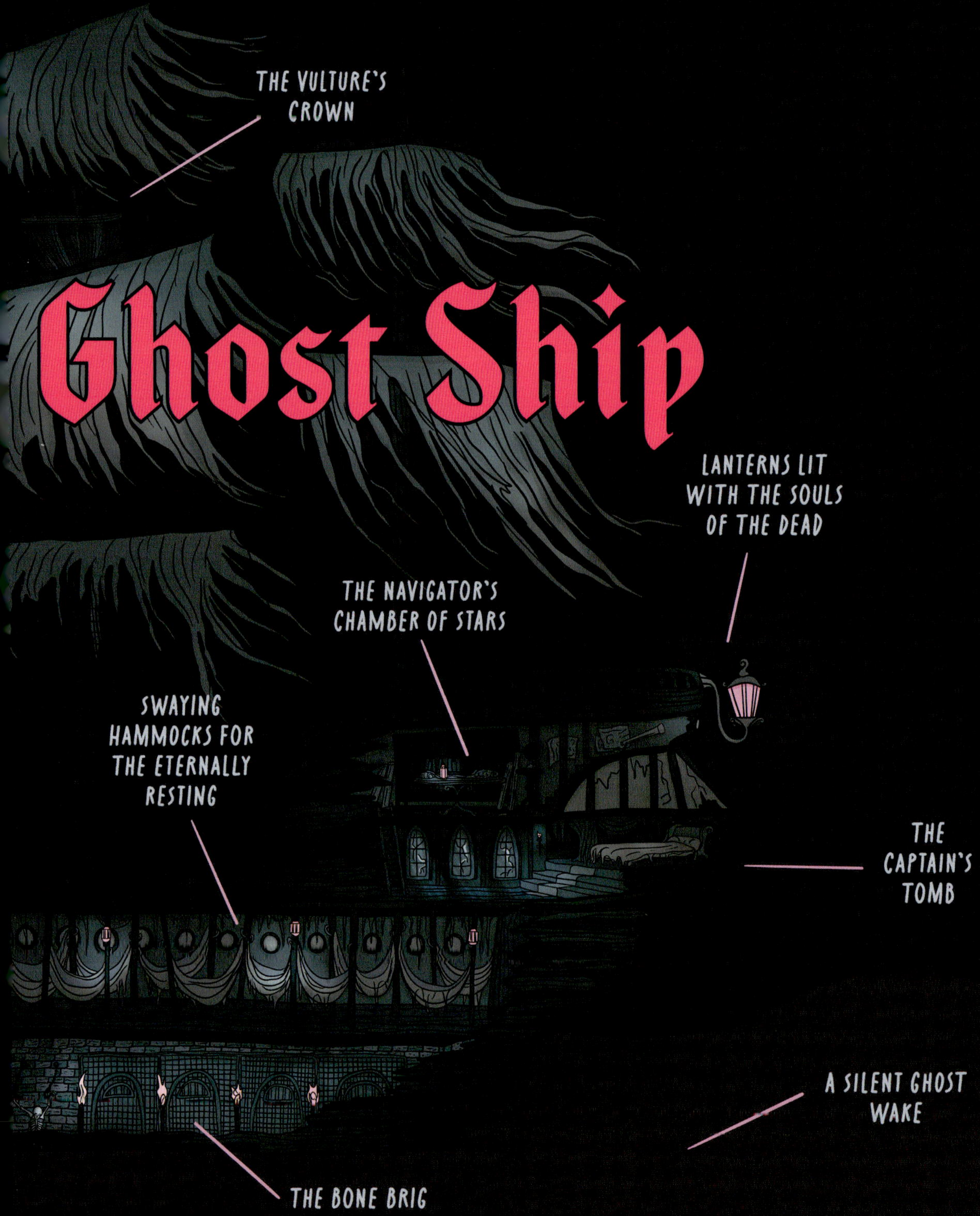
THE VULTURE'S CROWN
LANTERNS LIT WITH THE SOULS OF THE DEAD
THE NAVIGATOR'S CHAMBER OF STARS
SWAYING HAMMOCKS FOR THE ETERNALLY RESTING
THE CAPTAIN'S TOMB
A SILENT GHOST WAKE
THE BONE BRIG

The Americas

Canada

Full of bodies and blizzards, Canadian horror is colder, weirder, and more existential than most. Influenced by the people, the history, the isolation, the vast wilderness and contrasting metropolises, its horror reputation is built from its unique landscape and brand. Toronto's David Cronenberg reshaped horror with films like *Shivers* and *The Fly*, which unleashed body horror into the global bloodstream, and while it's common to think "Cronenberg" as soon as you think "Canada," Canadian horror has always been bigger than one man's bloody fingerprints.

In the seventies, they took part in the slasher boom with *Black Christmas* and *My Bloody Valentine*, then layered social commentary, gender identity, and emotional rage into cult hits like *Ginger Snaps*, as well as producing deeply metaphorical Indigenous horror pieces like *Blood Quantum*. Folklore—wendigos, skinwalkers, haunted forests—all contribute to the genre's voice. Today, with the Toronto International Film Festival's Midnight Madness and rising Indigenous, immigrant, and indie voices, Canada is a top global icehouse of horror.

Key Themes

- Isolation and hostile landscape
- Indigenous horror—erasure, disappearance, and reclamation
- Psychological, existential fear, and madness
- Body horror, gender identity, and transformation

Autopsy of Canadian Horror

THE LANDSCAPE: When you think of Canada, visions of cold isolation, brutal blizzards, northern remoteness without sunlight, frostbite, silt-gray wolves, furs, snow blindness, survivalists, and wilderness come to mind. Canadian horror uses its defining landscapes to bolster its horror giving it a unique and harsh style.

THE PEOPLE: The Indigenous peoples of Canada have endured centuries of colonial violence, land displacement, cultural erasure, missing and murdered women, and systemic oppression. All of which inform Indigenous horror stories from Canada.

Cronenberg Cronies

Horror's Swifties . . . okay, not an actual fan label (yet) but should be because Canada's David Cronenberg—the king of body horror—and now his son Brandon are two of the most iconic figures of the genre!

Toronto International Film Festival

More proof that Canadians have always valued the genre as a valuable form of artistic expression, and just plain fun, Midnight Madness is the award dedicated to the best horror, action, shock, or fantasy flick of the year at Toronto's renowned international film festival.

Defining Works

- *Black Christmas*
- *Shivers*
- *My Bloody Valentine*
- *The Fly*
- *Ginger Snaps*
- *Pontypool*
- *The Blackcoat's Daughter*
- *Blood Quantum*
- *Possessor*
- *Slash/Back*

THE UNITED STATES OF HORROR

NEW ENGLAND
THE MIDWEST
LVH
ORCA
Lincoln Valley High's
Senior Prom
1997
APPALACHIA
THE SOUTH
THE HOLY BIBLE
Miss American South

THE UNITED STATES OF HORROR

Horror is deeply woven into the American cultural identity. The Dust Bowl? Nuclear testing sites? Salem witch trials? And because of these events, our history, and the convergence of landscape, tradition, people, beliefs, and unmatched film industry, the United States is the most prolific, profitable, and influential horror creator on earth. It's the American scream.

No country produces more horror films per year than the US, because Hollywood turned horror into a genre-sustaining machine. Even indie horror thrives here thanks to streaming platforms, A24, Blumhouse, Shudder, and festivals like SXSW and Sundance. Horror here isn't fringe, it's mainstream. Jordan Peele turned sociopolitical horror into something that reached everyone, Stephen King is a one-man horror economy, and Halloween isn't just a holiday; it's an entire industry.

A lot of American horror is pure trope: exaggerated, stereotypical stigmas of the locals, their lifestyles, and their clashing worldviews. From Indigenous folklore to immigration, capitalism, religion, racism, war, suburbia, systemic violence, and more—much of it draws from the real, raw roots of the country.

American horror is also brilliantly colorful as it's a visual representation of the country's diverse geography. As every region has its own brand, distinct style, flavor, color palette, sound, and smell, so does the horror that comes out of it, and Hollywood has preyed on the culture of every part of the country and turned each into a full-blown caricature. From Appalachia folk horror to Southern gothic ghosts, California desert cults, and puritanical witch trials, this is a nation that turned its history into horror tropes. Whether it's camp or arthouse, conservative or subversive, religious or profane, glossy or gritty, American horror isn't one side dish, it's a combination splatter platter.

Get in, we're going on a road trip to see what makes up the United States of horror. SHOTGUN!

THE PACIFIC NORTHWEST

Kissing in cars at overlooks, Sasquatch, hitchhikers, wood-paneled station wagons, pine needles, winding forest roads, cabins in the woods, campfires, broken compasses, missing posters, damp mold, logging roads, unmarked trails, burnt coffee, radio static, flannel, cold lakes, ferry terminals, foghorns, tent zippers, wrong turns.

WEST COAST

Hollywood, cults, communes, acid trips, California fever dreams, satanic worship, sinister sunshine, wellness, plastic, mind control, perfection, beauty, dysmorphia, brainwashing, Manson murders, flower crowns, palm trees, infinity pools, rehab.

THE SOUTHWEST

Ghost towns, Area 51, radiation poisoning, desert highways, mirages, tumbleweeds, tinfoil hats, cacti, barbed wire fences, motel signs, survivalists, fallout shelters, empty canteens, burnt orange, incense, turquoise, petroglyphs, peyote, dry lightning, alien abductions, satellites, rusted trailers.

GREAT PLAINS

Dust, drought, locusts, cracked earth, ghost towns, black skies, white dresses, dead crops, windstorms, empty wells, scarecrows, banging barn doors, sun-bleached bones, bloody coughs, cracked lips, abandoned tractors, famine, static.

THE MIDWEST

Wheat fields, strip malls, religious extremism, wood chippers, scarecrows, prom night, crop circles, farms, barns, corn-fed killers, tornadoes, abandoned bikes, silos, slaughterhouses, church basements, diners, Bible camps, storm sirens, highways, pickup trucks, basement freezers, county fairs, American flags, wood paneling, frozen lakes, hunting season.

THE SOUTH

Bible Belt, Louisiana Voodoo, Hoodoo, bayous, gothic mansions, Spanish moss, decay, ghosts of slavery, plantations, beauty queens, Southern belles, gators, blood, humidity, rot, cicadas, cotton, fire, bourbon, peaches, crosses, chapels, porches, rocking chairs, gaslights, fireflies, hymns, rust, sermons, cottonmouths.

APPALACHIA

Cabins, gas stations, overalls, tobacco, chainsaws, sheds, chains, root cellars, shotguns, rust, moonshine, coal dust, mining tunnels, whistling, boot prints, banjos, woodsmoke, bloody hatchets, tent revivals, isolation, creaky porches, wind chimes, faded quilts, gutted deer, the woods.

NEW ENGLAND

Salem witch trials, Puritans, folklore, sacrifice, cemeteries, starvation, wild animals, old gnarled dark woods, colonial bonnets, goats, witches, ships, stone walls, hunting knives, symbols carved into trees, lighthouses, fog, dark academia, oil lanterns, the headless horseman, snow gently falling at a funeral, black veils, bustles, corsets, cloaks.

The Caribbean

The Caribbean, especially Haiti, influenced horror long before Hollywood. While it's not a region known for its mass production of horror films, its cultural contributions played a big role in shaping the genre. Vodou (the complex spiritual system rooted in the African diaspora and brought over via the transatlantic slave trade) contributed two major ideas: spiritual possession and the zombie. But Hollywood twisted Haiti's real history of slavery, colonialism, and survival into curses, "dark" magic, and mindless monsters to flatten traditions into racist fear tropes for Western audiences. Before it became a pop culture scare tactic, Vodou was and still is a vibrant, deeply spiritual religion that deserves to be seen in its full complexity. Let's dissect it.

Vodun, Vodou, Voodoo

VODUN: West African word for spirit.

VODOU: Haitian blend of African religion and Catholicism after slavery.

VOODOO: Americanized word used for Louisiana traditions and Hollywood.

Vodun to Hollywood Timeline

1500s–1700s: Enslaved Africans bring spiritual practices to the Caribbean.

1791–1804: Haitian Revolution spreads Vodou influence to Louisiana.

EARLY 1800s: Louisiana Voodoo develops focused on nature, healing, and spirits.

EARLY 1900s: Writers twist Vodou into exoticized myths with "dark magic" and "evil spirits."

1932: Hollywood's first zombie movie, *White Zombie*, hits theaters with a plot of Westerners going to deal with a Haitian "zombie master" named Murder.

LATE 1900s: Zombies shift into brain-eaters with Romero's *Night of the Living Dead*.

Zombi vs. Zombie

The original Haitian zombie wasn't a brain-hungry monster, and even though Western pop culture has used the character to carry its own metaphorical meanings (a tech-addicted brain-dead consumer or a victim of a widespread disease), the original creation of the zombi represents a person who is stripped of their soul and free will, a living symbol of slavery and colonial oppression, and a representation of one's loss of autonomy and humanity.

Vodou vs. Vo-Not

ORIGINS VS. POP CULTURE

A living religion practiced in Haiti, West Africa, and beyond.	Dark magic and curses used for scares and shock.
Focused on healing, ancestor worship, and spirit connection.	Focuses on evil spells, possession, and revenge.
Ceremonies involve music, dance, and honoring spirits.	Rituals are shown as scary, secret, and violent.
Spirit possession is sacred and joyful.	Spirit possession is demonic.
Vodou dolls are used for protection and healing.	Voodoo dolls are for causing pain and cursing.
Centered around community and public focused rituals.	Depicted as hidden cults with evil priests and priestesses.
Built from survival, resistance, and resilience.	Built from colonial fear, racism, and exoticism.

Brazil

When you think of horror, Brazil might not be the first place that comes to mind—but with its contemporary cult status among global horror lovers, we must claw open what Brazil has uniquely contributed to the genre.

Beneath the bossa nova, Copacabana glitz, and Carmen Miranda's fruit hats, something darker was starting to emerge in the 1960s. As Brazil dazzled the world with its colorful fever dream of music and nightlife, a different form of expression slowly crept its way out of the dense humid jungle (urban and rural): one filled with monsters and decay. Born from its contradictions—jungles and favelas, Catholicism and Candomblé, dictatorship and rebellion, the sacred and the profane, Brazilian horror is all of it swirling around and crunching in a bloody blender. From José Mojica Marins's Coffin Joe, through grindhouse, arthouse, and political allegory, to *Good Manners* (featuring an insanely unforgettable werewolf birth), and *The Nightshifter*, Brazilian horror continues to wield the genre like a machete against inequality and repression.

Key Themes

- Religious and spiritual practice
- Environmental horror
- Poverty and power
- Body and transformation
- Folklore

Autopsy of Brazilian Horror

Candomblé and Umbanda: Though often misrepresented, the Afro-Brazilian religions of Candomblé and Umbanda play trope roles in horror because of their connection to spirits, orixás, divination, possession, and mislabeled practices of witchcraft.

Folklore Spotlight: Saci is the one-legged trickster who may be hopping around your barn right now. Known for sucking on his signature pipe as well as the blood of animals.

Coffin Joe

José Mojica Marins, the father of Brazilian horror, who, as Coffin Joe (a reallllllly long-nailed, unibrow-sporting, Dracula cape–wearing heretic in a top hat), redefined horror in the sixties by blending satanic imagery, Nietzschean philosophy, and social critique. Coffin Joe may have been a bit silly looking in his vampiric getup, but with his pioneering horror film trilogy, TV shows, and appearances in comic books and music videos, he is an icon that flips the middle finger to Brazil's moral hypocrisy and one who claims the title of Brazil's National Boogeyman.

Defining Works

- The Coffin Joe Trilogy: *At Midnight I'll Take Your Soul*, *This Night I'll Possess Your Corpse*, and *Embodiment of Evil*
- *Good Manners*
- *The Nightshifter*
- *Hard Labor*
- *The Awakening of the Beast*
- *Medusa*
- *Bacurau*
- *Skull: The Mask*

Mexico

With its devastating beauty, rich pigments, dry wind-torn deserts, sweltering jungle paths, congested cities, vine-covered temples, cold-tiled haciendas with cracked adobe walls, bones dusted with dirt, skulls adorned with monarch-colored marigolds, smoke from burning agave plants and copal incense, the night clicking of the chapulines, and the ghosts of children running through fields next to lakes where their mother drowned them . . . we get Mexico—a visceral experience, an aesthetic, and a mood that penetrates all your senses at once.

The country is a living, breathing entity created from hundreds of years of culturally rich but turbulent history, filled with war, revolution, colonization, Catholicism intertwined with pre-Hispanic traditions, folklore, mythology, political, and social violence. All of which are baked into every inch of the land and its people—the voices of this vivid gothic landscape use a blend of enchantment and death to tell some of the scariest stories in the world.

Out of Mexico we get the works of horror giants like Carlos Enrique Taboada, Guillermo del Toro, Issa López, Juan López Moctezuma, Isabel Cañas, and Silvia Moreno-Garcia, creators whose works have infused the horror genre with unmatched macabre and the dark and magical Mexican gothic touch.

Can you tell it's my favorite?

Autopsy of Mexican Horror

LA LLORONA: The famous folktale of La Llorona, the drowning of her children by her own hand, and her cries heard at night around bodies of water has over thirty known versions told across Latin America, but she's most deeply embedded in Mexican folklore. The 1933 film *La Llorona* was the first Mexican horror film with sound.

DÍA DE LOS MUERTOS: The Mexican holiday that honors the dead through celebration, altars, offerings, food, and remembrance. While not a horror holiday, its imagery of skulls, candles, marigolds, and spirits often shows up in horror to represent grief, memory, and the veil between worlds.

CATHOLICISM: Catholicism shows up constantly in Mexican horror through themes like sin, guilt, punishment, and possession. Religious figures, symbols, exorcisms, and rituals are often used as scare tactics.

LUCHADOR FILMS: For the most radical and campy horror pop culture mashup yet, starting in 1952, Mexican lucha libre stars like El Santo and Blue Demon were given their own subgenre of horror when cast to fight off vampires, mummies, and werewolves on the big screen.

***EL VAMPIRO*:** Premiering just over twenty years after *La Llarona*, Abel Salazar and Fernando Méndez's classic Dracula-esque film, *El Vampiro*, kicked off the Mexican horror boom and is considered a masterpiece of horror cinema.

GUILLERMO DEL TORO: While many of his films are coproductions between Mexico, America, and Spain, the makeup of Mexican horror wouldn't be complete without the inclusion of Mexico's filmmaker, artist, and fantasy horror master Guillermo del Toro. With gothic fairy-tale visuals and allegorical undertones, del Toro fed us great works, some of which include *Cronos*, *The Devil's Backbone*, and *Pan's Labyrinth*.

Key Themes

- Colonialism and historical trauma
- Religious guilt and Catholic influence
- Death and the afterlife
- Generational pain and secrets
- Folk beliefs and supernatural legends
- Gender roles and repression
- Violence and corruption
- Poverty and social inequality

Defining Works

- Modern Mexican gothic must-read authors: Isabel Cañas and Silvia Moreno-Garcia
- *La Llorona*
- *El Vampiro*
- *Santo Contra los Zombies*
- *Even the Wind Is Afraid*
- *Alucarda*
- *Poison for the Fairies*
- *Santa Sangre*
- *Cronos*
- *The Devil's Backbone*
- *Pan's Labyrinth*
- *Tigers Are Not Afraid*
- *Huesera: The Bone Woman*

Argentina

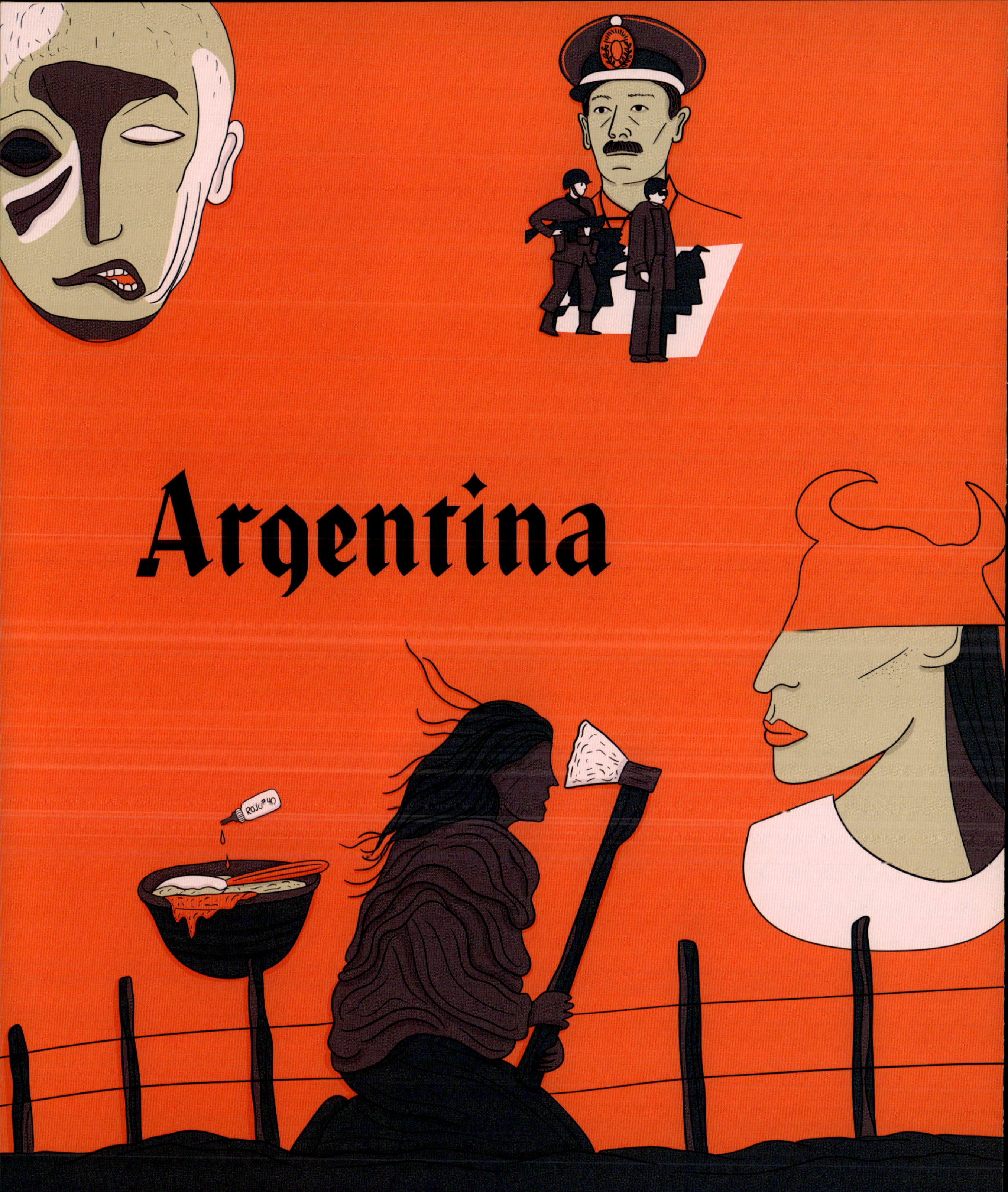

Before we talk about the blood Argentina has contributed to the global horror screen, we must talk about the blood they inked on the pages. The history of horror in Argentina begins with the classic literary works of Jorge Luis Borges, a pioneer of magical realism whose fantastical essays, poems, and short stories influenced the experimental and prolific works of Julio Cortázar. Their spirits still live and bleed through literary contemporaries like Mariana Enríquez and Agustina Bazterrica.

Argentina's film horror scene crept in during the midcentury with moody film-noir pieces like *El Vampiro Negro* and continued through the early seventies with films like *Nazareno Cruz y el Lobo*, a folkloric tale of a werewolf through a gaucho lens. From 1976 to 1983, Argentina's authoritarian regime stifled fiction and artistic expression, but when the genre reemerged, it took a new shape, an altered, heavier one, one which now used the art form to speak in metaphor, process the traumatic events of the country, and mourn the murder of thousands. The 2000s launched a resurgence with brutal, bold, and distinctly Argentinian-coded films like *Terrified* (*Aterrados*) and later Demián Rugna's *When Evil Lurks* (*Cuando acecha la maldad*), films that were grotesque, unrelenting, and soaked in rural rot.

Autopsy of Argentinian Horror

DIY PUNK CINEMA: Post-dictatorship, Argentinian filmmakers used horror as an outlet for their anger, and a new wave of cinema emerged. A postwar budget didn't deter filmmakers from bringing their creations to life—using cake batter and red food coloring to make DIY blood, for instance. They had a distinct revolutionary style that said, "we won't be silenced no matter our circumstances." This punk attitude garnered a massive cult following.

THE NATIONAL REORGANIZATION PROCESS, or "The Dirty War" (an outsider label) refers to the period of military dictatorship in Argentina from 1976 to 1983 when over thirty thousand people "disappeared" at the hands of the military. Horror has become a tool for Argentinians to explore the genocide, guilt, repression, and trauma of this period.

Key Themes

The National Reorganization Process

- Disappearance
- Spiritual possession
- Political possession
- Isolation
- Urban gothic

Defining Works

When Evil Lurks – Argentina's new horror landmark and most successful international horror release to date. It was acquired by Shudder as a flagship global title.

Literature

- The works of Jorges Luis Borges and Julio Cortázar (not horror authors but highly influential on the genre)
- *Tender Is the Flesh* - Agustina Bazterrica
- *Our Share of Night* - Mariana Enríquez

Film

- *Nazareno Cruz y el Lobo*
- *When Evil Lurks*
- *Terrified*
- *Luciferina*
- *History of the Occult*
- *The Returned* (*Los Que Vuelven*)
- *The Silent House*
- *White Coffin*

THE Americas' Most Haunted

Eastern State Penitentiary

Once the most famous prison in the world, Philadelphia's Eastern State Penitentiary pioneered solitary confinement—and drove inmates mad in the process. Even though it closed in 1971, the ghosts of those who died of disease, death, murder, suicide, and torment keep its crumbling cellblocks at full capacity.

The Stanley Hotel

Long before Steven King's *The Shining* (inspired by his own stay), the ghosts of the Stanley Hotel had already checked in. Since its build in 1909, mediums, ghost hunters, and paranormal-obsessed guests have reported children laughing, pianos tinkling, and a resounding warning to steer clear of room 217, King's choice of lodging that one fateful night.

Isla de las Muñecas

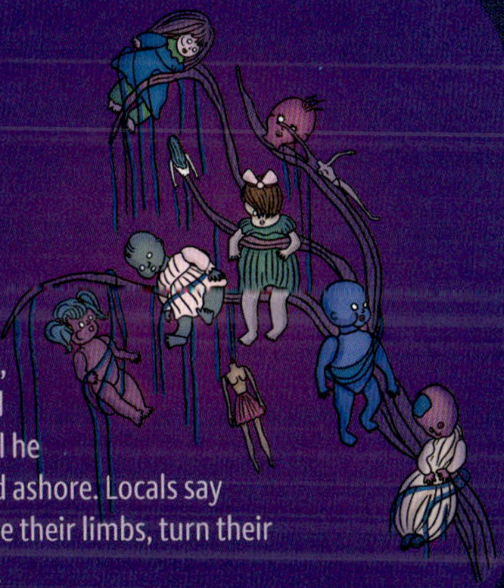

Deep in the canals of Xochimilco, Mexico, you'll find an island draped in decaying dolls. Hung by Don Julián Santana Barrera, he claims they're possessed by the ghost of a young girl he found mysteriously washed ashore. Locals say the dolls are known to move their limbs, turn their heads, and open their eyes.

Key West, Florida

Don't be fooled by the sunshine—Key West has some dark haunted history. Primarily taking shape in Robert the Doll, a cursed toy (and mean girl) locked in a plexiglass case in the Fort East Martello Museum said to blink, move, and dramatically ruin the lives of those who mock him.

The Bell Witch Cave

In the early 1800s in Tennessee, the Bell family was tormented in their home by a violent, shape-shifting force thought to reside in a cave on their land. What started as sounds of loud knocking and dragging chains, quickly turned into physical attacks and full vocal confrontations. When John Bell died of "natural causes" three years later, the presence diminished.

La Recoleta Cemetery

In the heart of Buenos Aires, you'll find a gothic maze of crumbling mausoleums and elaborate tombs housing the who's who of Argentina. Among the marble angels and crypts, you may catch glimpses of ghosts, even the one of Rufina Cambaceres, who was accidentally buried alive there in 1902.

Waverley Hills Sanatorium

What's now called the Most Terrifying Building in America was once a tuberculosis hospital in Kentucky that saw tens of thousands die within its walls. It's famous for its "body chute," a tunnel used to discreetly remove the piling dead.

Gettysburg

The site of the Civil War's bloodiest bloodbath of them all, so intensely filled with death, memory, loss, grief, and pain that ghosts seem to radiate from the ground. Phantom cannon shots, gunfire, and lost soldiers are witnessed here . . . some say the battlefield itself still feels alive.

Winchester Mystery House

Built by Sarah Winchester, heiress to the rifle fortune, this sprawling labyrinthine mansion with staircases to nowhere, doors that open into walls, and over 160 rooms was designed to confuse the ghosts of those killed by Winchester rifles—ghosts she believed were haunting her family, ghosts she thought couldn't find her if she just kept building.

Banff Springs Hotel

Another must-stay on your haunted hotel journey, this towering castle is perched in the Canadian Rockies and is crawling with ghosts. The most famous being the young bride who fell to her death on the hotel's staircase on her wedding day in the 1920s. She's been spotted dancing in her gown ever since. A phantom bellhop has also appeared to lend a hand to guests.

La Casa Matusita

In the middle of Lima, Peru, this unassuming building is said to drive people mad. Legends claim a séance gone wrong or a dinner party turned massacre left the place cursed. Locals say to avoid the second floor, where unexplained activity is still reported.

Contemporary Cryptids

THE WORLD'S SNEAKIEST HORROR CREATURES

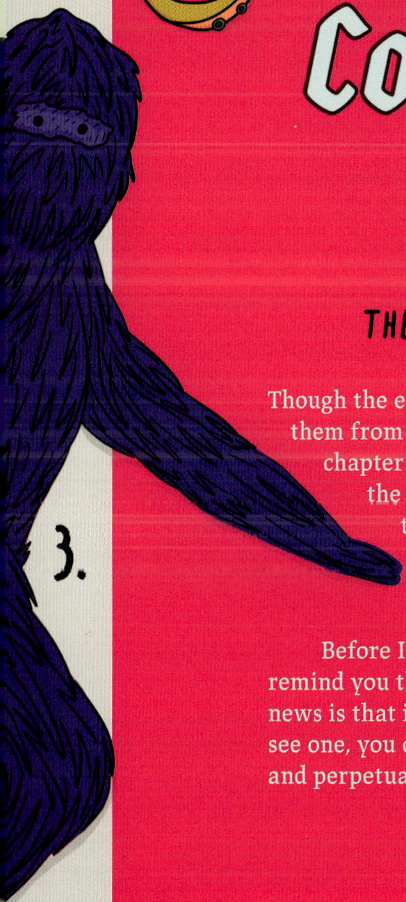

Though the existence of cryptids is still up for debate, this hasn't stopped them from consistently creeping into horror stories. As we saw in chapter 1, these frightening fantastical beasts first took shape from the world's oldest folklore, but they have persisted through the centuries, proving that no matter who you are, where we're from, or how much time passes, humans can't help but obsess over what may or may not exist, and spin the scariest tales about the wildest things we can imagine.

Before I send you little cryptozoologists out on your safari, I must remind you that these creature's existence is highly disputed. The good news is that if you see one, you could be the first; the bad news is, if you see one, you could be the last. It's all fodder for the lore though. Go forth and perpetuate horror!

5.

6.

1. THE KRAKEN
Icy Nordic sea beast of legend. Strength: Can snap masts like matchsticks. Last seen: Off the coast of Greenland . . . allegedly.

2. THE JERSEY DEVIL
Winged goat-faced Jersey hell spawn. Strength: A scream that makes your ears bleed. Last seen: Galloway Township, New Jersey, 2015.

3. SASQUATCH AKA BIGFOOT Towering, shaggy, and shy. Strength: Outdoor skills and permanent blur filter. Last seen: South Carolina, 2024.

4. LOCH NESS MONSTER
Scotland's serpentine legend lurking since 565 AD. Strength: Launched a cryptid empire with one blurry photo. Last seen: Loch Ness mass search, August 2023.

5. MOTHMAN
Red-eyed Appalachian harbinger with a ten-foot wingspan. Strength: Knows the future. Last seen: Near O'Hare Airport, Chicago, 2017.

7.

6. THUNDERBIRD
Supersized sky beast with a block-the-sun wingspan. Strength: Can carry livestock . . . and kids. Last seen: Soaring over Derry Township, Pennsylvania, January 2024.

8. MONGOLIAN DEATH WORM
Acid-spitting, electrifying, sand-surfing nightmare. Strength: Best name in the game. Last seen: Gobi Desert, 1920s.

7. YETI
Himalayan snow stalker with zero chill. Strength: Climbs Everest barefoot. Last seen: Nepal, 2019.

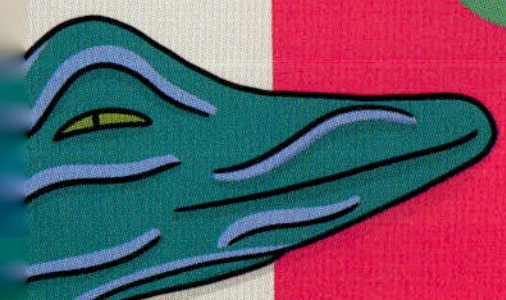

9. THE DOVER DEMON
Alien headed, spindly limbed, furless creep with bad posture. Strength: Caused mass hysteria after one night out. Last seen: Dover, Massachusetts, April 1977.

10. CHUPACABRA
Latin America's livestock vampire with mange and fangs. Strength: Can easily clear a chicken coop. Last seen: Rural Texas, 2023.

8.

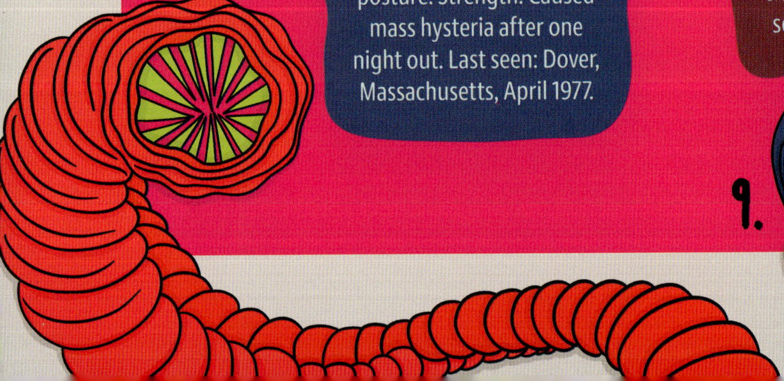

9.

10.

Urban Legends

Come, sit around the campfire, let's tell some scary stories. Not the ones of yore with beautiful creatures in the woods with good moral-bestowing intentions, though. Tonight we're going to share some urban legends—modern stories with modern ghosts and modern killers who could lunge out of a mirror or throw your organs on ice at any moment. Here's a smattering from around the world to share at your next sleepover. *For adults too.*

SLENDER MAN (USA)

The modern internet-made boogeyman created in 2009. Slender Man is an extra tall, faceless figure in a black suit with long tentacles protruding from his back who stalks and abducts children. Supposedly fictional . . . but don't let him lure you in.

THE CRYING BOY PAINTING (UK)

In the 1980s, a string of house fires swept across the UK—and in the charred remains, firefighters kept finding one thing in common, a painting of a sad little boy with tears streaming down his face, perfectly intact. The artwork, known as *The Crying Boy*, became legend that spread like wildfire. Tabloids ran with it, calling it cursed, and whether the legend was true or not, no one wants that kid hanging on their wall anymore.

THE NIGHTMARCHERS (HAWAII)

The huaka'i pō are spirit warrior processions adorned with drums and decorated dress traveling through the night. If you look them in the eye or let your presence be known, it will be the last thing you do.

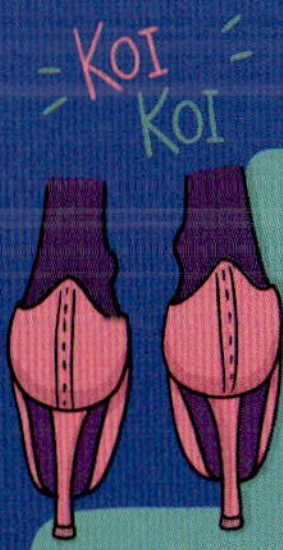

MADAM KOI KOI (NIGERIA AND GHANA)

The legend of a vengeful ghost schoolteacher who always appears in her signature red heels. Her spirit is said to haunt boarding schools, with her heels clicking *koi koi, koi koi* down the hallways at night as she gets closer and closer . . . looking for a student out of bed to attack.

TEKE TEKE (JAPAN)

The ghost of a schoolgirl cut in half by a train that haunts railway stations and roads. Moving on her elbows, she makes a *teke-teke* sound as she chases people—if she catches you, she cuts you in half with her scythe to make you look just like her.

THE VANISHING HITCHHIKER (USA)

A driver picks up a quiet hitchhiker, usually a young woman, on a dark road. When they reach their destination, she's vanished from the backseat. The driver then learns that the passenger died years ago, just where they picked her up.

THE BLACK VOLGA (EASTERN EUROPE)

In the sixties and seventies, a black Volga was rumored to roam the streets, especially near schools. If it pulled up beside you, you vanished—snatched by the devil, the KGB, or organ traffickers. No one ever saw who was driving.

BLOODY MARY (INTERNATIONAL)

They say if you stand in front of a mirror in the dark and say *Bloody Mary* three times, she'll appear—bloody faced, screaming, and reaching through the glass to kill you.

THE BACKSEAT KILLER (USA)

The story always begins with a woman driving home at night—a truck starts tailing her, flashing its brights, swerving, speeding up. She makes it home, terrified, only to find out the driver wasn't trying to kill her but warn her. Someone was in her backseat . . .

THE BLACK-EYED CHILDREN (USA)

They show up at night, kids with pale skin, old clothes, and pitch-black eyes. They knock on doors or tap on car windows, asking to be let in. People say if you do, you'll never feel the same again, and that's if you live.

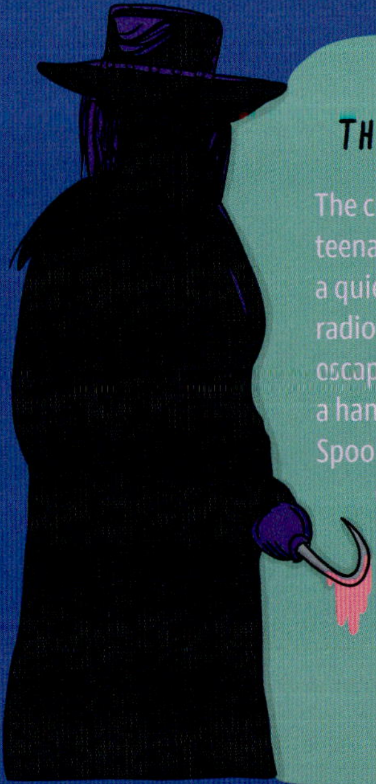

THE HOOK MAN (USA)

The classic legend of the teenage couple parked on a quiet lovers' lane when a radio alert warning of an escaped killer with a hook for a hand interrupts their kissing. Spooked, they drive off fast, only to find a bloody hook dangling from their car door. He was right outside all along.

WELCOME BACK, TRAVELERS! I SEE some of you are still a little green from that ghost ship tour, so I'll give you a moment. In the meantime, did you enjoy your haunted trip around the world? What was the scariest destination for you? Who did you land on as your favorite horror powerhouse? And how many of you have chosen to never leave your house again? Well . . . at least you have years of horror books and films to consume.

Well! Jet lag be dammed, I'm really into dissecting things after all that. So why don't we just keep cutting . . . Actually, why don't we just slice the entire genre up into parts? Oh, and . . . did somebody drop their knife?

You're going to want that where we're going.

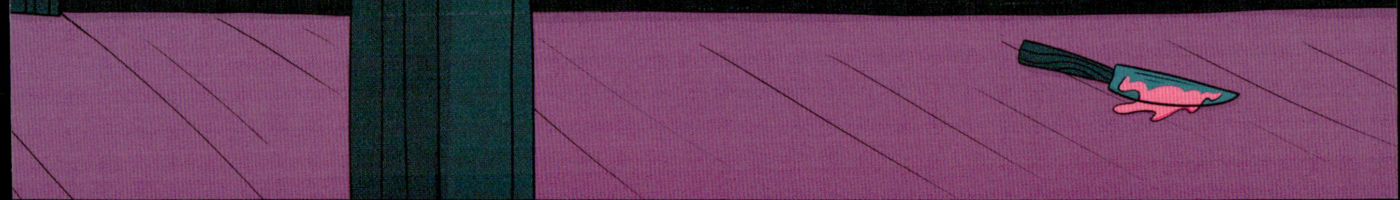

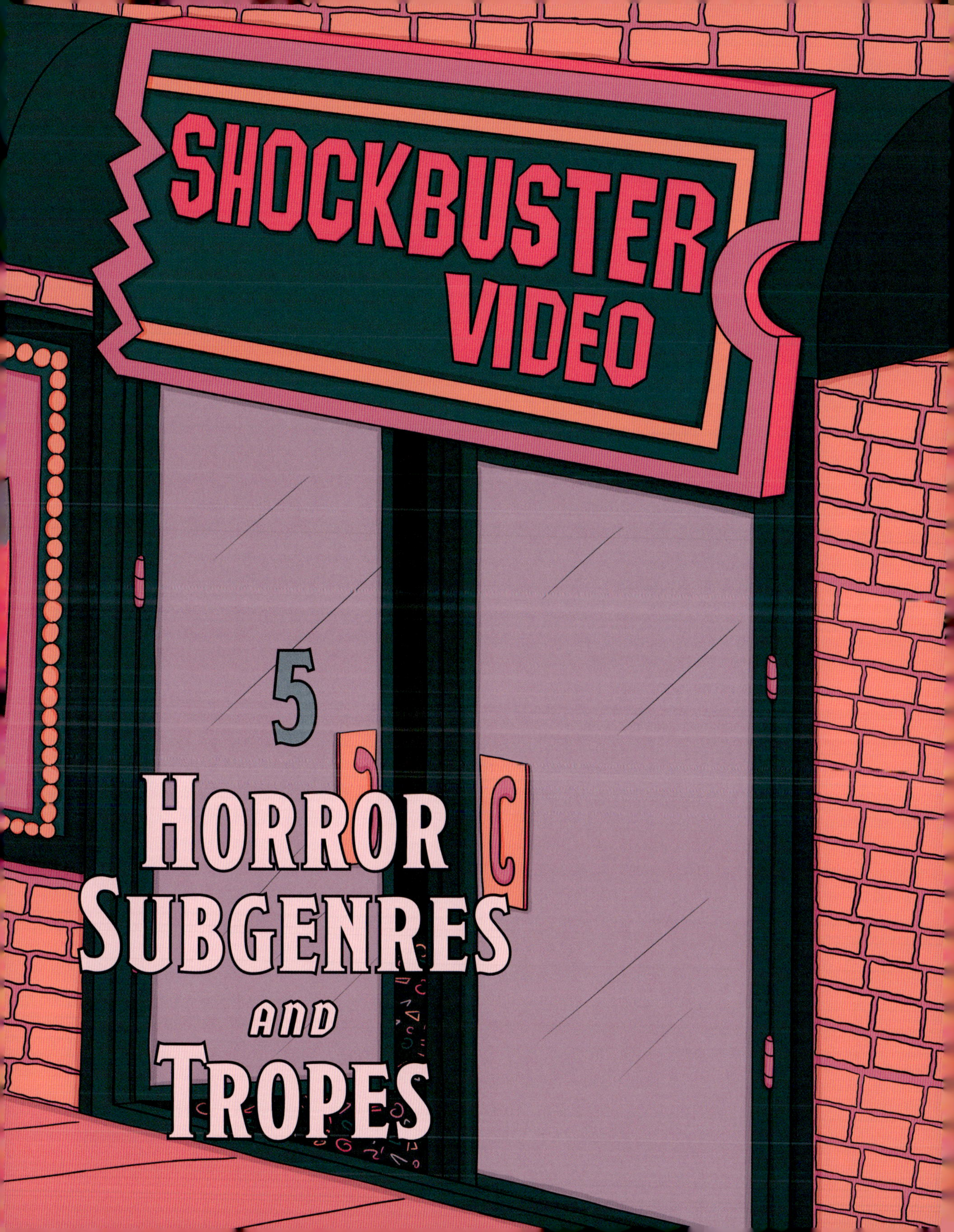

5 Horror Subgenres and Tropes

WELCOME TO SHOCKBUSTER, where you can rent any movie, as long as it's a horror movie! No, don't go! Horror is one of the most diverse genres, and there's more here than senseless blood and guts, I promise! Horror contains multitudes of subgenres to choose from, all oozing with their own signature characters, styles, environments, items, plots, and tropes! Oh, the tropes, what would each horror subgenre be without its defining tropes?!

So go ahead, grab your candy, mill about, and rent as many movies as you like, each section of the store covers a different subgenre. Be careful, though; someone with a mask and butcher knife has been hanging out in the slasher aisle lately, and the Satanists started another movie club in the religious section, so be vigilant there, they're always trying to recruit new members. And finally, remember to be kind and rewind, or else we'll have those creepy children over there kill you.

Welcome to the subgenres and tropes of horror!

THE Gothic

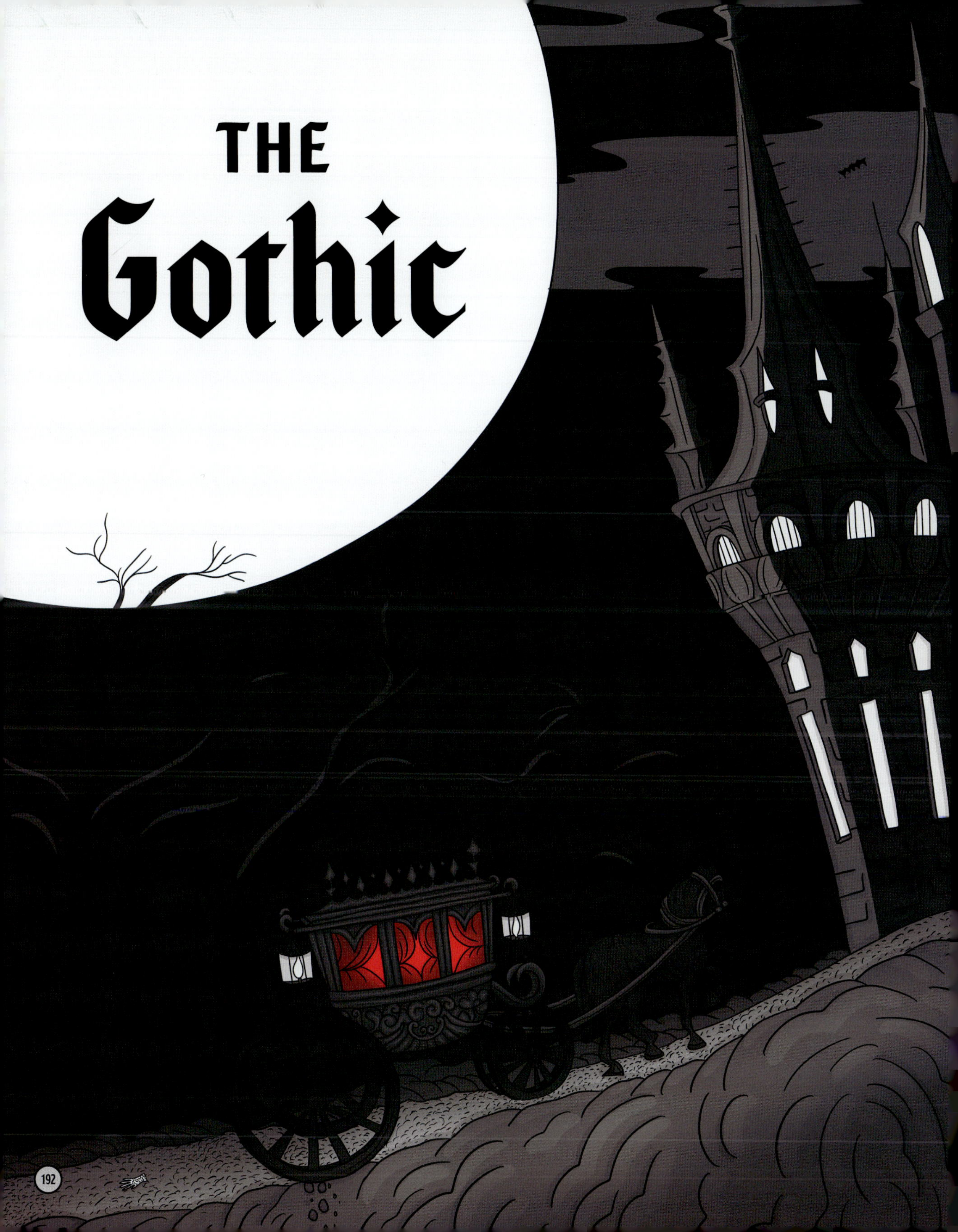

THE Birth OF Modern Horror

Before slashers, found footage, and demonic dolls, there was the gothic—horror's moody ancestor, born from crumbling castles, secrets, ghosts, and utter exasperation. The genre emerged from the macabre moors in 1764 with Horace Walpole's *The Castle of Otranto*, and has rung in our ears like a blood-curdling scream ever since.

Gothic horror was the first to fuse supernatural fear with psychological dread. It's dripping in drama and atmosphere—stormy weather, candlelight, fogged cathedral windows, and crimson-corseted satin gowns laced around skin so pale it could be mistaken for dead. It's fixated on the past: ancestral sins, diseased souls, inherited trauma, and family secrets (or families themselves) rotting under floorboards. It loves a heroine on the brink, a Byronic villain in the shadows, and a house that's its own eerie character.

By the 1800s, Mary Shelley's *Frankenstein*, Bram Stoker's *Dracula*, and Poe's entire catalog had staked gothic as the genre of haunted minds and haunted places. But the gothic didn't stay trapped in the crumbling cold castles of Victorian Europe. The subgenre became universal, and it spread like a spiderweb—adopted by every shadowy corner of the melancholic world for storytelling.

In the American South, it transformed into Southern gothic, where genteel manners masked rot, and history refused to stay buried. In Mexico, it bloomed into Mexican gothic, where colonial mansions fester with fungi, bloodlines, and colonial guilt. Gothic horror evolved, and not just geographically, but emotionally. What began as a physical aesthetic descriptor of crumbling castles and stormy landscapes became something deeper: a global language for describing internal environments, repression, and the psychological aftermath of trauma.

Gothic isn't defined by where it came from, it's defined by how it feels—oppressive, decaying, dramatic, and haunted by the past. It persists because it was never really about the stone castle, it was always about what can be found hiding inside our bleeding stone hearts.

A Visual Guide to the Gothic

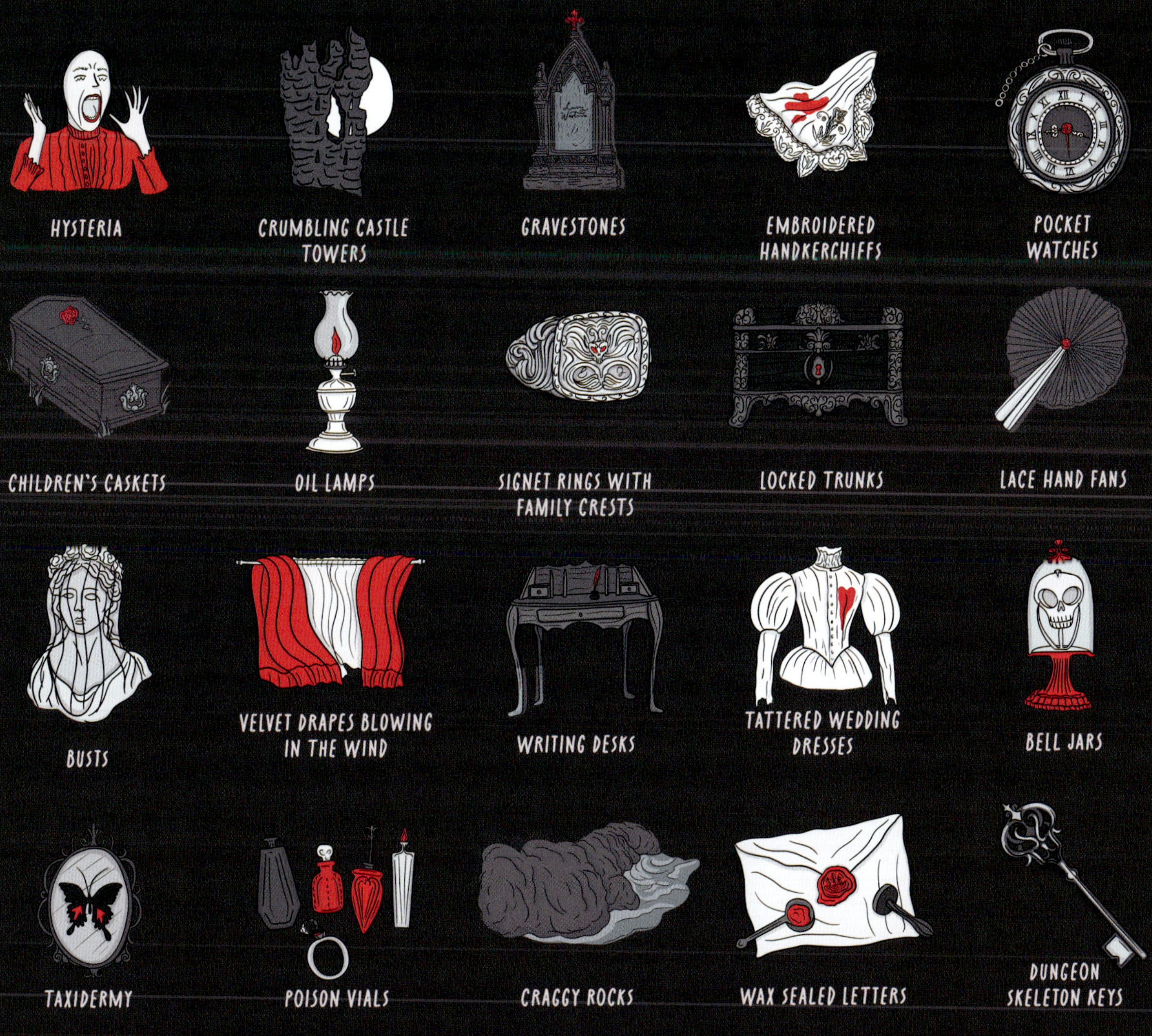

PORTRAITS AND PALE PALLOR
MANOR HOUSES
FEVER DREAMS, FITS, HALLUCINATIONS, AND SPELLS
MOURNING VEILS
CANDELABRAS
CORSETS AND NIGHTGOWNS
FAINTING COUCHES
CARRIAGES
THUNDERSTORMS
EXHAUSTION, MELANCHOLY, EXASPERATION, AND DESPAIR
VAMPIRES
BLACK LACE GLOVES
SHEET-DRAPED FURNITURE
HAIR CLIPPINGS IN LOCKETS
PARASOLS
DAMP STONE WALLS
FOG-COVERED MARSHES AND MOORS
PARANOIA AND SCRATCHING IN THE WALLS
MUSIC BOXES
IVY-CHOKED WALLS
WEEPING GHOSTS
GOVERNESSES
EERIE ATMOSPHERES
LOCKED ROOMS
ETHER
TROUBLED CHILDBIRTH
OPULENCE
ROMANCE AND TERROR
CRACKED MONOCLES
DEATH

THE Goth Kids

Mary Wollstonecraft Shelley

There's no greater gothic tale than the one of Mary Shelley and her Modern Prometheus—or as we know him, Dr. Frankenstein. The dark creation story begins when sixteen-year-old Mary Godwin, daughter of pioneering feminist Mary Wollstonecraft (dead just eleven days after Mary was born) and radical philosopher William Godwin, ran off with Percy Shelley—the poster boy of all first loves—a twenty-two-year-old, already married, creditor-dodging, jobless activist and poet. Allegedly she lost her virginity to him in the churchyard on, or near, her mother's grave. If true, I'd bet my corset it was raining.

Aside from these questionable actions (but very on-brand for an emo teen in the 1800s), she was a highly observant thinker who had been scribbling down her dreams since childhood. Now publicly running around with Percy after his first wife's suicide, the emotional baggage of losing their first child, and most likely a lot of laudanum, they decided to take a trip. Seeing as Lord Byron was a close friend, they chose Byron's estate as their destination. The year was 1816, and the gothic gods bestowed them with the gift of a volcanic eruption in Indonesia that resulted in such dark and dreary conditions in Europe it was named "the year without a summer." So instead of outside activities, they chose to pass the time telling ghost stories, fireside. Lord Byron proposed that each of them write their own ghost story. Percy, Byron, and Byron's physician produced stories quickly, but Mary was at a loss for her own.

Days passed and the long philosophical conversations continued, many surrounding the origins of life due to Erasmus Darwin's life-generating experiments at the time. The impact of these discussions on Mary "haunted her midnight pillow," possessed her, and terrorized her with the thought of how "frightful must it be; for supremely frightful would be the effect of any human endeavor to mock the stupendous mechanism of the Creator of the world." These obsessive thoughts, along with her experience of loneliness, dismissal, and mistreatment from Percy, were the spark of life to her own ghost story and the waking dream scribbled that became one of the most masterful and heartbreaking science fiction horror stories ever written. Years later upon Percy's passing, when his calcified heart remained intact after cremation, Mary kept it wrapped in a silk cloth by her side until her own death in 1851.

Bram Stoker

Bram Stoker didn't invent the vampire, but he made them iconic. He took centuries of Eastern European folklore, mixed it with Victorian paranoia, and gave us the blueprint for pretty much every bloodsucker thereafter. Born in Dublin in 1847, Stoker was a sickly kid who spent a lot of time bedridden (so goth). He later became a theater critic and ended up as the personal assistant to Sir Henry Irving, a Shakespearean actor some say was the inspiration for the Count, though others say it was the bloodthirsty Impaler, Vlad. Stoker published *Dracula* in 1897, and he died in 1912 of either syphilis or the most gothic-coded illness of all time—"exhaustion." It wasn't until *Nosferatu* (the 1922 film that illegally ripped off *Dracula*) and Universal's 1931 *Dracula* that Stoker's vampire became *the* vampire—sexy, brooding, and crawling up the walls.

Edgar Allan Poe

If horror had a sad, unhinged uncle who never(more) left the house and dressed exclusively in black, it'd be our American gothic darling Edgar Allan Poe. Born in 1809, orphaned by age three, and dead by forty under bizarre, macabre circumstances (found dead in someone else's clothes likely due to disease, depression, or alcohol), he was the godfather of the modern horror short story. While others were focused on the external horrors of ghosts and monsters at the time, Poe dragged us into the unraveling psyches of the guilty, the obsessed, and the mad through his poem "The Raven," "The Tell-Tale Heart," and 116 other deliciously dark tales. Throughout his weird and chaotic life in which he feuded with everyone and married his thirteen-year-old cousin, he gave birth to both psychological horror and detective fiction, leaving a legacy that will continue to impact the genre forever.

Ann Radcliffe

Long before Shelley, Stoker, and Poe, Ann Radcliffe was out here inventing the entire gothic aesthetic. Haunted castles, moody villains, mist-covered mountains, crumbling abbeys, heroines on the verge of hysteria . . . all her. She was the gothic genre's original architect. Born in 1764, Radcliffe had zero formal literary training and only started writing out of boredom while her husband was away. Her 1794 work *The Mysteries of Udolpho* made her a sensation. It was dramatic, suspenseful, and packed with all the gothic tropes everyone would go on to copy for the next century. The Radcliffe twist, though, is that her work was all about the fear of the unknown, not the fear of the undead. The ghosts and supernatural entities of her stories were always explained away with logical reason. She published five major novels and then disappeared, ghosting the whole literary world herself for the remainder of her days.

Body Horror

Hope you're not squeamish, because body horror isn't just here to scare you, it's here to make your skin crawl. This subgenre is obsessed with what happens when the human body breaks down, mutates, melts, merges, or turns against itself in unnatural and violently distorted ways, because deep down, we're all a little terrified of our own bodies—how fragile and foreign they can be, how easily they change, and how little control we really have over what's growing, festering, or falling apart inside us.

Think puss-oozing wounds, invasion, contagion, mutation, mutilation, disease, extra limbs, teeth where there shouldn't be, and transformations so grotesque you'll start questioning if your stomach is just gurgling from hunger or if it's an alien form rapidly growing inside you. It's gross, gratuitous, and completely unhinged. So! If your bones are still intact and your face hasn't split open yet, YAY! You're ready to peel the skin of body horror back. Let's begin with its six major tropes!

INVASION

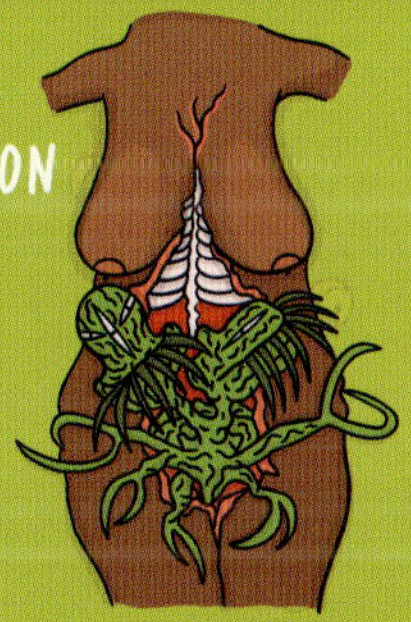

TRANSFORMATION

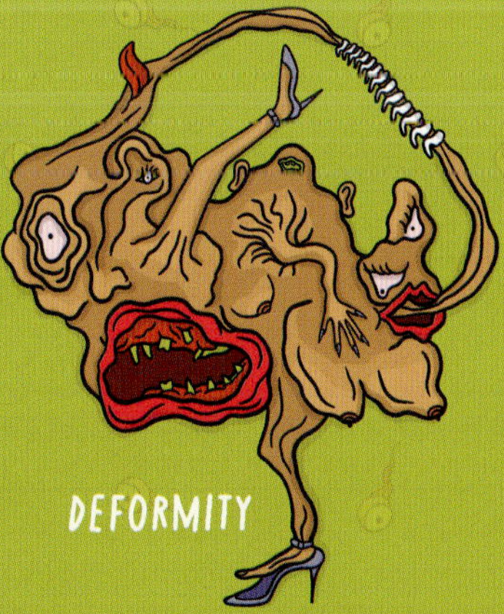

DEFORMITY

PARASITISM

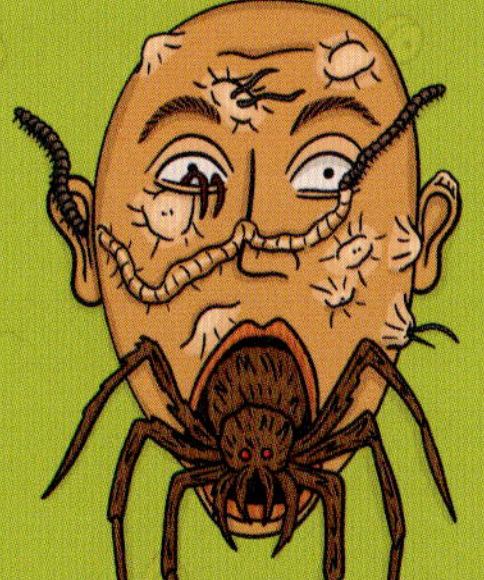

DISEASE AND DECAY

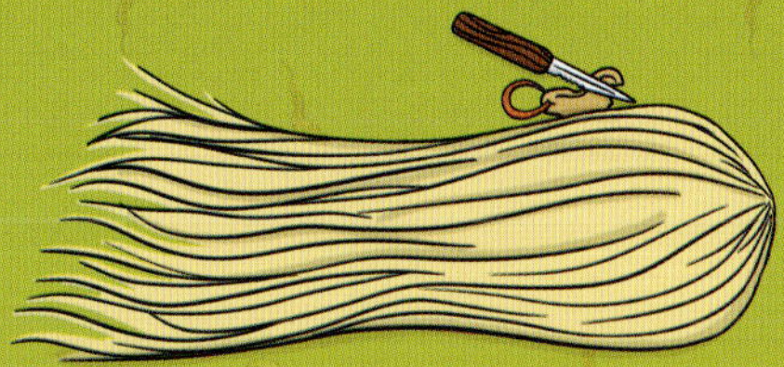

MUTILATION AND DISMEMBERMENT

The Bodies

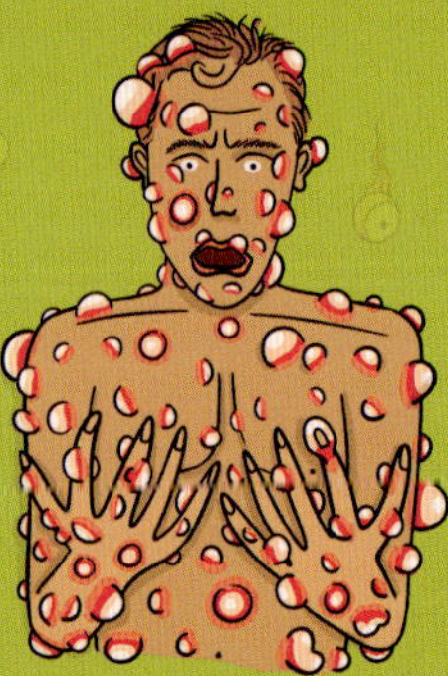
THE INFECTED

THE WILLING HOST

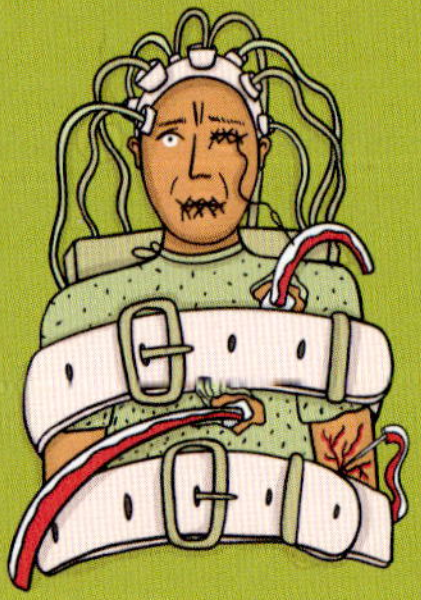
THE EXPERIMENTED

THE TRANSFORMED

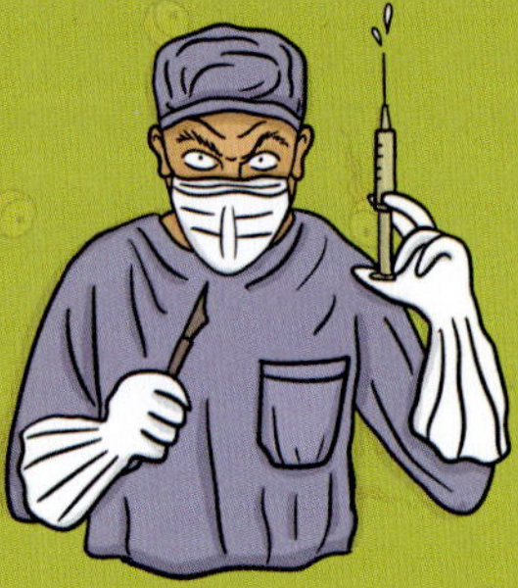
THE SICKO SURGEON

Symbols of the Flesh

WHAT THE PARTS OF THE BODY METAPHORICALLY REPRESENT IN HORROR.

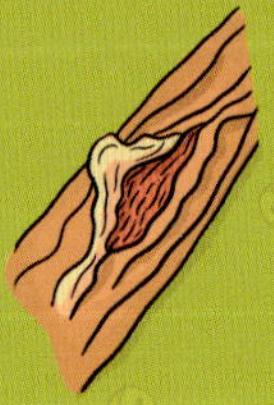
PEELING SKIN
Identity loss

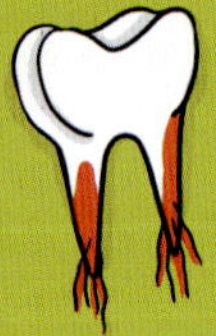
EXTRA TEETH
Evolution

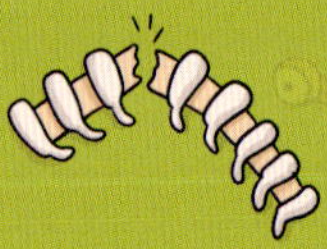
CRACKED SPINE
Corruption

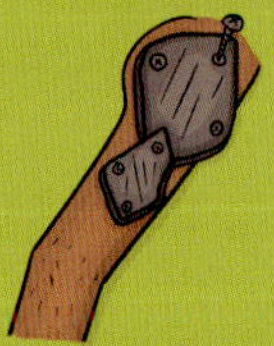
METAL FUSED TO SKIN
Dehumanization

WOUNDED MOUTH
Repression

PARASITIC LUMP
Autonomy loss

Erotic Horror

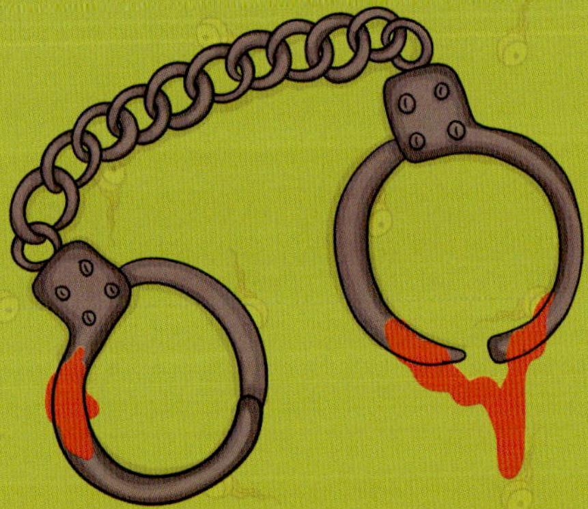

Erotic horror—the slutty, smutty sister of body horror. With biting, bondage, and body fluids, this subgenre exhibits the overlap of fear and desire. We're talking kinks like monster erotica to lesbian vampire romance and everything in between. It's an exploration of extreme pleasure in pain, lust, power dynamics, control, and violent attraction. Sometimes it's overt: writhing tentacles, seductive killers, or blood-soaked sex. Other times, it's subtle—with phallic and vaginal imagery sneaking into creature design or architecture to symbolize patriarchal guilt, repression, or sexual trauma.

DYSTOPIAN HORROR

You need antibiotics, but the hospital's across the city. Search the area for supplies—find them all to survive. Miss one? Better luck next apocalypse.

- The hospital
- 1 backpack
- 2 handguns
- 3 ammo boxes
- 5 water bottles
- 1 gas mask
- 1 pair of shoes
- 5 first aid kits
- 5 granola bars
- 1 crowbar
- 1 pocketknife
- 4 pill bottles
- 4 gas cans
- 1 wild dog
- 5 purple medicinal plants
- 1 satellite phone
- 1 pair of socks
- 1 tarp
- 1 set of jumper cables
- 1 city transit map

SLASHER

Welcome to Slasher Ridge—where the teens are horny, the power's out, and someone just heard a noise outside the cabin. Slasher horror is the genre's bloody playground, built on really dumb decisions, (sometimes masked) psychos, and a body count that climbs with every sequel . . . of which there are many because the killers never really die, do they? Grab the sharpest household object you can find and let's slash this subgenre open to perform an autopsy of all its bloody parts!

THE SLASHERS

THE RECLUSE

Classic creepy outsider, usually angry or jealous of young, beautiful creatures reminiscent of the ones who bullied him. Loves a trench coat.

THE WHITE-COLLAR PSYCHOPATH

He may have an expense account, but this psycho will iron his crispy white sheets before and after spraying your blood all over them.

THE SCORNED REVENGE KILLER

Spent years planning the perfect fairy-tale wedding only to find out Prince Charming was romancing the whole gated community. Wipes him and his entire Rolodex out.

THE BOYFRIEND

We all know this jackass.

THE MASKED KILLER

Of course you have your ghost face–masked killers et cetera, but then there's the mask-wearing-hunting-and-killing-for-fun-with-no-remorse kind of killer. No motive, just loves to kill people . . . and in a dolly mask nonetheless.

Slasher Weapons

Survival Horror

Congratulations!! You graduated/got engaged/reached a milestone/are experiencing a major life event! This means . . . you're going on vacation with your friends to celebrate!! Now choose one place to vacay—each has its perks. Unfortunately, each has its downside as well . . . Nothing's perfect, right?

CHOOSE YOUR OWN ADVENTURE

OMG, you chose **THE SKI TRIP!** Upside, so cute and so chic. Downside is that whether from falling, frostbite, or razor-sharp chairlift wires, you and your friends won't be making it out with your limbs or lives.

Oooh, **EURO BACKPACKING TRIP!** Great choice. Upside, hostels are cheap! Downside, you and your friends will be paying with your organs.

Ahhh, **THE LAKE HOUSE**, so quiet and serene. Upside, moonlit canoe rides on the glassy lake and long soul-connecting chats on the dock, skinny-dipping, and maybe even a card game or two. Downside, the weird neighbors just showed up and plan to use you as firewood.

THE CABIN IN THE WOODS, a true classic. You have excellent taste. Upside is, you're alone in the woods! Downside is, you're not alone in the woods.

CAMPING! Great idea! Upsides—wildlife sightings, s'mores, scary stories, and finally the perfect opportunity to get out of the group chat and unplug. Downside—the only thing getting unplugged is your life support.

And finally, **THE TROPICAL MYSTERY LOCATION!** The upside, a beautiful locale and an all-inclusive resort. The downside, not only did your plane crash, but the resort is actually a sick battle royale game arena, and only one person is leaving this island.

THE CHARACTER TROPES OF SURVIVAL HORROR

CHOOSE YOUR PLAYER, THEN CHECK YOUR SURVIVAL RATE.

THE JOCK

The dumb, hot party boy. Hard to kill at first because there's a lot of hair gel and muscle to get through. 0 PERCENT.

THE CHEERLEADER

The Jock's blond, popular sidepiece who trips in her heels, screams the loudest, and always stupidly says "hello?" into the dark. If she's the final girl, she dumps the jock and quits the squad. 50 PERCENT.

THE BEST FRIEND

Loyal and sidelined, he never gets the girl, is almost always the only minority, and always dies first. 0 PERCENT.

THE NERD

Smart, quirky, and artsy, she's always annoyed with the group, usually the final girl, and sometimes hooks up with the jock in secret. 98 PERCENT.

THE STONER

Thinks it's all a prank until he's baked, barefoot, and beheaded. He's the comedic relief-turned-corpse, and he's probably still holding the joint. 5 PERCENT.

THE SKEPTIC

Way too cool to believe anything is going on. Mocks the supernatural, gets killed when out for another smoke. Dies via slaughter just like his signature leather jacket. 20 PERCENT.

THE CLUELESS COP

On the night shift, eating his sandwich, just one call from clocking out. Shows up too late, sees too little, dies before helping anyone. Badge does nothing. 0 PERCENT.

THE RED HERRING

Creepy stare, twitchy hands, maybe a limp or a hospital bracelet. Warns the group but in riddles. Unhinged and unsettling, he looks like a killer but never is. 99 PERCENT.

THE HOST

Sweet, elderly, and armed only with extra towels and spare keys. Just came to check in, dies violently on the porch. 0 PERCENT.

WHAT *TROPE* WOULD MAKE YOU *CHOKE?*

WOULD YOU SURVIVE THE CLASSIC HORROR WAYS TO DIE?

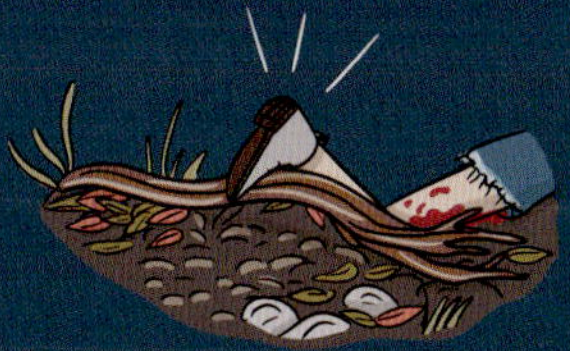

THE TRIP AND FALL

DEFYING WARNING SIGNS

SHOWERING ALONE

SAYING "I'LL BE RIGHT BACK"

SPLITTING UP

FUMBLING YOUR KEYS

CHOOSING AN ISOLATED VACATION SPOT

GOING TO THE BASEMENT

THINKING THE KILLER WAS DEAD

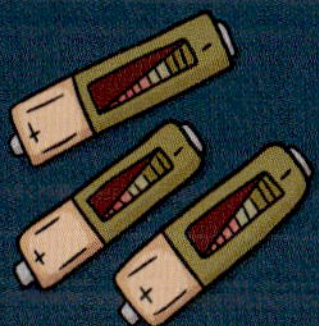

FLASHLIGHT DIES

CELL PHONE GIVES AWAY YOUR HIDING SPOT

ESCAPING ONLY TO WAVE DOWN THE KILLER FOR HELP

HAVING SEX

CAR WON'T START DURING A CHASE

INCLEMENT WEATHER

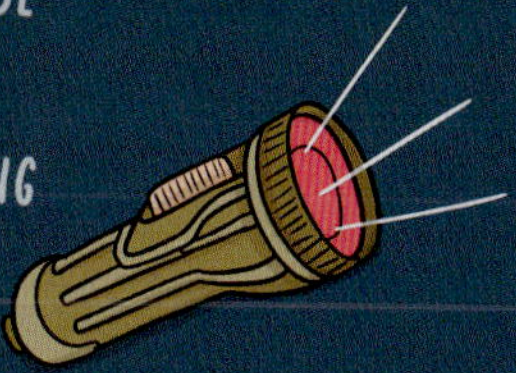

INVESTIGATING A NOISE

FORGOT INHALER

IF YOU DIDN'T TRIP AND FALL FOR ANY OF THESE DEATH TROPES, YOU MUST BE THE FINAL GIRL . . .

Autopsy of the Final Girl

The trope that survives all other tropes.

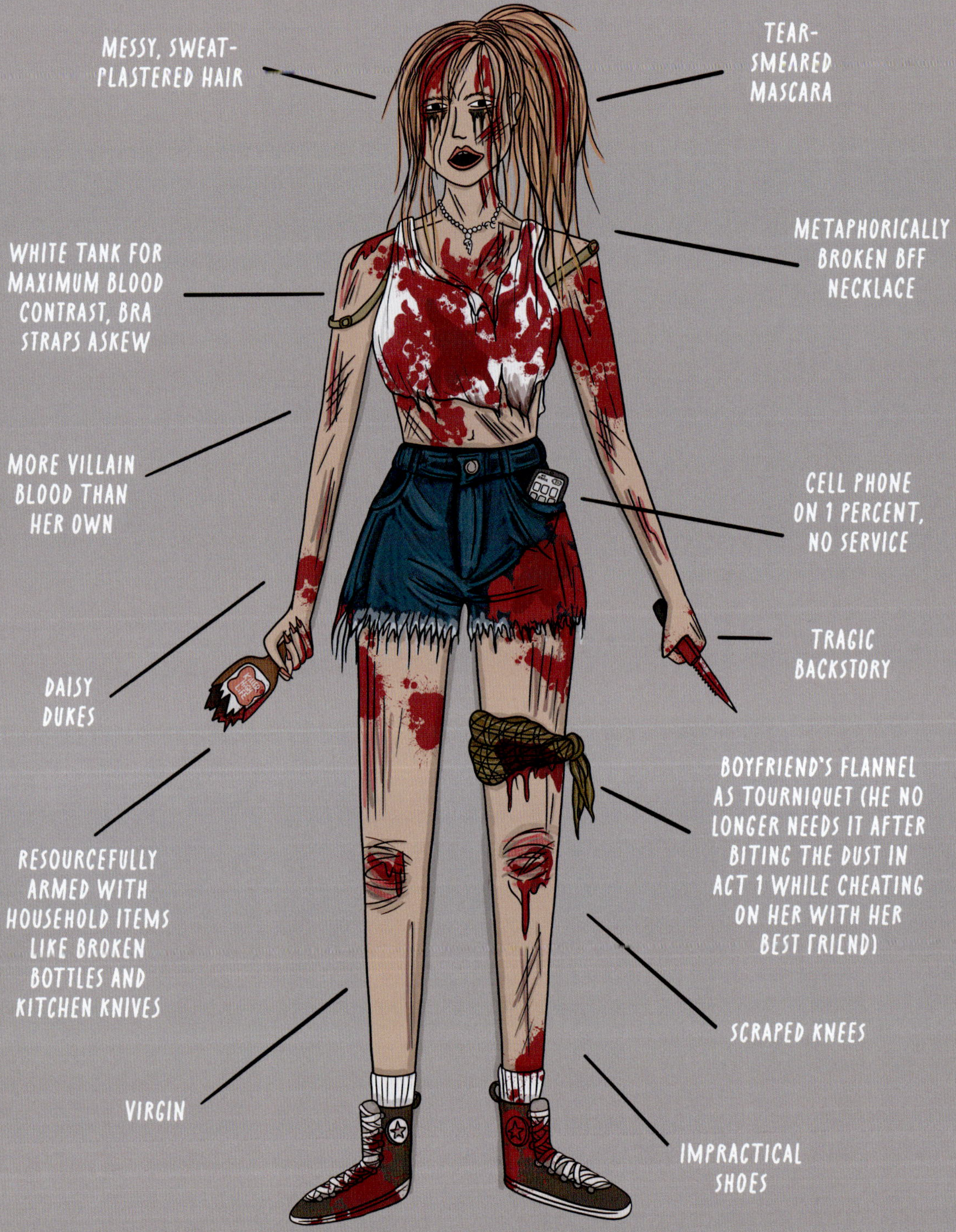

KILLER LOOKS: THE STYLES OF HORROR

Subgenres are just the bones, babe. The style? That's the skin, the face, the drip, the dress. I'm Horror Barbie and I'm here to show you how horror looks. Let's unbox the vibe, the mood, and the visual language behind horror's most iconic and transcendent styles!

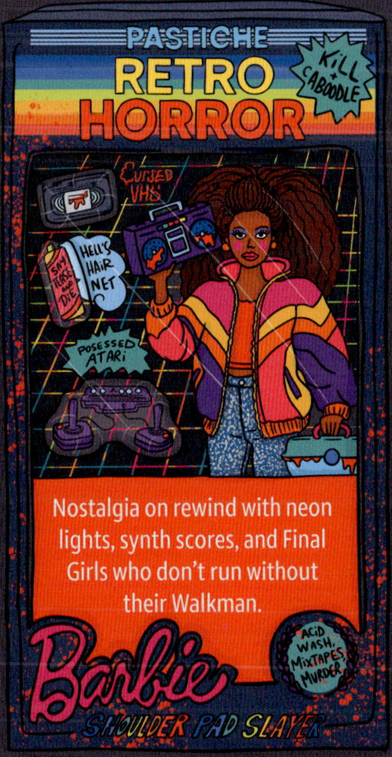

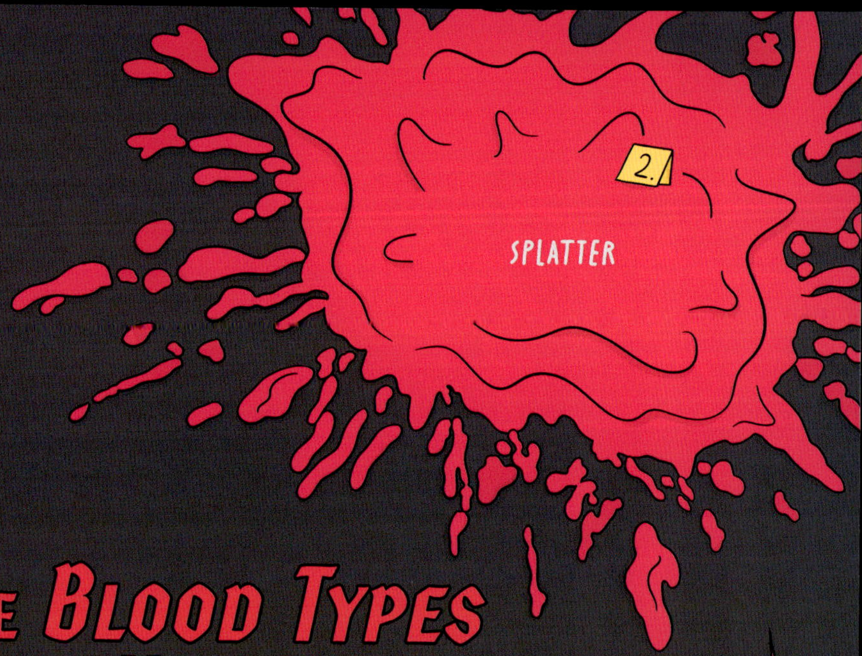

THE BLOOD TYPES OF HORROR

With its requisite appearance in horror, blood could be its own subgenre. Let's examine this bloody tropey crime scene and all the ways the leading, bleeding lady of the horror genre shows up . . . after it leaves the body, that is.

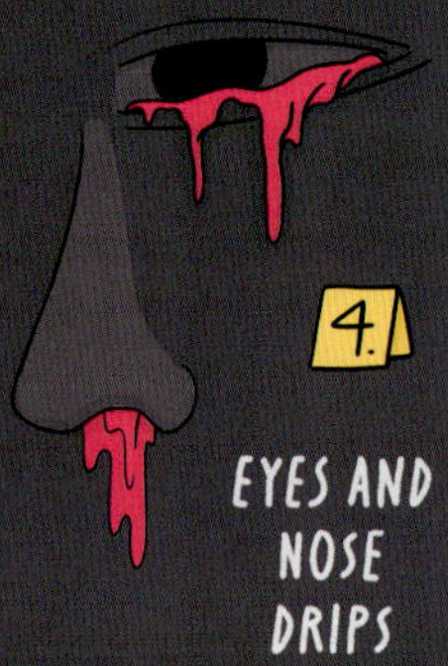

Supernatural Horror

Can you feel the spirits stirring? If you start to feel cold, don't worry, that's just someone who died here, passing through your body.

In this realm, whoever is present won't chase you down. They'll just watch. And wait. And then they'll slowly haunt. Supernatural horror is about the weight of what's left behind—unfinished business, unresolved trauma, and the victims that won't rest or be silenced until someone pays. Usually the next occupant.

Occupant of what, you ask? Well, at the center of supernatural horror is one of the genre's oldest and most iconic tropes: the haunted house. It's more than four walls and creaky floors—it's a mirror for the people inside it, and sometimes a living thing all its own. The house remembers. It's haunted by grudges and grief. It doesn't just contain horror—it's made of it. It's where pain soaks into the velvet curtains like rancid tobacco smoke, secrets echo in the long carpeted corridors, and the past waits for you in the eyes of every portrait watching as you roam by with your candelabra.

So go ahead. Open the door. Step inside and explore. It sounds like someone may be playing piano . . . Just remember, even if you'd like to stay, this house no longer belongs to the living.

IRON CRESTING AND FINIALS
DORMERS
THE NURSERY
SALONS
STRANGE PHENOMENA
CLAW-FOOT TUBS
SLEEPING CHAMBERS
FIREPLACES
PARLOR
THE LIBRARY
THE STUDY
GRAND STAIRCASE
GHOSTS
CANDLELIT CORRIDORS

RELIGIOUS HORROR

Welcome in, my child . . . you felt it, didn't you? The pull. That tingle down your spine when the church bells tolled through the cobblestone streets of Rome. Your quickened pulse when the hymns poured out the cathedral's bloodstained glass windows. The burning on your scalp as you neared the sacred items of God? Not everyone hears the call . . . but you did.

Here in the sacred order of religious horror, we worship fear in its holiest form—guilt, shame, damnation. We honor the classics: spinning heads, screaming exorcisms, and satanic rites. Every film is a sermon. Every demon, a reminder that the devil doesn't need permission to enter—he's already inside. You may even be carrying his child. You don't remember that night you showed up on our doorstep asking for help, do you? Don't worry—initiation doesn't hurt much. Just a little possession, maybe a light animal sacrifice, and the lingering fear that your soul's been marked since birth. Standard stuff really. Now take this tannis root and kneel. Cross yourself (or don't—it's too late anyway) and repeat after us: In religious horror we trust. In faith we fear. Amen.

Satanist's Supply List

Religious Horror Sites

The Six Signs Of Possession

Religious Horror Icons

What's In My Bag?

(EXORCIST EDITION)

CHRISTMAS *Horror*

Deck the halls with blood and bodies! One of the *hallmarks* of horror is perversion. It loves to take our *nicest* things and twist them into something *naughty*. Even the sacred is fair game in horror, in fact, the more precious something may be, the more likely it is to fa-la-la-la-all victim to the genre. Though the folktale stories that inspired our most popular Christmas tales are often dark, leave it to the horror genre to take the most peaceful, gentle night of the year, and smash a snow globe against its skull. Open the advent calendar to find the twelve tropes of Christmas horror!

1

GHOSTS

Dickens's *A Christmas Carol* was inspired by the British tradition of telling ghost stories during Christmas and winter solstice, when nights were long and the veil was believed to be thinnest.

2

KRAMPUS

The horned, demonic terror from Alpine pagan lore punished the naughty so Saint Nick could keep his hands clean.

RELIGION

Religion is already its own horror subgenre—so a holiday rooted in one is a tinsel mine for tropes. Think midnight mass, nuns, and all the sacrilegious festive fun to be had.

3

KILLER SANTA

This guy will let himself down your chimney, slice and dice you, and still eat the cookies you left out for him.

4

5

CAMP

Christmas horror is often pure "camp"; it's over the top, maximalist, gaudy, theatrical, flamboyant, and exaggerated.

6

CURSED GIFTS

The perfect opportunity to unload any cursed items on your enemies.

7

SILENT NIGHT?

Carols, sleigh bells, children laughing? Expect all your comforting classic seasonal sounds to be twisted into haunting melodies and harbingers of death.

8

FESTIVE WEAPONS

Why would you use a basic weapon when you could strangle with Christmas lights or stab with candy canes?

9

WINTER WEATHER

Snowy icy blizzards, killer snowmen, and isolation. Plus, blood looks great on snow. 'Tis the season!

10

PUNNY TITLES

Better Watch Out, *Violent Night*, *Black Christmas*, *All the Creatures Were Stirring*? It's not true Christmas horror without a punny Christmas title.

11

THE NAUGHTY LIST

If you're naughty, expect more than coal in your stocking this year.

12

FAMILY DYSFUNCTION

Have you ever wanted to murder your family at the holidays? Christmas horror helps you follow through.

FOLK HORROR

Maybe you've been invited, or maybe you took a wrong turn in the woods. Either way, you're now in a village that's not on any map, surrounded by smiling strangers telling you you're just in time for "the choosing."

Folk horror is all about isolation, old gods, and the underlying fear that something's going unsaid. This subgenre thrives on traditions gone askew and a worshipped force needing appeasement. We get pagan rituals, sacrifices, sacred lands, and controlling cults. The bloodline must continue, and the crops always need to be fed.

If you've found yourself here . . . don't break the circle, don't question the harvest, don't drink the tea or eat the "meat," and for the love of whatever god is worshipped here, get out before the festival.

WELCOME, OUTSIDER

Whether you're here for the week or the rest of your life (could be one and the same), the village map and calendar will help guide your stay.

1 MAY DAY	2 BARN RAISING	3	4 GROUP HUNT	5	6 PRAY TO THE OLD GODS	7 SEWING CIRCLE BYO SKINS
8	9 FEED BONE TREE BLOOD	WASH BLOODY WHITE LINENS WITH WASHBOARD	11	12 GOAT SLAUGHTER	13 THE DRINKING	14
TOWN MEETING	ATONE FOR IMPURE THOUGHTS	17	BLOOD MOON	19	20	SUMMER SOLSTICE SACRIFICE
22 OFF SITE RECRUIT	23	BUNDLE STICKS WITH JUTE	25	SKIN RABBITS	HARVEST	
29	BATCH BREW TEA	31	BURN EFFIGY	2	3 THE CHOOSING	REPLENISH FIELDS SOW SEEDS FEED CROPS

THERE ARE PLENTY OF ACTIVITIES TO JOIN THIS MONTH!

The Folk Horror Paper Doll

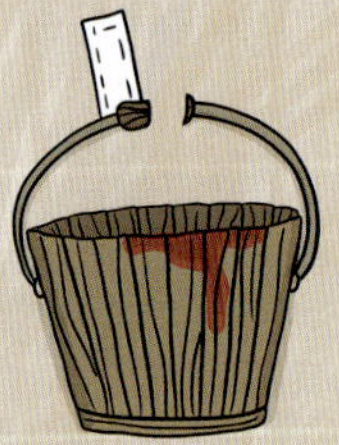

You Know You've Joined a Folk Horror Cult If You're . . .

CHURNING A LOT OF BUTTER

ONE OF MANY DATING "THE PROPHET"

CARVING SYMBOLS IN TREES

ACQUIRING A TASTE FOR GOAT'S BLOOD

DRINKING HERBAL "KOOL-AID"

SLAUGHTERING OUTSIDERS

Autopsy of the Creepy Kid

THE LITTLEST MOST PERSISTENT HORROR TROPE

THE CREEPY KID STARTER PACK

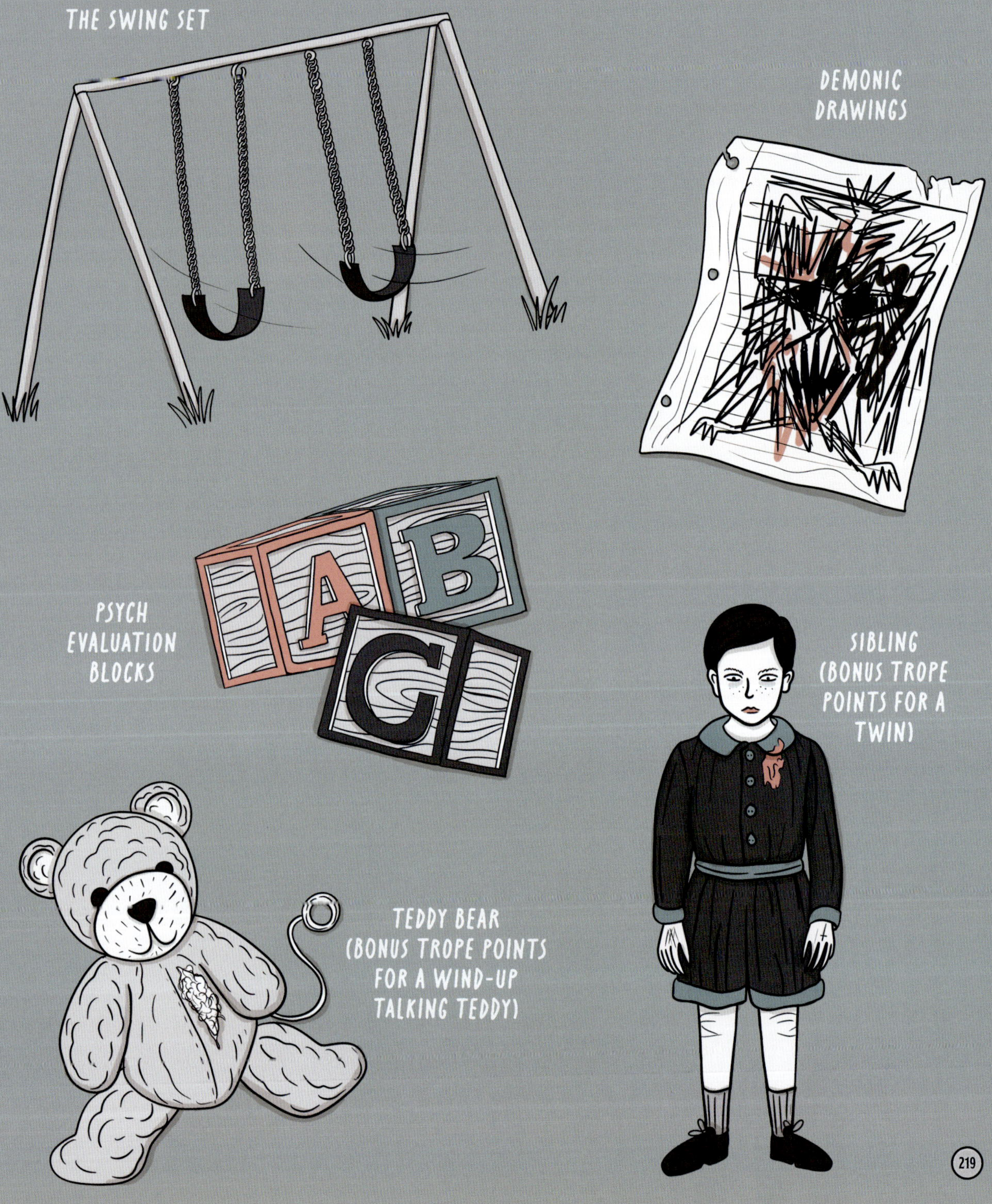

FOUND FOOTAGE

If you're reading this, you've stumbled upon some found footage. But all that's left is the tape . . . no narrator, no polished shots, just the firsthand account of what happened to them, and I think I hear some panicked breathing . . .

Like this tape, found footage recordings are usually discovered after the fact. They're left behind in a haunted house, temple ruins, buried in a backpack, or uploaded by someone who never logged back on. You're witnessing things exactly how they happened, right up until the moment the person filming disappeared . . . probably in the place you're standing right now.

This subgenre leans hard into supernatural horror—demons, ghosts, curses, and things that don't appear to the naked eye or ear, only on camera. It's raw, gritty, occasionally shaky, and real enough to make you question if what you're watching actually happened . . .

So . . . still curious? Go ahead. Hit play. Chances are what you're about to see is one of the most common found footage setups below. Just don't expect everyone in the footage to be found. And honestly, I'd get out of here before what got them, gets you.

THE DOCUMENTARY MAKERS

THE PARANORMAL NIGHT CAM

THE NEWS CREW

THE LIVE STREAM

THE COUPLE'S VACAY

THE HOME VIDEO

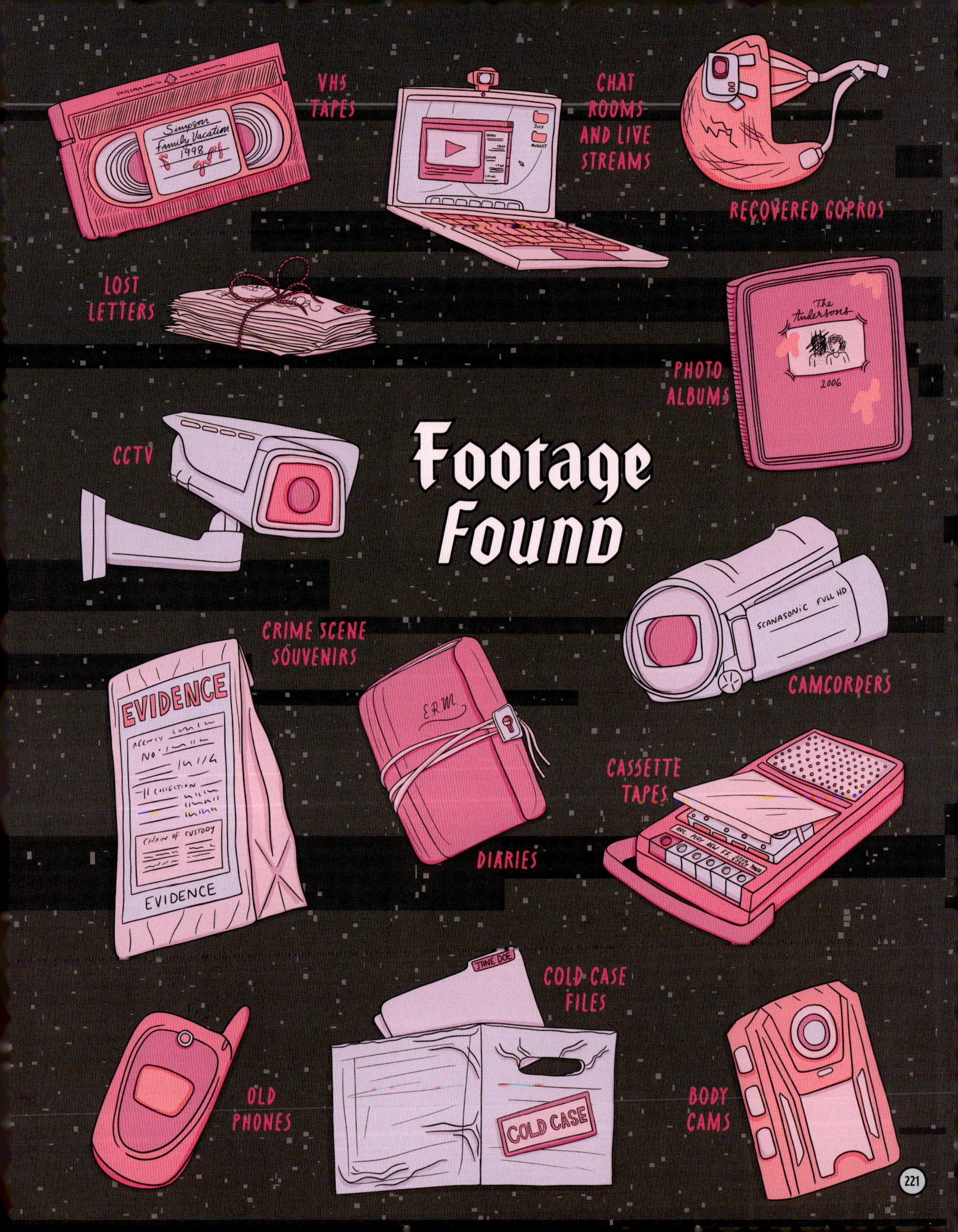

Footage Found
VHS TAPES
Simpson Family Vacation 1998
CHAT ROOMS AND LIVE STREAMS
RECOVERED GOPROS
LOST LETTERS
PHOTO ALBUMS
The Andersons
2006
CCTV
CAMCORDERS
SCANASONIC FULL HD
CRIME SCENE SOUVENIRS
EVIDENCE
CHAIN OF CUSTODY
EVIDENCE
E.R.M.
DIARIES
CASSETTE TAPES
COLD CASE FILES
JANE DOE
COLD CASE
OLD PHONES
BODY CAMS

PSYCHOLOGICAL HORROR

You're not in danger. You're just tired. Stressed. Paranoid. Overthinking, right? That shadow in the corner isn't moving. That voice isn't real . . . is it? Psychological horror doesn't need butcher knives and chainsaws—it uses your own mind as its weapon. It's about losing control, questioning what's real, and your psyche unraveling one thought at a time. The subgenre feeds on gaslighting, memory gaps, déjà vu, identity collapse, and the dread that something is very wrong—but only you seem to notice.

THE CORE ELEMENTS OF PSYCHOLOGICAL HORROR

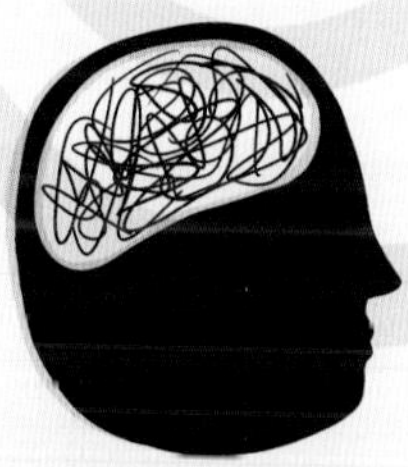

INTERNALIZED FEAR - MENTAL TORMENT, EMOTIONAL CHAOS

UNRELIABLE NARRATION - A FRACTURED PERCEPTION

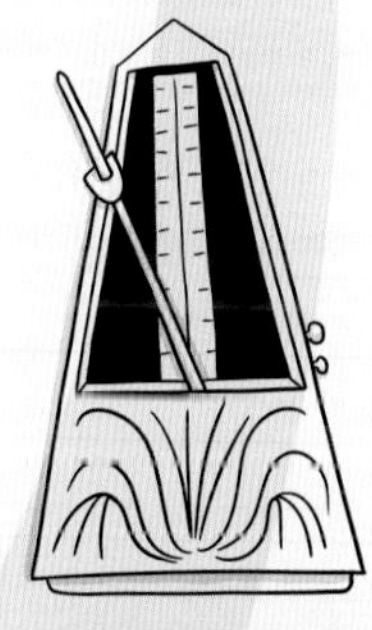

SLOW SUFFOCATING TENSION - MIND UNRAVELING TAKES TIME

ISOLATION AND ALIENATION - PHYSICAL AND EMOTIONAL SEPARATION

MANIPULATION AND CONTROL - MIND GAMES AND GASLIGHTING

IDENTITY CRISIS AND MADNESS - A LOST SENSE OF SELF

ARE YOU *WATCHING* PSYCHOLOGICAL HORROR OR ARE YOU *GOING CRAZY*?

Cosmic Horror

Like psychological horror, cosmic horror preys on the mind—but on a much bigger scale. It's about the suffocating fear that we're small, powerless, and never truly in control. Think ancient gods, sublime forces, and existential dread so vast it fractures the mind. In cosmic horror, the universe finds you insignificant. It doesn't care if you live, die, or lose your grip on reality.

CREATURE

Did you feel that? The ground shook a second ago . . . there are ripples in your water glass . . . why have the birds stopped chirping? Did those trees over there just splinter and fall?! . . . I think something's coming . . .

Creature features are horror at its LOUDEST! Massive monsters, mutated science projects, and ancient beasts awakened from the earth's core by bad human choices. It's chaos, destruction, and the perfect way to feel as insignificant as the ants we casually squish under our feet.

It's the realm where monsters crawl out of the ocean, thaw out of the Arctic, and stomp through our cities rendering us completely defenseless. It's where our weapons become laughable, our nets tear like paper, our cages snap like twigs, and our armies look like toy soldiers.

This is the home of Godzilla, King Kong, giant insects, toxic swamp lurkers, killer sharks, and anything with too many teeth. Sometimes the creature is a force of nature, sometimes it's mankind's hubris getting body

FEATURES

slammed by a four-hundred-foot lizard. Most likely it's a metaphor for nuclear warfare, invasion, and . . . racism? Turn to chapter 6! You might outrun it, but most likely you'll find yourself pulverized among the rubble.

Everywhere Monsters: THE INSIDIOUS CREATURE TROPE

This trope appears when the movie monster isn't confined to a single colossus—it's inside everything, and everyone. The threat can be in plain sight spreading like a virus through crowds—it's not one beast you can outrun—but a growing infestation that turns entire towns, cities, or worlds into apocalyptic hunting grounds. The horror comes from realizing there's nowhere left to run, every house could be invaded, every stranger and friend could be one of them, and survival means trusting no one.

The Subgenre Mash Up

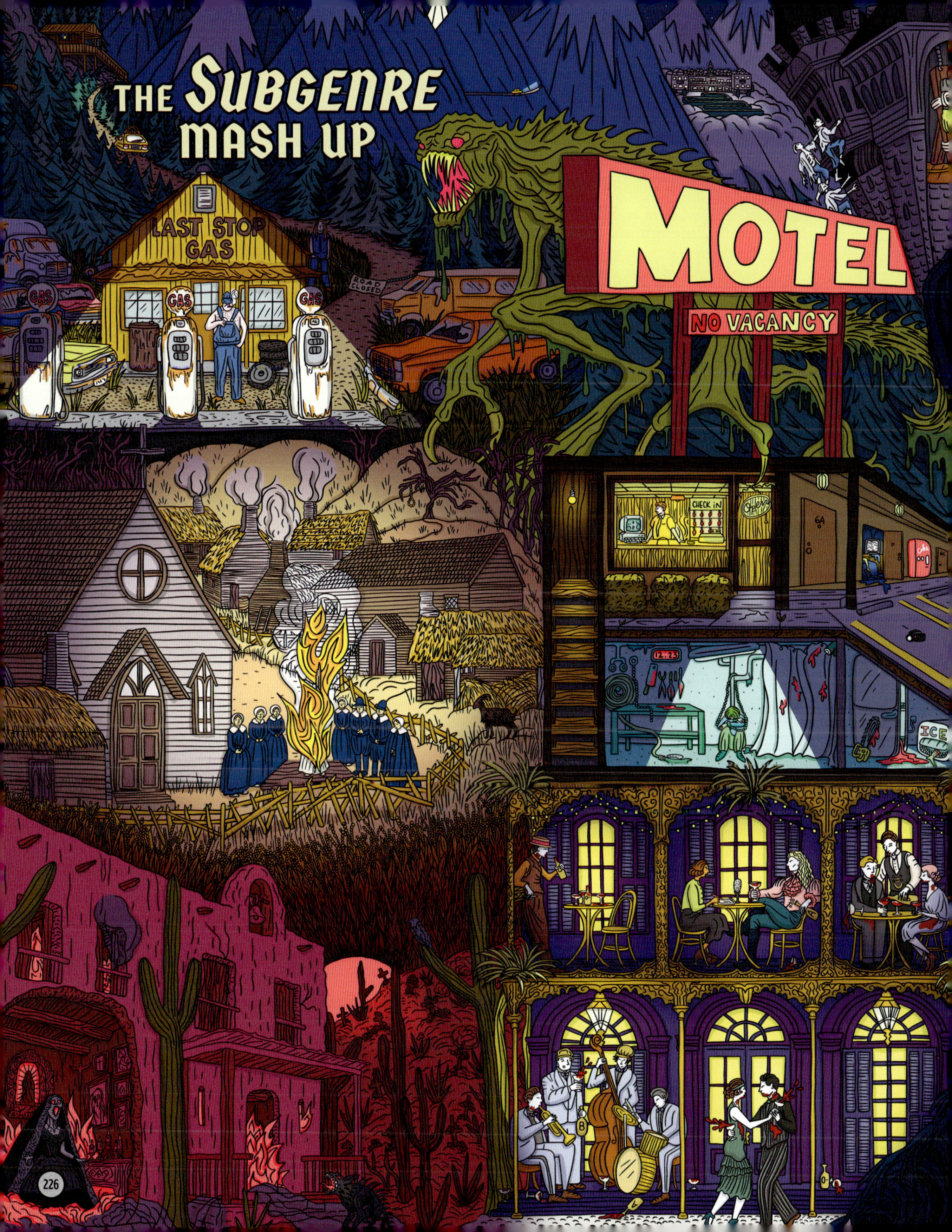

CAN YOU FIND?

- 1 rat
- 1 remote
- Rotten food with flies
- 3 cigarettes
- 1 foot
- 1 bell
- 5 ghosts
- 1 camcorder
- 1 hand
- The word *help*
- 2 ladders
- 1 interview
- 1 hedge maze
- 1 goat
- 34 candles
- 1 cabin in the woods
- 1 knife
- Half a cat
- 1 Bible
- Edgar Allan Poe

SHOCKBUSTER
VIDEO

WELCOME BACK! TO THOSE WHO returned their rentals, thank you. To those who didn't, I know you're trying to be the Final Girl and all, but here at Shockbuster, all our VHS tapes are cursed so . . . see you never.

Well then! Did you see that there's so much more to horror than gore? What was your favorite subgenre? Character trope? Did you join a cult? Ah yes, they can be very persuasive, I get it.

In fact, real-life events and experiences *like* cult recruitment have shaped the horror genre so deeply that it can practically be read like a chronological history book. So, if you dare, take a seat, and open your texts . . .

YEAR:
00
10
20
30
40
50
60
70
80
90

6

Horror Through the Decades

Is it history or horror? The history of horror? The horrors of history? Is it all the same thing?! Whatever the answer, one thing's for sure, the two have always been, and always will be, engaged in a dance macabre.

When we look back decade by decade, we see that horror isn't just about trends or tropes—it's a time capsule. Every era has its own unique flavor of fear, shaped by what was happening in the real world at that time. From war, plague, social unrest, scientific breakthroughs and breakdowns, horror caught it all, dressed it in claws, blood, and shadows, and handed it back to us.

The horror genre is a mirror. At times, a deeply unflattering one, but a mirror, nonetheless. It reflects everything we're scared of, angry about, or dying from. Horror is where we reclaim events that we have no power over. It's how we raise our voices, rebel, resist, rejoice, and reconcile. It's emotional exorcism and a kind of revisionist history—a way for humans to rewrite, reclaim, and interact with their past, present, and future, through metaphor, story, and style.

Horror isn't just relevant—it's reactive. It shifts with us. It mutates alongside our fears. It's how we make sense of the world.

If you care to see for yourself, proceed forward into the time machine, and if you get motion sickness, please try not to stain our leather seats.

1900s ~ 1910s

POST-INDUSTRIAL REVOLUTION

Machines had replaced people, urban slums swallowed communities, and factory life dehumanized the worker. Horror responded with narratives of man vs. machine, human obsolescence, mechanical monsters, and cold isolation in crowded industrial spaces.

WORLD WAR I (1914–1918)

The first modern war unleashed real-life body horror: trench foot, gas burns, "shell shock," and rotting corpses in no-man's-land. Soldiers came home transformed—body parts missing, minds shattered. Horror echoed this with broken bodies, haunted psyches, and a rising fear that war had turned men into monsters.

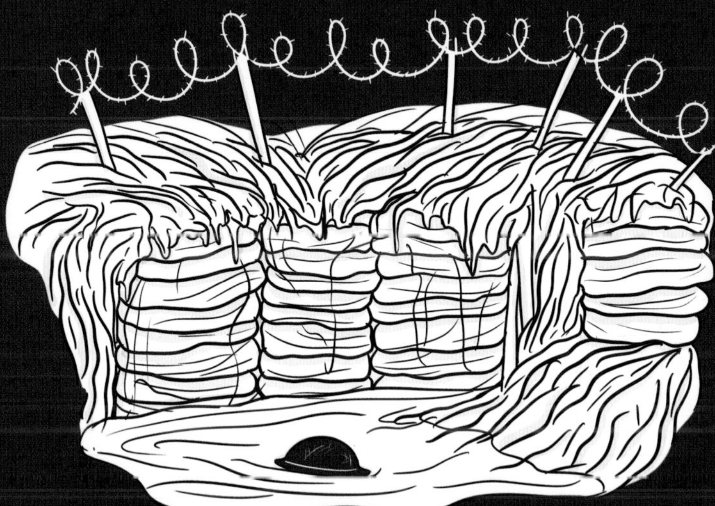

MIND DISSECTION

In the early 1900s, Freud introduced psychoanalysis to the American public, cracking open the human mind and diving into dreams, repression, and the unconscious, all which became horror's new playground.

CLASS ANXIETY

Two existing social roles of the time fueled horror—the crumbling aristocrat and the "freakish" underclass. Prejudices turned into fears. Influenced by sideshows, horror portrayed disabled, disfigured, or nonconforming bodies as monstrous, villains or victims were shown as unclean, malformed, or "less evolved." Physical difference signaled moral danger, echoing elite anxieties about poverty and collapsing class divides.

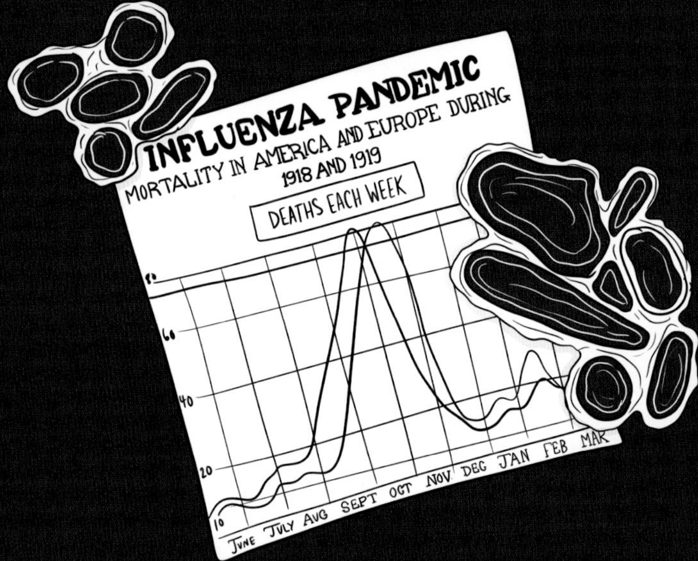

SPANISH FLU PANDEMIC (1918)

The deadliest pandemic in history killing over fifty million (more than World War I) and striking just as soldiers returned home. Horror absorbed the terror of contagious breath, masked faces, mass graves, and bodily breakdown. Death was viral, public, and infectious, fueling early depictions of fear toward an invisible enemy.

CONSUMPTION CHIC

Tuberculosis was one of the deadliest diseases of the early 1900s. Its symptoms—wasting, dilated pupils, pale complexion—were romanticized as tragic and beautiful, some women even poisoning themselves to achieve the look. This ideal fed directly into gothic imagery and the myth of the beautiful vampire. The bloody handkerchief remains an enduring omen in horror.

THE TRIANGLE SHIRTWAIST FACTORY FIRE

When over a hundred women were trapped and burned alive behind locked doors, fire became an iconic horror image. Scorched Victorian dresses, congested factories, and working-class bodies—especially in stories where women's labor and lives were disposable—set the cogs in motion for tragedy-inspired terror.

NOSFERATU

F. W. Murnau's *Nosferatu* brought vampires to the screen shaped by postcolonial paranoia, and inspired by the recent plague, it made them foreign, contagious, and morally corrupting. The monster arrived by ship, carrying death into "clean and pure" cities. The vampires, mummies, and golems of the 1900s embodied fears of immigration, disease, and foreign influence.

1920s – 1930s

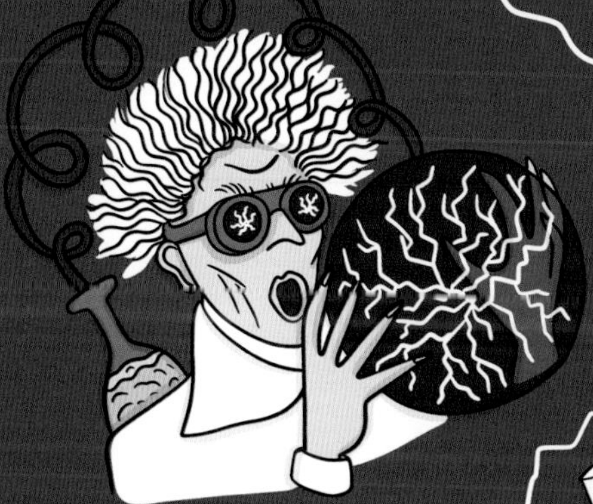

SCIENCE = DANGER

As science advanced—electricity, surgery, genetics—horror warned through stories like *Frankenstein* that playing god makes you the monster.

THE GREAT DEPRESSION

Horror used monsters to symbolize the poor, desperate, and outcast struggling to survive.

UNIVERSAL MONSTERS

Out of the decade's darkest events came horror's golden age, with each iconic monster standing in as a metaphor for the real events and fears of the time.

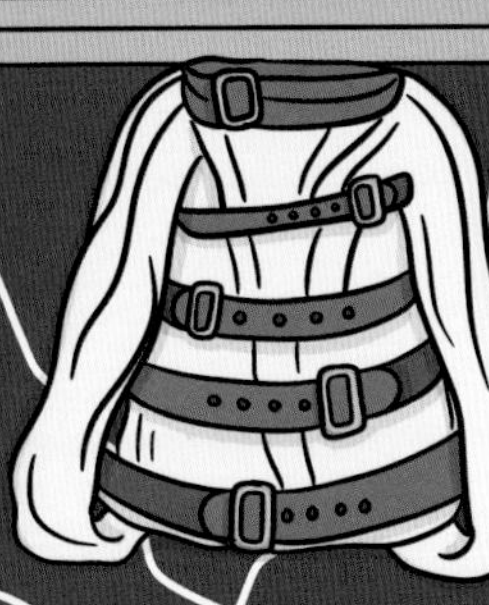

INSTITUTIONALIZATION RISES

"Hysterical" women and the poor are isolated and mistreated. Horror adopts the asylum and turns the mentally ill into monsters. Lobotomies are introduced.

KING KONG

Brought from a "savage" island to New York where he's exploited, feared, and ultimately destroyed. The iconic "monster" was never just spectacle, but a deeply racialized allegory reflecting the racist anxieties of the time.

RISE OF FACISM AND THE OUTSIDER

As dictators gained power, horror gave us evil leaders with mass mind control. As immigrants arrived, xenophobia and antisemitism gave monsters foreign accents.

THE "DANGEROUS" WOMAN

As women gained power and Prohibition banned pleasure, seductive women became monsters in horror punished for beauty, desire, and independence.

1940s

WORLD WAR II (1939–1945)

Atomic bombs, genocide, and large-scale destruction made real life more terrifying than anything horror could imagine. The genre pulled back, shifting to subtler themes instead of overt manufactured fear.

HUMAN AS MONSTER

The Holocaust forced a global reckoning with the monstrous potential of humanity. Horror began shifting away from fictional creatures and toward man as the real threat, with Nazis becoming one of the genre's most enduring villain archetypes.

GOTHIC REVIVAL

Mass death sparked a return to Spiritualism, and horror stories returned to ghosts, hauntings, and attempted connection with the afterlife to process loss.

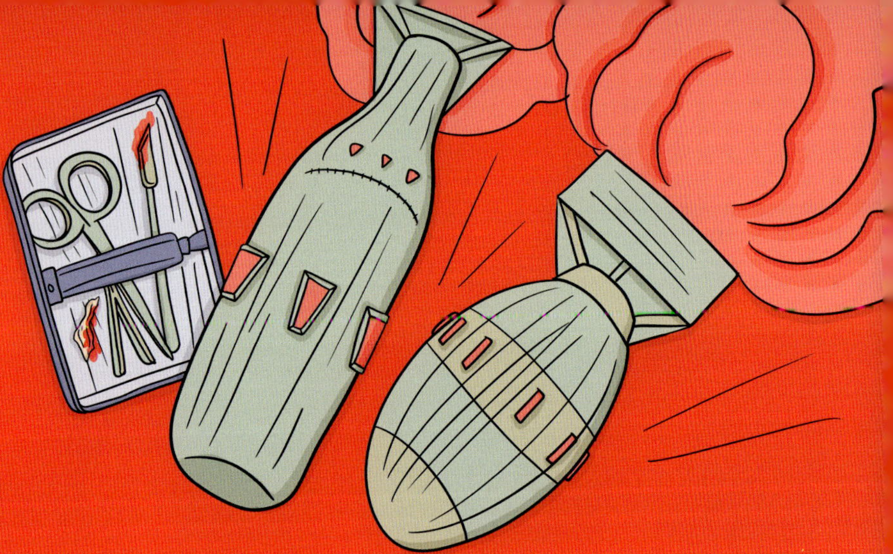

THE MAD SCIENTIST EVOLUTION

World War II's grotesque medical experiments, bomb building, radiation poisoning, and psychological warfare shifted horror's mad scientist archetype from eccentric to cruel and inhuman.

CENSORSHIP TIGHTENS

The Hays Code—a set of industry imposed moral guidelines—cracked down on violence, sex, and immorality in media, so horror leaned harder on metaphor. Dracula could still ooze seduction, as long as it stayed symbolic . . . and he was staked in the end.

WOMEN ARE DISMISSED

After aiding the war efforts, women were pressured back into domestic roles—horror reflected this by punishing powerful independent women with madness, monstrosity, and death.

SHIFT TO INTERNALIZED HORROR

After the war, veterans faced incapacitating PTSD and identity crises. Horror mirrored this by turning inward to explore madness, amnesia, and mental unraveling.

1950s

INVASION

Aliens became stand-ins for outsiders—communists, immigrants, and anyone seen as a threat to American values. Horror reflected invasion panic by metaphorically turning any "other" into something from another world.

THE HOUSEWIFE

After the war, women were sent home and chained to expectations. Horror punished independence and any ambition beyond domesticity. The automaton housewife—smiling, repressed, and under enough pressure to blow her husband away while heating his dinner, has endured as a metaphorical horror trope since the fifties.

COLD WAR AND THE ATOMIC BOMB

The bombs were dropped in the forties, but the fallout bled into the fifties when the mushroom cloud became horror's defining symbol. As nuclear testing and Cold War tension grew, horror reflected the constant fear of total annihilation—redefining terror as man-made, sudden, and unstoppable.

MCCARTHYISM AND THE RED SCARE

Witch hunts spread as fear of the "un-American" took hold. Neighbors turned on each other and suspicion ruled. Horror wiretapped into the paranoia with stories of surveillance, betrayal, enemies in disguise, and the fear of always being watched.

SUBURBAN CONFORMITY

The fifties demanded perfection—matching lawns, cookie-cutter homes, and dinner at 5:00 p.m. Identities that didn't fit the mold—queer, rebellious, or non-white—were pushed out. Horror turned that tension into fear: pod people, impostors, and total identity suppression.

MONSTROUS DESTRUCTION

As atomic fears grew, so did the monsters. Radiation-spawned creatures embodied the consequences of war and fears of mutation and otherness.

GODZILLA

In America, the atomic bomb birthed paranoia. In Japan, the trauma took monstrous form—becoming Godzilla, the towering, radioactive icon of the twentieth century. Forged from real-life devastation, Godzilla was created in postwar Japan as a metaphor for nuclear destruction, reflecting the trauma of Hiroshima and Nagasaki.

HORROR'S MOST LITERAL METAPHOR: A direct metaphor for nuclear destruction following the atomic bombs the US dropped in 1945, Godzilla appeared—unstoppable, devastating, and man-made.

KAIJU: Japanese monster movies made in the 1950s as a direct response to World War II—used to process occupation, loss, and powerlessness. Kaiju cinema explicitly used horror to reclaim the narrative after invasion.

RADIATION: Godzilla's mutated size and scales glowing with radiation symbolized the effects of nuclear fallout.

DESTRUCTION: Godzilla's ability to easily reduce metropolises to dust mirrored the devastation the nuclear bombs brought to Japanese cities.

Historical Masks

BORN OUT OF NECESSITY, KEPT ALIVE BY HORROR.

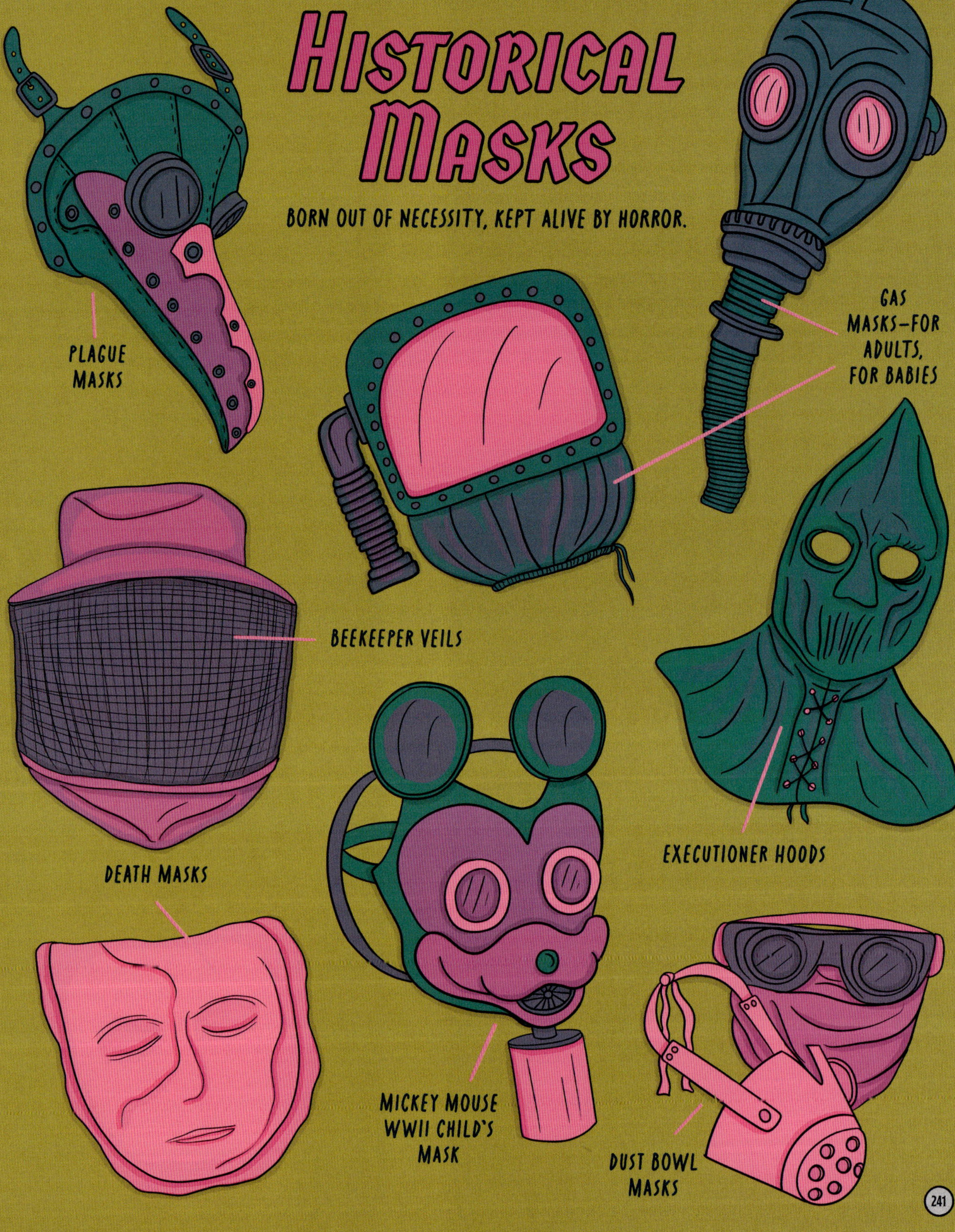

1960s

THE VIETNAM WAR (1955–1975)

As the first televised war, death was brought directly into American living rooms—body bags, napalm, civilian casualties over frozen TV dinners. Horror responded with bleaker stories—no clear villains, no justice, just senseless violence, moral confusion, and bodies that didn't stay dead . . .

CIVIL UNRESTED

As war and civil unrest raged, horror brought the fallen back to life to comment. Released the same year as Martin Luther King Jr.'s assassination, *Night of the Living Dead* (1968) became horror's first explicit racial allegory—its Black lead killed in a manner that reflected America's history of racial violence.

COUNTERCULTURE AND PSYCHEDELIA

Acid trips and mind expansion cracked horror wide open. Stories got more absurd, the blood on the walls got brighter, and scary stories fell down the rabbit hole into surreal, drug-fueled nightmares.

CIVIL RIGHTS MOVEMENT

As the country boiled with protest and resistance, horror tapped into the tension and chaos by amplifying stories of identity fear and power shifts. Desegregation, violent inequality, riots, and rebellion echoed through the genre as loudly as the marches in the streets.

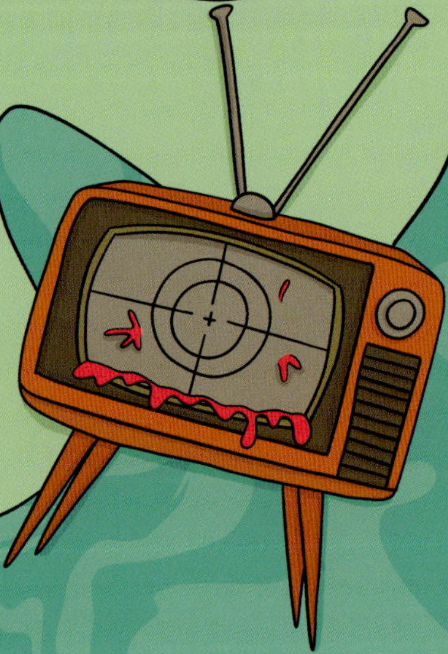

ASSASSINATIONS AND NATIONAL GRIEF

When leaders—JFK, MLK Jr.—were killed on live TV, the hope they embodied died with them. Fear of sudden, senseless violence sank into the cultural psyche. Horror began to exploit that vulnerability by building up assumingly invincible protagonists, only to slaughter them without a second thought—most famously in the shower of the Bates Motel.

NUCLEAR FAMILY BREAKDOWN

The perfect 1950s family started to crack. Divorce, teen rebellion, and shifting gender roles splintered the white picket fence. In horror, the family portrait was replaced by monsters, and the TV dinner was served cold and moldy.

1970s

GOVERNMENT DISILLUSIONMENT

After Vietnam and Watergate, the government was no longer the hero—just another source of betrayal. Distrust went mainstream, and horror followed suit with corrupt authorities, secret experiments, and controlling institutions that couldn't be trusted.

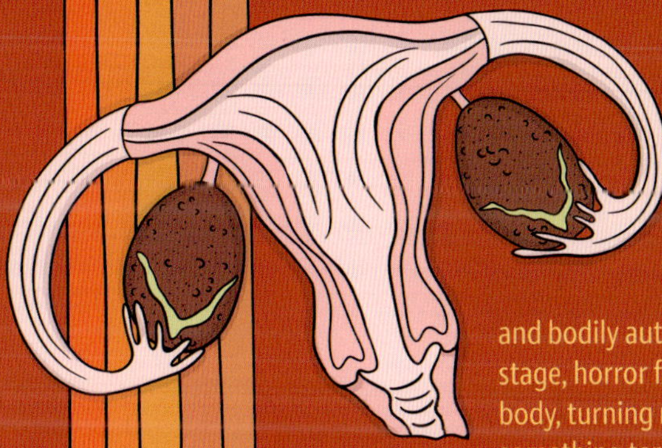

ROE V. WADE (1973)

As the fight for abortion rights and bodily autonomy took center stage, horror fixated on the female body, turning reproduction into something terrifying where what grows inside could destroy you.

SATANIC PANIC AT THE DISCO

As traditional Christian values unraveled post-1950s, the church door swung open for demons. Occult practices reentered pop culture, and horror was *possessed*—with films like *The Exorcist* sparking a boom in religious horror and igniting the beginnings of the Satanic Panic.

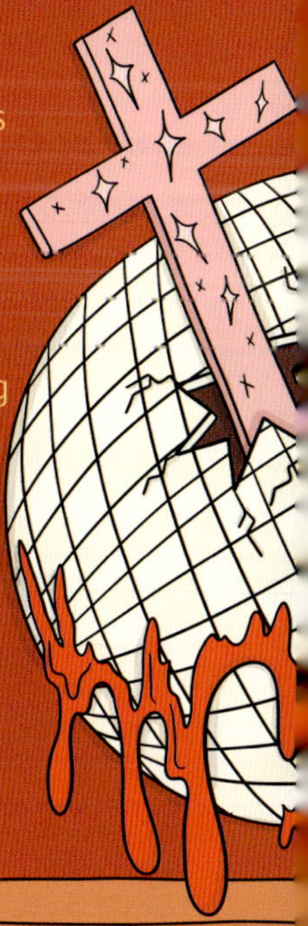

WOMEN'S LIBERATION MOVEMENT

As women pushed back against traditional roles, workplace equality and rejecting the self-sacrificing mother—horror responded with tropes that punished that rebellion. Female rage, autonomy, and sexuality were framed as dangerous. Horror turned this growing independence into a source of fear. The witch remains alive and well.

GRIT TO GRAIN

The postwar economic crisis punctured the picture-perfect image of the fifties and sixties, and urban decay visually infected idyllic life. Horror embraced this, using cities as bleak backdrops full of crime and grime. The seventies Super 8 filmmaking added to the gritty realism, an aesthetic still mimicked today to achieve the raw, visceral tone of the decade's unique horror look.

CULT MANIA

Heaven's Gate, the Symbionese Liberation Army, and, most famously, the Peoples Temple led by Jim Jones who shepherded followers from Indiana to California, to Jonestown, Guyana, and eventually their death via a vat of cyanide-laced grape Flavor Aid—resulting in the mass suicide of over nine hundred members—rocketed horror narratives of groupthink and brainwashing like a spaceship following the Hale-Bopp comet to the top. Not to mention it was the decade of the iconic and very charismatic Charles Manson and his merry group of manipulated murderers.

RECORD-RISING CRIME

After Ed Gein's inspirational reign in the fifties, Berkowitz, Bundy, and Gacy (who really didn't help the case for scary clowns) took over, causing serial killers to become cultural icons. Horror leaned into home invasions, masked killers, and playgrounds becoming prey grounds. Their unpredictability, lack of remorse, and public visibility redefined horror villains again—not just as monsters, but as real people.

BLAXPLOITATION

Hollywood was still ignoring Black stories, so Black audiences carved out space of their own. Out of rising frustration and cultural pride came Blaxploitation horror—loud, stylish, and unapologetically Black. Films like *Blacula* put Black leads front and center, even if the genre was exploitative.

1980S

SURVIVAL OF THE PUREST

In the eighties, slashers exploded, and the Final Girl trope was codified. Women were allowed to live but only after suffering, proving themselves "good," smart, and able to endure trauma.

REAGANOMICS

Tax cuts for the rich and slashed social programs widened wealth gaps. Horror reflected this with monsters of greed—vampires, cannibals, and slashers in power suits feeding on the powerless.

BUY, DIE, REPEAT

With malls exploding in popularity, horror followed, using ads and sales to lure and turn these temples of capitalism into death traps. Rabid consumer culture was villainized, the shopping spree was weaponized, and brainless zombie crowds wandered neon-lit food courts trying to fill insatiable appetites.

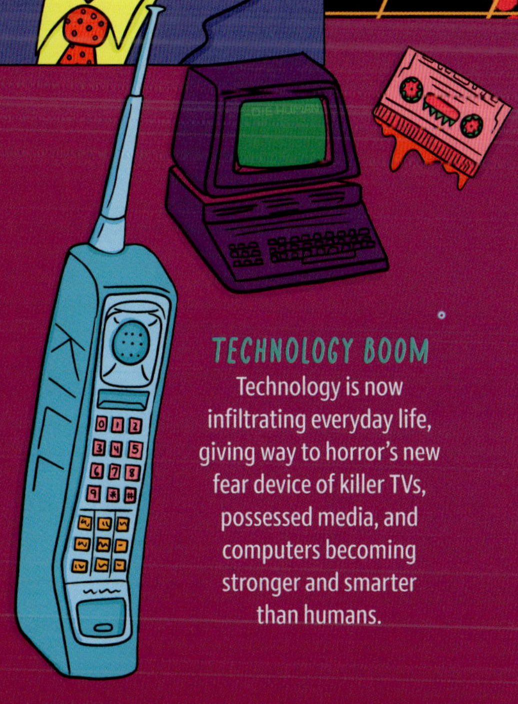

TECHNOLOGY BOOM

Technology is now infiltrating everyday life, giving way to horror's new fear device of killer TVs, possessed media, and computers becoming stronger and smarter than humans.

WAR ON DRUGS

Nancy Reagan's "Just Say No" initiative era turned addicts into monsters. Horror adopted it as an archetype and set scenes in crack houses, framing drug use as dangerous, dirty, and deserving of punishment.

SATANIC PANIC PEAKS

The 1980s feared rebellion. Reagan's conservatism, televangelist crusades, and the rise of MTV collided to paint any pop culture nonconformity—sex, drugs, heavy metal, and D&D as the work of the devil. Horror reflected rebellion with demon-possessed teens, killer kids, and brutal punishments for stepping out of line. The 1983 McMartin preschool case was one of the most infamous drivers of Satanic Panic, which claimed kids were abused by satanic cults during care. Sensational media coverage stoked national hysteria that the devil was infiltrating even the most trusted institutions.

HIV/AIDS CRISIS

As fear of infection and queer stigma spread, horror responded with body horror, contamination, and isolation tropes, turning illness into a threat and queerness into something feared and misunderstood.

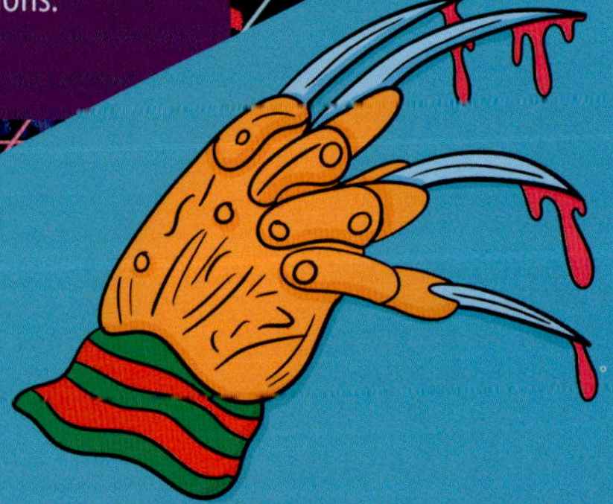

FREDDY KRUEGER

Often regarded as a queer allegory and "the gayest horror movie ever made," *A Nightmare on Elm Street 2* has Freddy possessing teen Jesse who struggles with urges he can't explain. Taking place in S&M bars, locker rooms, and hosting themes of hidden identity, Freddy becomes a symbol for internalized fear and repression, mirroring 1980s anxieties around queerness and being outed.

1990s

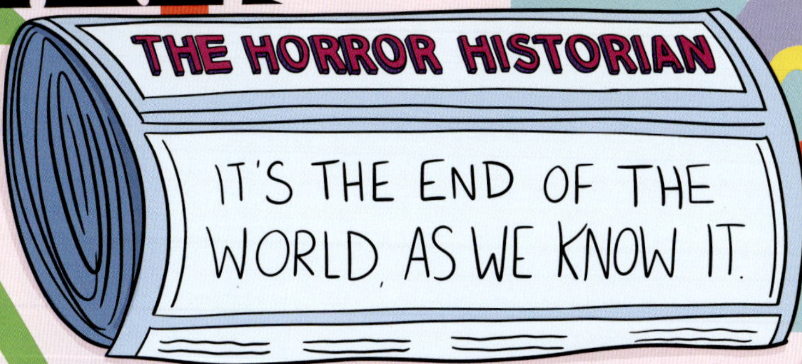

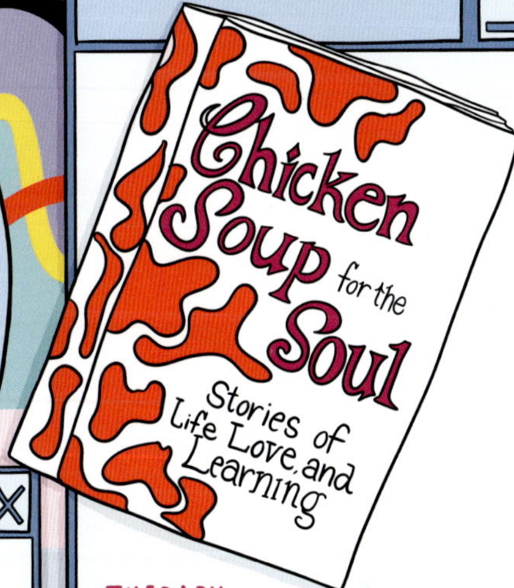

THERAPY GOES MAINSCREAM

The nineties saw a massive cultural embrace of therapy—from self-help books to Oprah and Dr. Phil, trauma became a trendy public conversation and psychology went full pop. Horror followed suit with protagonists haunted by grief and guilt, and their inner wounds becoming the external monsters they feared.

COLUMBINE

The 1999 Columbine shooting reshaped horror overnight. It sparked national debates over violent media, censorship, and teen identity. Horror reflected the fear that the killer could be a friend, a student, or any kid with a grudge. The high school setting exploded in the genre, turning classrooms and hallways into kill zones.

Y2K

Y2K ANXIETY

End-of-millennium fears were uniquely nineties. As the year 2000 approached, widespread panic spread over computers crashing, machines misfiring, global systems failing, and planes falling from the sky. In horror, tech glitches became doomsday fodder, symbolizing the rising fear of digital dependence.

OKLAHOMA CITY, WACO, AND RUBY RIDGE

The Oklahoma City bombing shattered the idea that terror was foreign—it was homegrown, white, and radicalized. Waco and Ruby Ridge exposed a rising distrust in government, fueling modern domestic militia movements. Horror stories pivoted to explore anti-government ideology, conspiracies, and extremism. Doomsday prepping and apocalypse-minded isolationism exploded—underground bunkers, cult compounds, and survivalist tropes detonated across the genre.

HELLO, CLARICE

In the nineties, women didn't just survive horror—they owned it. Third-wave feminism and the backlash to the eighties' morally policed Final Girl pushed complex, emotionally loaded female leads into the spotlight. From Clarice to Sidney to Buffy, women were no longer just victims. But power came with pressure. These femtagonists were often doubted, hunted, or underestimated, echoing real-life dynamics in workplaces, schools, and society at large.

THE REAL WORLD

By the late nineties, media was nonstop—twenty-four-hour news, reality TV, and paparazzi made real fear into real entertainment. Shows like *COPS* and *The Real World* blurred the line between watching and being watched. So horror started recording too, giving rise to the found footage boom and the paranoid reality that someone's always watching.

QUEER CODING GETS DECODED

The nineties marked a shift and queer subtext started becoming explicit text. Post-AIDS activism; "don't ask, don't tell"; and rising visibility pushed LGBTQ+ identity into horror's spotlight. Monsters still lurked in metaphor, but queer characters, empowered by real life, began to step out of the shadows.

2000s

9/11 AND TERRORISM

The 2001 attacks shattered America's illusion of safety and immunity as a global superpower, instantly refocusing public bias around who's to blame—both in real life and in horror. Sudden destruction, religious extremism, and the fear that terror could strike anytime seeped into the genre. Horror leaned into the Islamophobia that followed—Middle Eastern people were cast as "the other" in politics, pop culture, and horror alike. Islamic dress and desert imagery signaled danger, while villains resembling Al-Qaeda and Taliban extremists became shorthand for evil. Again, *foreign* became synonymous with *threat*, fueling horror's newest wave of its oldest trope—cultural demonization.

BIG BROTHER BUSH

After 9/11, the US expanded its powers under the guise of security. The Patriot Act enabled mass surveillance, wiretapping, and profiling with little oversight. With the government acting with unchecked authority, trust in institutions eroded, and horror reflected the fear of protector turned predator. Government overreach and surveillance paranoia crept into the genre.

TORTURE PORN

Images from Abu Ghraib and Guantanamo exposed state-sanctioned torture—and horror used it. Films like *Saw* fetishized pain, forcing audiences to watch what was being inflicted. Torture became a cheap shock tactic in horror, with violence cranked up purely for spectacle.

BODY MODIFICATION CRAZE

Piercings, tattoos, and plastic surgery went mainstream—the body was no longer sacred, it was editable. Horror ran with it, evolving body horror into a space where identity was fragile, changeable, and flippantly manipulated. The cloning of Dolly the sheep introduced the potential of designer bodies, human duplication, and another opportunity to play god. Horror had a heyday with the new body of work to play with.

BIOTERROR

The 2001 anthrax attacks triggered mass paranoia, mask-wearing, and fear of everyday objects. Horror tapped in with virus outbreaks, airborne contamination, and the return of invisible killers. Major outbreaks like SARS and swine flu fed pandemic paranoia, sparking horror's zombie revival. Infection was everywhere, and with capitalism booming, the undead again went viral.

CHAIN MAIL

Before social media, there was chain mail—2000s era email-born urban legends that cursed you if you didn't hit forward. Horror's new killer didn't need to break in; they were already in your inbox.

AN INCONVENIENT TRUTH

Hurricane Katrina and rising climate change awareness blew eco-horror wide open. Disaster films flooded the genre with storms, tidal waves, wildfires, and quakes, all framing nature as a violent vengeful force striking back.

2010s–NOW

QUEER FEAR

Queer themes in horror are no longer subtext. Earlier decades coded and hinted, but by the 2010s, queer creators and stories are out. Transgressive, tender, angry, or joyful, horror doesn't just include queer identity, it leads with it.

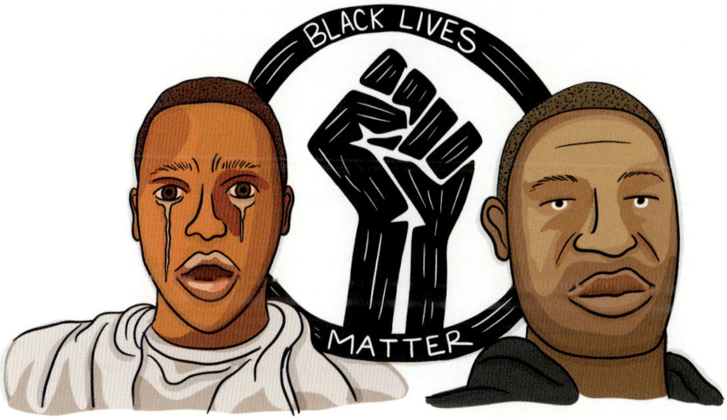

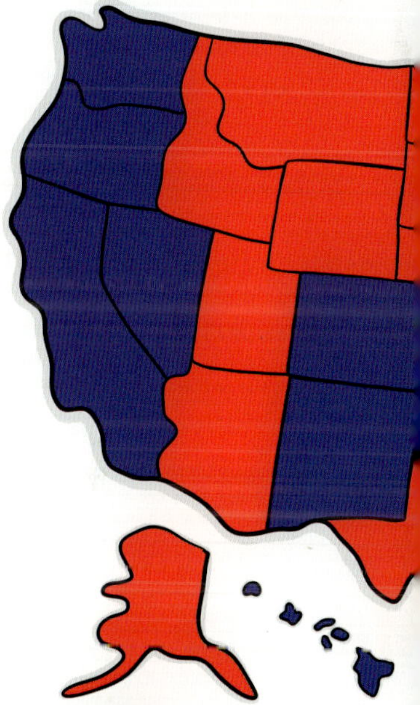

BLACK LIVES MATTER

The rise of the Black Lives Matter movement, especially after the 2020 murder of George Floyd, sparked a national reckoning around police brutality, systemic racism, and the lived realities of Black Americans. Horror responded by making race, racism, bias, displacement, and generational trauma explicit central themes and gave rise to a wave of justice and revenge horror. BLM ignited a shift, and horror became a platform to confront America's racial violence head-on.

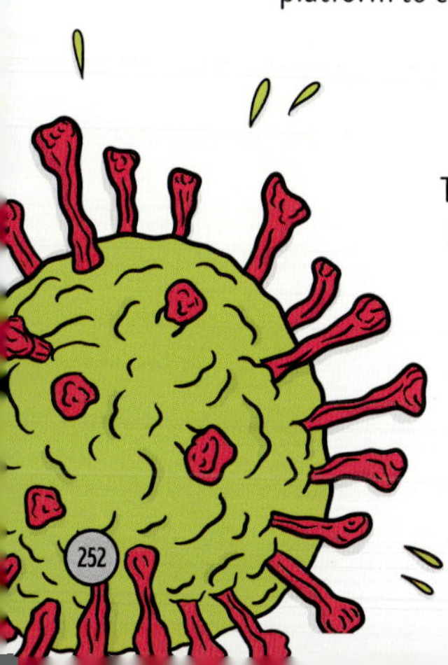

COVID-19

The pandemic trapped us and escape fantasy in horror disappeared. Horror stole our freedom just like the pandemic did. Recognizing the impact of the real-life horrors humanity was facing—extreme claustrophobia, involuntary isolation, masked figures, loneliness, grief, existential crisis—these themes seeped into every story the genre told.

UNPACKED

Anxiety, depression, and neurodivergence are normalized. Mental illness isn't backstory; it's the core narrative. No more metaphor. Horror now spirals, dissociates, and experiences painful altered realities with its protagonists in real time at the hands of mental illness.

GET READY WITH ME

Digital horror takes a new form. Earlier decades feared technology failing or being smarter—now horror fixates on what it does to you. It's brain-eating social media toxicity, hypervisibility, algorithm obsession, consumerism, performative identities, and the pressure to always be "on." Horror is influenced by influencers—slipping back into mindless conformity and the dangers of "the blind following the beautiful." Follow for more!

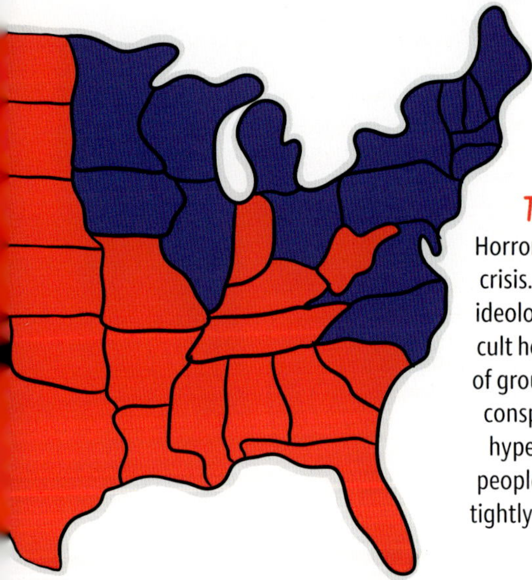

TRUMP ERA DIVISION

Horror exploits the national identity crisis. America is split by race, class, ideology—even truth itself. Folk and cult horror surge, tapping into fears of groupthink, us-vs.-them paranoia, conspiracy, and extremism. Horror hyperbolizes what happens when people cling to a contested belief so tightly that they're willing to sacrifice others for it.

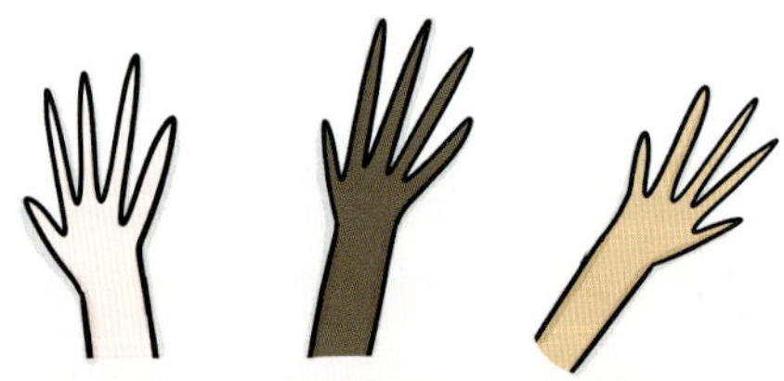

PROMISING YOUNG FINAL GIRL

The #MeToo movement unleashed decades of rage, and horror absorbed the fallout. Women didn't just outlive the monster. They became it. Now horror isn't about strong women, it's about autonomy and body reclamation, transformation, and revenge. It's emotional, physical, and unapologetic.

FULL CLIMATE COLLAPSE

By the 2010s, the effects of climate change weren't a warning—they were a reality. Eco-horror shifted its tone to mirror a world already unraveled, where the air is poison, the soil is lifeless, and humans must pay for their actions.

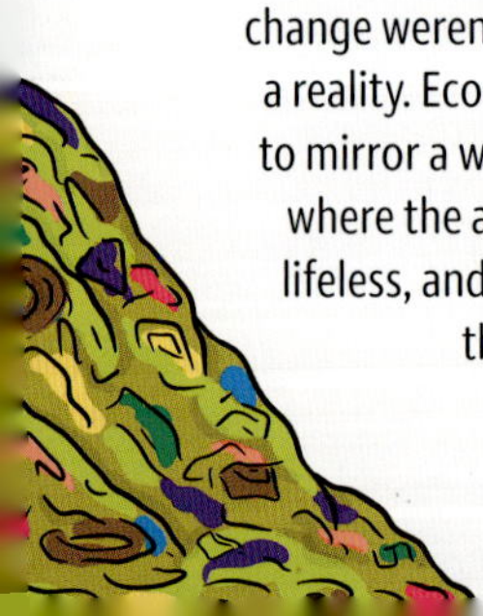

YEAR:
00 10 20 30 40 50 60 70 80 90

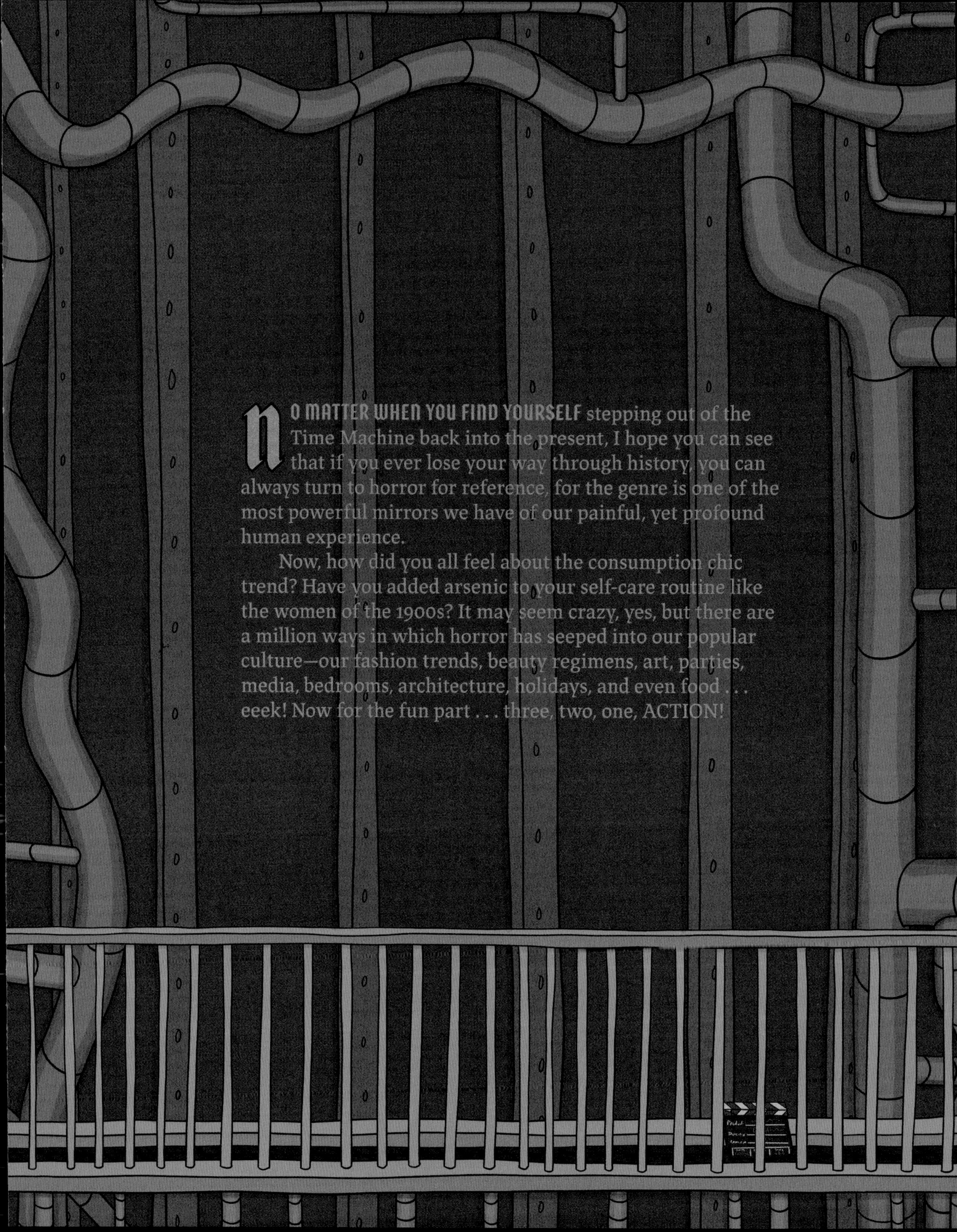

NO MATTER WHEN YOU FIND YOURSELF stepping out of the Time Machine back into the present, I hope you can see that if you ever lose your way through history, you can always turn to horror for reference, for the genre is one of the most powerful mirrors we have of our painful, yet profound human experience.

Now, how did you all feel about the consumption chic trend? Have you added arsenic to your self-care routine like the women of the 1900s? It may seem crazy, yes, but there are a million ways in which horror has seeped into our popular culture—our fashion trends, beauty regimens, art, parties, media, bedrooms, architecture, holidays, and even food . . . eeek! Now for the fun part . . . three, two, one, ACTION!

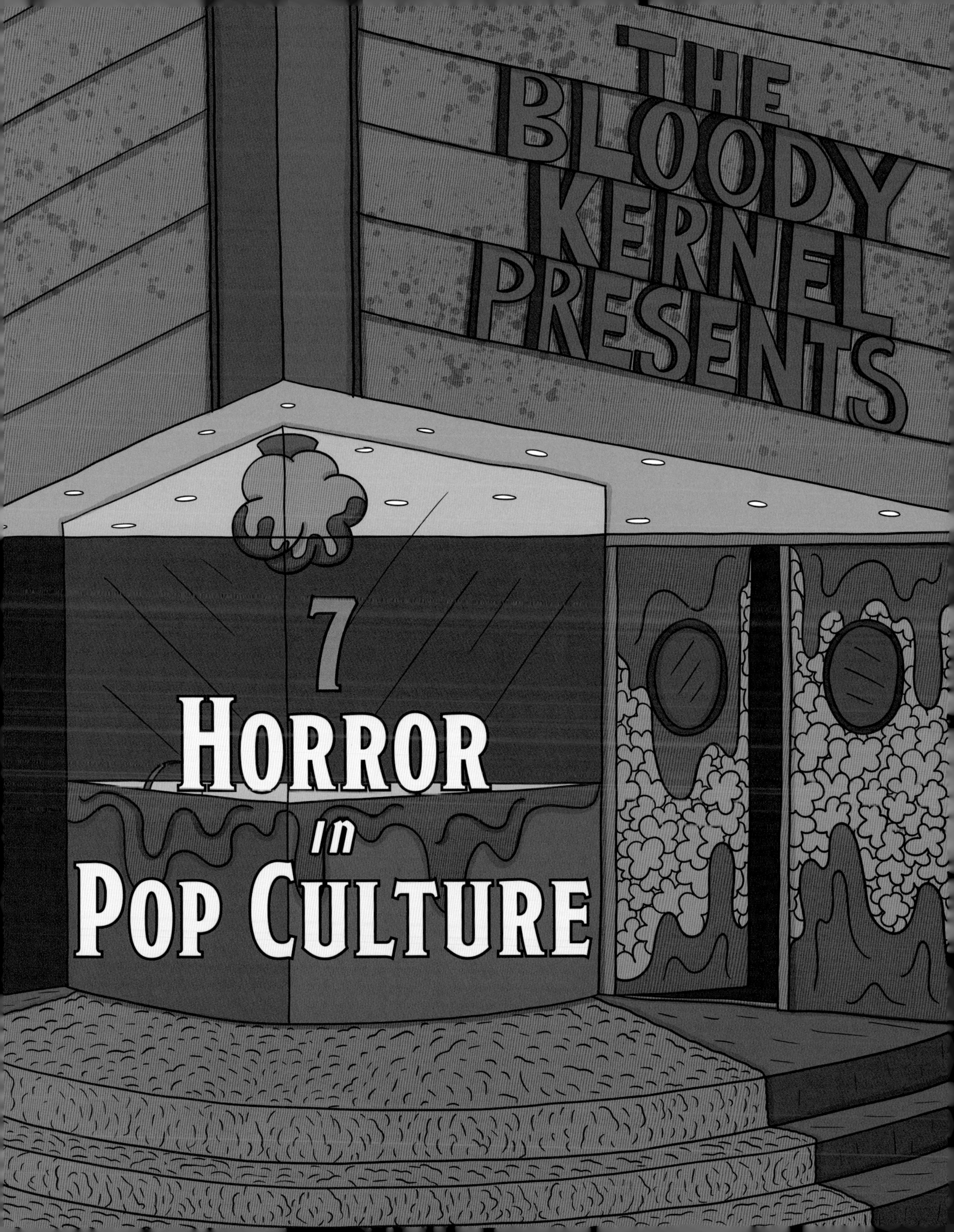
THE BLOODY KERNEL PRESENTS
7
HORROR in POP CULTURE

AHH, I SEE YOU'VE FOUND the Bloody Kernel. The haunted multiplex that appears only on the darkest of autumn nights. If you dare approach, you can purchase a ticket at the box office. It may look like no one is in there, but rest assured, we employ the spectral. Tonight, we dive into pop culture, showing the most iconic films, TV shows, and literature of the horror genre. Now scurry like a little rat and take your seat. You don't want to miss the trailers! Oh! And grab a popcorn on the way in. It's free, and better yet, instead of butter, we smother our kernels in blood.

Now that you're seated and the doors are locked, I have news. When the credits roll and the lights come up, don't think you're free to leave what you've witnessed behind. We will show you how the horror genre isn't just isolated to the movie theater, but how it bleeds into every corner of our lives and culture—from our cereal boxes to cartoons, fashion, toys, music, video games, memes, collectibles, and even our vernacular. Horror has been so deeply integrated into our lives that we've designated an entire time of year to celebrate it. One where devout horror and non-horror fans alike let it creep in like a slow fog over our outfits, screens, ears, and decor. We gather as a community to welcome it, bask in it, worship it, and consume it, just like it consumes us, until we're absolutely scared shitless and loving it. Showtime! Please silence your hell phones.

Horror's Hit Films

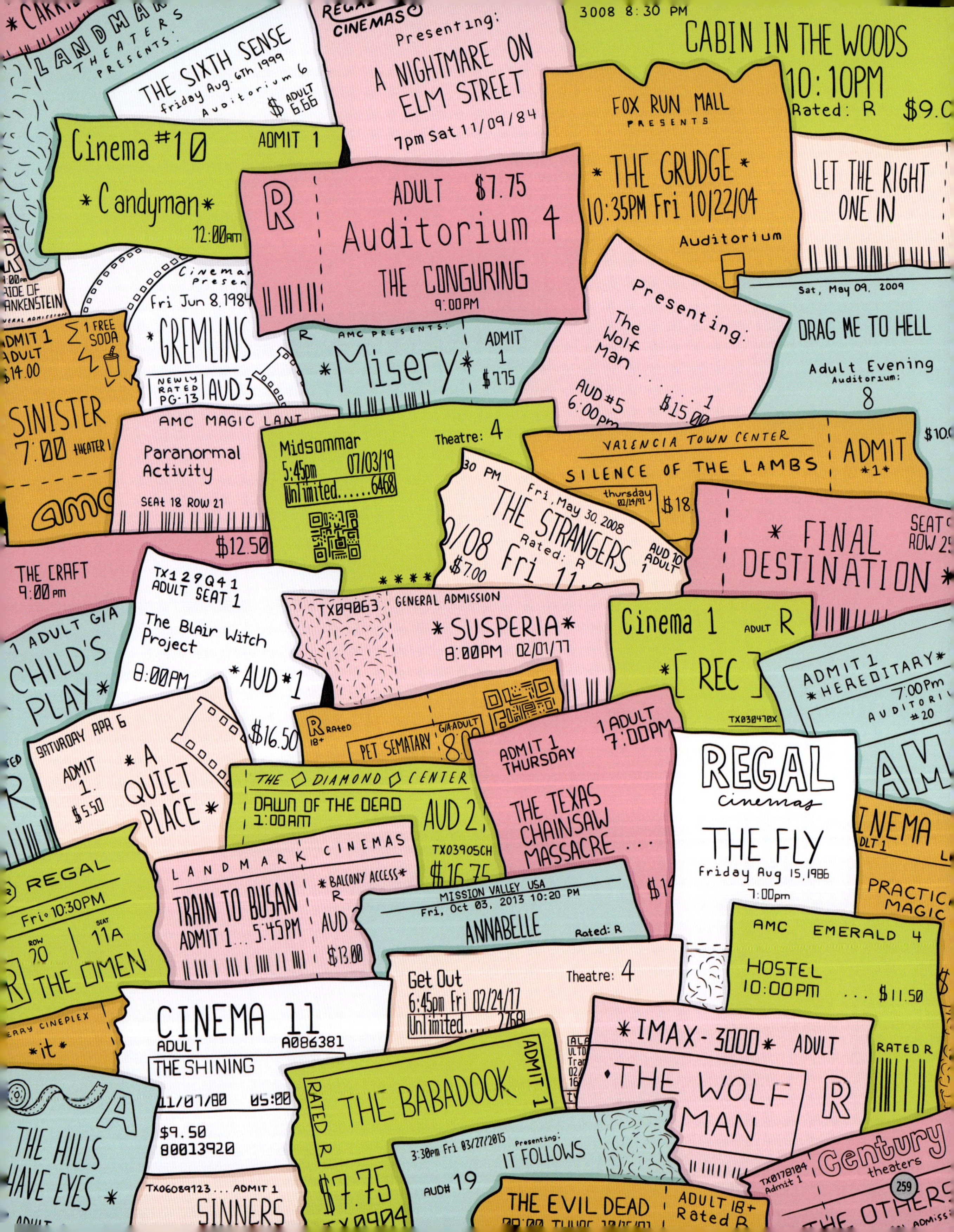
LANDMARK THEATERS PRESENTS:
THE SIXTH SENSE
friday Aug. 6th 1999
Auditorium 6
ADULT $6.66
REGAL CINEMAS
Presenting:
A NIGHTMARE ON ELM STREET
7pm Sat 11/09/84
3008 8:30 PM
CABIN IN THE WOODS
10:10PM
Rated: R
Cinema #10
ADMIT 1
Candyman
12:00am
R
ADULT $7.75
Auditorium 4
THE CONJURING
9:00PM
FOX RUN MALL PRESENTS
THE GRUDGE
10:35PM Fri 10/22/04
Auditorium
LET THE RIGHT ONE IN
Fri Jun 8,1984
GREMLINS
NEWLY RATED PG-13
AUD 3
AMC PRESENTS:
Misery
ADMIT 1
$7.75
Presenting:
The Wolf Man
AUD #5
6:00pm
$15.00
Sat, May 09, 2009
DRAG ME TO HELL
Adult Evening
Auditorium:
8
ADMIT 1
ADULT
$14.00
1 FREE SODA
SINISTER
7:00 THEATER 1
amc
AMC MAGIC LANTERN
Paranormal Activity
SEAT 18 ROW 21
Midsommar
5:45pm 07/03/19
Unlimited......6468
Theatre: 4
VALENCIA TOWN CENTER
SILENCE OF THE LAMBS
thursday 02/14/91
$18
ADMIT *1*
Fri, May 30, 2008
THE STRANGERS
Rated: R
$7.00
AUD 10
ADULT
FINAL DESTINATION
SEAT
ROW
$12.50
THE CRAFT
9:00pm
TX129Q41
ADULT SEAT 1
The Blair Witch Project
8:00PM
*AUD*1
$16.50
1 ADULT G/A
CHILD'S PLAY*
TX09063
GENERAL ADMISSION
SUSPERIA
8:00PM 02/01/77
Cinema 1
ADULT R
*[REC]
TX030470X
ADMIT 1
HEREDITARY
7:00pm
AUDITORIUM
#20
SATURDAY APR 6
ADMIT 1.
$5.50
A QUIET PLACE
R RATED 18+
PET SEMATARY
G/A ADULT
1 ADULT
7:00PM
ADMIT 1
THURSDAY
THE TEXAS CHAINSAW MASSACRE...
REGAL cinemas
THE FLY
Friday Aug 15, 1986
7:00pm
THE DIAMOND CENTER
DAWN OF THE DEAD
1:00AM
AUD 2
TX03905CH
$16.75
REGAL
Fri 10:30PM
ROW 20
SEAT 11A
R THE OMEN
LANDMARK CINEMAS
TRAIN TO BUSAN
ADMIT 1... 5:45PM
BALCONY ACCESS
R
AUD 2
$13.00
MISSION VALLEY USA
Fri, Oct 03, 2013 10:20 PM
ANNABELLE
Rated: R
CINEMA
PRACTICAL MAGIC
AMC EMERALD 4
HOSTEL
10:00PM ... $11.50
Get Out
6:45pm Fri 02/24/17
Unlimited......2768
Theatre: 4
CINEMA 11
ADULT A086381
THE SHINING
11/07/80 05:00
$9.50
80013920
it
IMAX-3000 ADULT
*THE WOLF MAN
R
RATED R
RATED R
THE BABADOOK
ADMIT 1
$7.75
A
THE HILLS HAVE EYES*
TX06089123... ADMIT 1
SINNERS
3:30pm Fri 03/27/2015
Presenting:
IT FOLLOWS
AUD# 19
THE EVIL DEAD
ADULT 18+
Rated R
TX0178104
Admit 1
Century theaters
THE OTHERS
259

WES CRAVEN

ALFRED Hitchcock

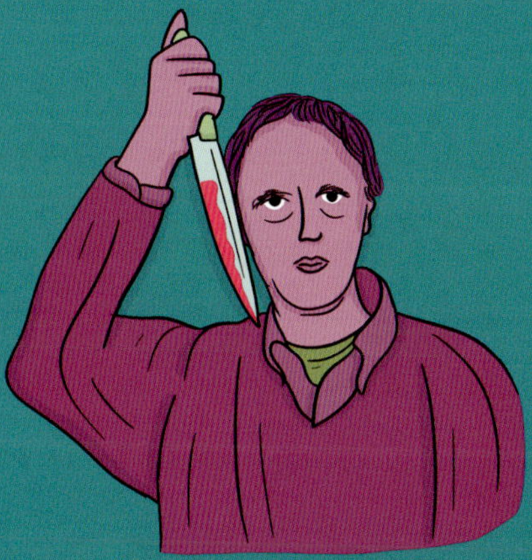
DARIO ARGENTO

GUILLERMO DEL TORO

DIRECTORS OF Darkness

THE VISIONARIES BEHIND THE CAMERA WHO BURNED THEIR NIGHTMARES INTO OUR MINDS.

GEORGE A ROMERO

JAMES WAN

DAVID CRONENBERG

JOHN CARPENTER

ROB ZOMBIE
SAM RAIMI
TIM BURTON
JORDAN PEELE
TOBE HOOPER
M. NIGHT SHYAMALAN
MIKE FLANAGAN
ROBERT EGGERS
ARI ASTER

SCREAM QUEENS
SARAH MICHELLE GELLAR
I Know What You Did Last Summer, Buffy the Vampire Slayer, Scream, The Grudge
FAY WRAY
King Kong
NEVE CAMPBELL
Scream, The Craft
MIA GOTH
Suspiria, X, Pearl, MaXXXine
JAIME LEE CURTIS
Halloween, The Fog
SIGOURNEY WEAVER
Alien, Ghostbusters
JANET LEIGH
Psycho, The Fog
DREW BARRYMORE
Scream
HEATHER LANGENKAMP
A Nightmare on Elm Street
CLASSIC KINGS
LON CHANEY JR.
BELA LUGOSI
CHRISTOPHER LEE
VINCENT PRICE

Pop Scream!!!

FAMOUS HORROR QUOTES THAT HAUNT POP CULTURE—CAN YOU NAME THEM ALL?

1. "WHAT'S YOUR FAVORITE SCARY MOVIE?"

2. "BE AFRAID. BE VERY AFRAID."

3. "IT'S ALIVE!"

4. "THEY'RE HERE . . ."

5. "HERE'S JOHNNY!"

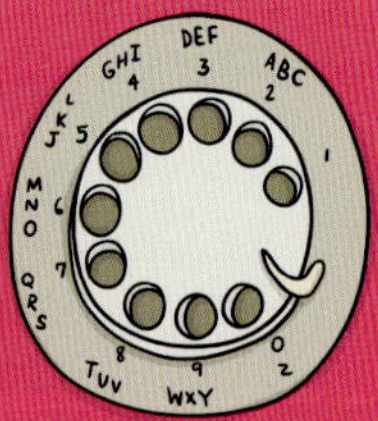

6. "WE'VE TRACED THE CALL; IT'S COMING FROM INSIDE THE HOUSE."

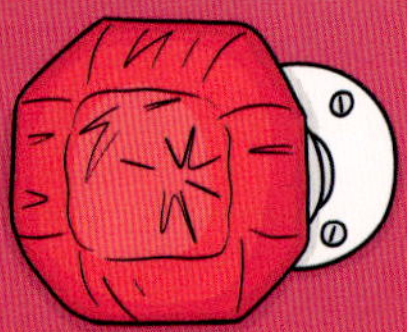

7. "I SEE DEAD PEOPLE."

8. "YOU'RE GONNA NEED A BIGGER BOAT."

9. "WE ALL GO A LITTLE MAD SOMETIMES."

10. "IN SPACE, NO ONE CAN HEAR YOU SCREAM."

11. "I ATE HIS LIVER WITH SOME FAVA BEANS AND A NICE CHIANTI."

12. "WHAT ARE YOU WAITING FOR, HUH?!"

ANSWERS: 1. *Scream*, 2. *The Fly*, 3. *Frankenstein*, 4. *Poltergeist*, 5. *The Shining*, 6. *When a Stranger Calls*, 7. *The Sixth Sense*, 8. *Jaws*, 9. *Psycho*, 10. *Alien*, 11. *The Silence of the Lambs*, 12. *I Know What You Did Last Summer*.

ICONIC POP CUL

BAD GUYS WITH BRANDS THAT

TURE Villains

REACH FAR BEYOND THEIR BEGINNINGS.

KILL COUNT: 39 TO 79

KILL COUNT: 45

KILL COUNT: 80

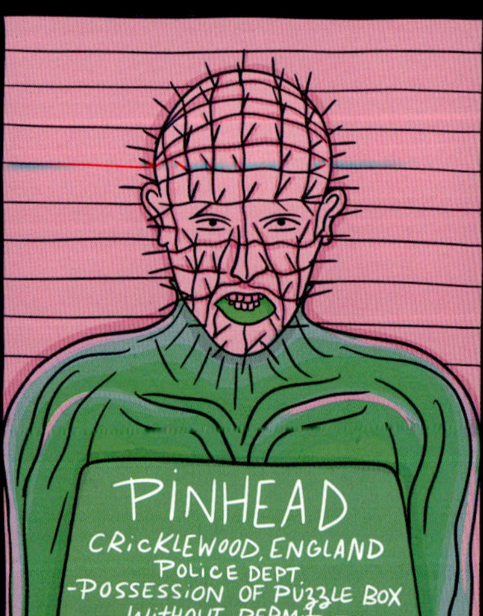

KILL COUNT: 320+

KILL COUNT: 203

QUINT'S HARPOON RIFLE
Jaws $84,000 (2015)

LAMENT CONFIGURATION PUZZLE BOX
Hellraiser €11,970 (2024)

BOB GLEASON'S ORIGINAL ACRYLIC PAINTING
used as the poster art for *Halloween* $84,000 (2016)

THE ICONIC COSTUMES AND COLLECTIBLES PEOPLE HAVE DIED FOR.

EVIL CLOWN DOLL
Poltergeist $656,250 (2023)

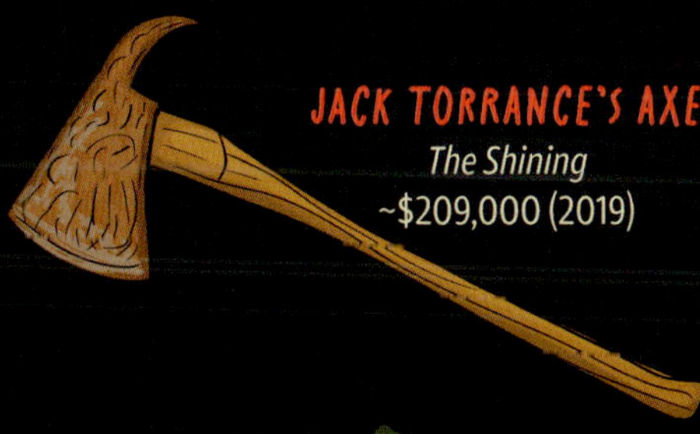

JACK TORRANCE'S AXE
The Shining ~$209,000 (2019)

GILL-MAN MASK
Revenge of the Creature $80,500 (2009)

ZUNI FETISH DOLL
Trilogy of Terror $217,600 (2019) The most expensive horror movie prop ever sold publicly.

ELLEN RIPLEY'S SPACE SUIT
Alien $204,800 (2018)

NIGHTGOWN WORN BY MIA FARROW
Rosemary's Baby
$4375 (2014)

NORRIS SPIDER HEAD MODEL
The Thing $587,500
(2023)

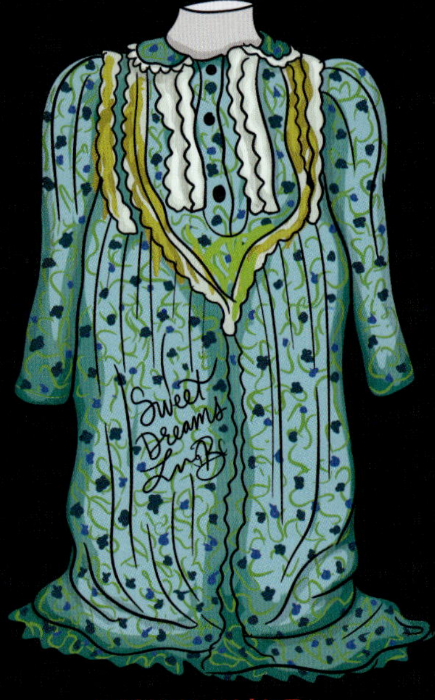

REGAN'S VOMIT-SOAKED NIGHTGOWN
(signed "sweet dreams" by Linda Blair)
The Exorcist $79.85 (2018)

HOCKEY MASK
worn by Kane Hodder (signed "To Tom, you're next!") *Jason Goes to Hell* $225,000 (2021)

BLOOD-SPLATTERED PROM DRESS
Carrie (2013)
$25,200
(2025)

ORIGINAL GHOSTFACE COSTUME
Scream $270,900
(2024)

FREDDY KRUEGER'S HERO BLADE GLOVE
A Nightmare on Elm Street 3: Dream Warriors
$135,000 (2021)

NECRONOMICON EX-MORTIS
(stunt copy)
Evil Dead II
$132,000
(2024)

THE MONSTER MAKERS

H. R. GIGER The Swiss surrealist artist best known for his creation of the Xenomorph in *Alien*. Trained in architecture and industrial design, Giger fused flesh, bone, and machinery into haunting, erotic nightmares with his signature airbrushed "biomechanical" style. His work wasn't just art, it was body horror meets goth, meets opera, meets metallurgy, and was so radically impactful on the genre, he won an Oscar for it.

MILICENT PATRICK One of horror's earliest and most overlooked monster makers. A trained artist and Disney animator, she designed the iconic headpiece for *Creature from the Black Lagoon* but was erased from the credits by her jealous boss. She broke the prosthetic ceiling as one of the first female special effects artists in Hollywood and brought a unique eerie elegance to the monstrous art form.

TOM SAVINI The artist whose medium was blood. A Vietnam combat photographer turned actor, director, stuntman, and FX legend, Savini brought blood, guts, and realism to horror with groundbreaking makeup work in *Dawn of the Dead*, *Friday the 13th*, and more. If you've ever seen a head explode or a zombie feast that felt extremely real and visceral, it was the work of Tom Savini.

Ghost Writers

THE MODERN LITERARY ICONS OF THE HORROR GENRE.

STEPHEN KING

There was no need for a pseudonym as King rightfully took the throne as the genre's most recognizable and prolific author of the last century.

ANNE RICE

As *The Queen of the Damned* herself, Rice redefined vampires with *Interview with the Vampire*, stoking modern vampire (and witch) lore into a pop culture fueled wildfire.

H. P. LOVECRAFT

Father of cosmic horror, his creations and Cthulhu mythos haunt every intersection of sci-fi horror pop culture.

SHIRLEY JACKSON

Master of quiet dread, she gave us *The Haunting of Hill House*, *The Lottery*, and more, cementing psychological horror in the modern literary canon.

CLIVE BARKER

The dark prince of flesh, fantasy, and *Hellraiser*, Barker's works keep horror erotic, gory, and deliciously twisted.

LITERATURE

Welcome to the stacks of rats, bats, witch hats, and slasher whacks. If you're looking for the top one hundred horror stories of all time, right this way. If you get lost, look to the Booey Decimal System, or consult Edgar . . . if you can find him. He's easier to spot by the light of his lantern rather than his body . . . for he doesn't have one. Reader, beware! You're in for a scare!

THE WILLOWS
THE EXORCIST WILLIAM PETER BLATTY
Psycho ROBERT BLOCH
SOMETHING WICKED THIS WAY COMES RAY BRADBURY
WORLD WAR Z
fledgling OCTAVIA E. BUTLER
Kindred OCTAVIA E BUTLER
The Hacienda Isabel Cañas
THE GIRL WITH ALL THE GIFTS M.R. CAREY
THE Bloody Chamber ANGELA CARTER
The Upper Berth Francis Marion Crawford
HOUSE OF LEAVES MARK Z. DANIELEWSKI
THOMAS HARRIS
THOMAS HARRIS
Hannibal THOMAS HARRIS
the Final Girl Support Group GRADY HENDRIX
THE FOG JAMES HERBERT
THE RATS JAMES HERBERT
NOS4A2 JOE HILL
The Woman in Black Susan Hill
The legend of Sleepy Hollow Washington Irving
THE HAUNTING OF HILL HOUSE SHIRLEY JACKSON
we have always lived in a castle shirley jackson
THE LOTTERY SHIRLEY JACKSON
The Monkey's Paw W.W. Jacobs
SALEM'S LOT Steven King
Pet Sematary STEVEN KING
The Shining STEVEN KING
CHRISTINE STEVEN KING
CUJO STEVEN KING
Doctor Sleep Steven King
the changeling Victor Lavalle
THE PHANTOM OF THE OPERA GASTON LEROUX
ROSEMARY'S BABY IRA LEVIN
The Stepford Wives Ira Levin
Let the Right One In John Ajvide Lindqvist
THE CALL OF CTHULHU H.P. LOVECRAFT
Rebecca Daphne Du Maurier
SWAN SONG ROBERT R. McCAMMON
THE ROAD CORMAC McCARTHY
Mexican Gothic Silvia Moreno-Garcia
BELOVED TONI MORRISON
Haunted Chuck Palahniuk
THE RAVEN EDGAR ALLAN POE
THE TELL-TALE HEART EDGAR ALLAN POE
THE FALL OF THE HOUSE OF USHER EDGAR ALLAN POE
Annabel Lee Edgar Allen Poe
The Cask of the Amontillado Edgar Allan Poe
The Masque of the RED DEATH Edgar Allan Poe
the black cat E.A.P.
The Ruins Scott Smith
THE STRANGE CASE OF Dr Jekyll + Mr. Hyde ROBERT LEWIS STEVENSON
DRACULA BRAM STOKER
Ghost Story Peter Straub
RING KOJI SUZUKI
the Other thomas tryon
The Island of Dr. Moreau H.G. Wells
THE INVISIBLE MAN H.G. WELLS
The Ghost Stories of Edith Wharton
THE PICTURE OF DORIAN GRAY OSCAR WILDE
THE KEEP F. PAUL WILSON

Horror Onstage

The stage is sacred ground for horror, trust me, I'm a theater kid. It's where ghosts glide through the catwalks and pull levers to fog-machine-choked trapdoors. In 1606, we got *Macbeth* or "The Scottish Play" (say "*Macbeth*" in a theater and you're cursed) complete with witches, murder, and madness. From there, horror evolved from Shakespearean tragedy to sing-along cult musicals splattered in buckets of pig's blood. *The Phantom of the Opera* made the masked monster romantic, *Sweeney Todd* served us street meat, *Carrie* and *Evil Dead: The Musical* turned stages into splash zones, at midnight *The Rocky Horror Show* brought us up to the slab, *Little Shop* sang us into a monster's jaws, and *The Woman in Black* earned the title of the longest-running horror play in London's West End history. Lately, theater has embraced the immersive format à la haunted house and now you too can become the ghost who fuels the theater's superstitious players . . . or you can just die by chandelier. Either method will bring the drama and persist in pop culture until the curtain falls.

A GALLERY OF HELL

The collection before you holds the most iconic works of art horror history. Pieces like *The Scream* and *The Nightmare* aren't just dusty, forgotten paintings, they're living horror relics, their imagery continually devoured à la Saturn's son, then regurgitated through movies, TV, video games, parodies, T-shirts, animation, metal album covers, and even memes to describe "OMG the worst day ever!" As we ceaselessly stitch these images into Halloween costumes, print them on keychains, and ink them into our skin, we perpetuate horror imagery's place in pop culture, and leave marks on our lives no amount of turpentine can erase.

THE SCREAM
Edvard Munch

JUDITH BEHEADING HOLOFERNES
Caravaggio

SATURN DEVOURING HIS SON
Francisco Goya

GARDEN OF EARTHLY DELIGHTS
Hieronymus Bosch

THE GATES OF HELL
Auguste Rodin

THE NIGHTMARE
Henry Fuseli

THE SOUND OF VIOLENCE

In horror, it's all about sound, and besides silence—arguably the scariest sound of all—we've learned how to hear fear before it even arrives.

THE INSTRUMENTS OF HORROR

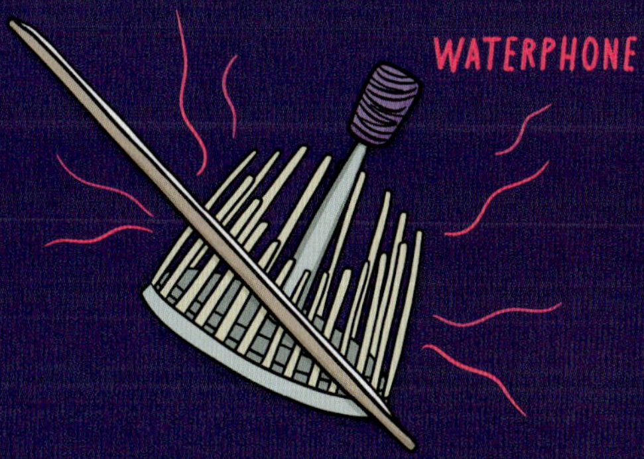

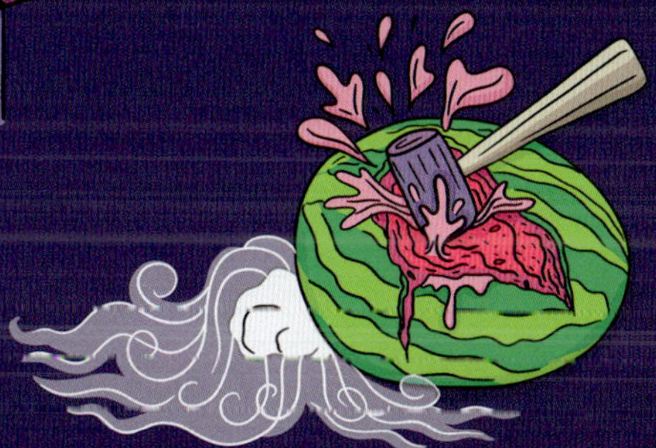

FOLEY ARTIST TOOLS

Before super advanced sound FX, Foley artists were using instruments like metal on dry ice, creaking doors, and melons for the perfect skull smash.

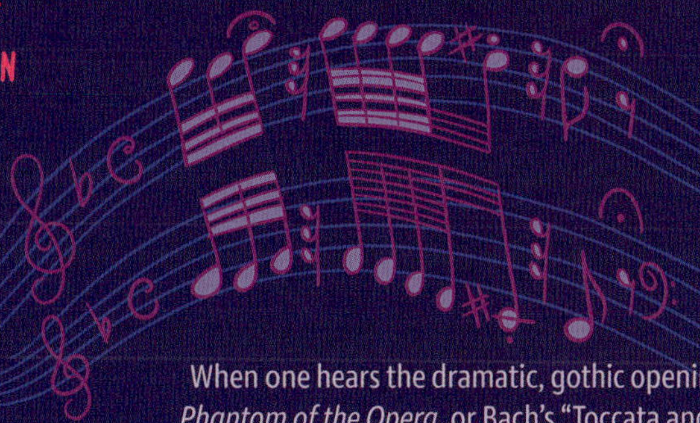

When one hears the dramatic, gothic opening notes of *Phantom of the Opera*, or Bach's "Toccata and Fugue in D minor," there's no mistaking the full-body chill you're in for.

The *DANCE MACABRE* began in medieval Europe as allegorical artworks showing skeletons leading people of all classes into death. In 1874, composer Camille Saint-Saëns turned the idea into a symphonic poem, using instruments to mimic rattling bones and death itself.

THE MOVES AND MELODIES OF HORROR

THE ADDAMS FAMILY's snaps" are pop culture's catchiest reflex, and the "Monster Mash," which beat Elvis to number one in 1962, eternally carved horror's place on the dance floor.

"THRILLER," Michael Jackson's fourteen-minute, $1-million mini-movie powered the best-selling album of all time, and moonwalked horror into pop culture superstardom, resurfacing every year as the ultimate Halloween anthem.

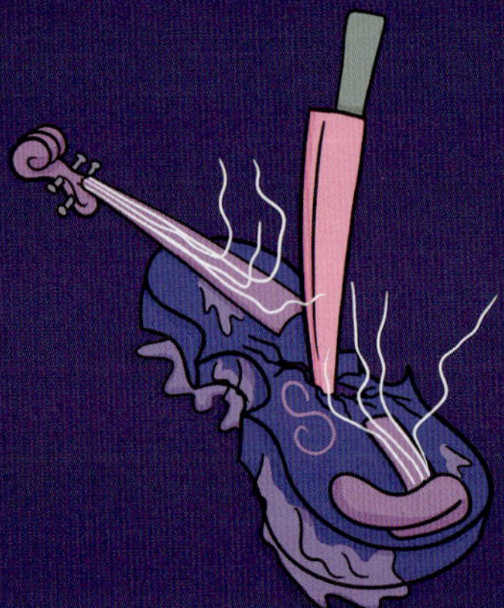

THE SCORES OF HORROR

Bernard Herrmann's *PSYCHO* suite gave us the shrieking *REE-REE-REE* violins of the shower scene, a sound so iconic it's been endlessly parodied across pop culture ever since.

With *JAWS*, John Williams proved you only need two notes to create one of pop culture's most quoted sounds of all time.

The iconic *HALLOWEEN* theme, written by director John Carpenter on a synthesizer in just a few days because of budget constraints, became the most recognizable horror score of all time. Likely due to its unsettling five-four time signature.

GOTH

Horror doesn't just live in movies and books—it seeps into how we design, build, dress, and soundtrack our lives. That's where goth comes in. It's horror's longest-running cultural remix, a subculture that borrowed the genre's favorite imagery and turned it into fashion statements, music scenes, and iconic architectural symbols. Think of it as a horror lifestyle brand with equal parts cathedral, corset, and Bauhaus record.

AUTOPSY OF A GOTH

- Black hair & makeup
- Piercings
- Choker
- Veil
- Corset
- Metal crosses, spikes & rings
- Gloves
- Fishnets
- Lace
- Chunky boots

GOTH FASHION is ready-to-wear horror imagery. It's the embrace of drama and darkness, transformed into style, self-expression, and identity. It began with Victorian mourning traditions of black dress and evolved through the decades, with high-fashion designers like Jean Paul Gaultier, Alexander McQueen, and Rick Owens becoming contemporary pallbearers for the aesthetic—death-marching the look down runways and making goth couture.

GOTH MUSIC grew out of horror's atmosphere—Bauhaus's "Bela Lugosi's Dead" turned Dracula into an anthem, while Siouxsie and the Banshees and Robert Smith of The Cure gave goth its sound and look, which gloriously festered in underground clubs like London's Batcave. Horror imagery shaped the scene, and in turn, goth music left sound waves all over pop culture.

GOTHIC ARCHITECTURE was designed for reverence, its scale drawing beholder's eyes toward God. But its ominous traits—jutting spires that pierce dark skies, vaulted ceilings dripping with drama, flying buttresses, bloodred rose windows, cold stone, and shadows attracted horror instead, branding gothic cathedrals and castles as enduring pop culture symbols of the haunted.

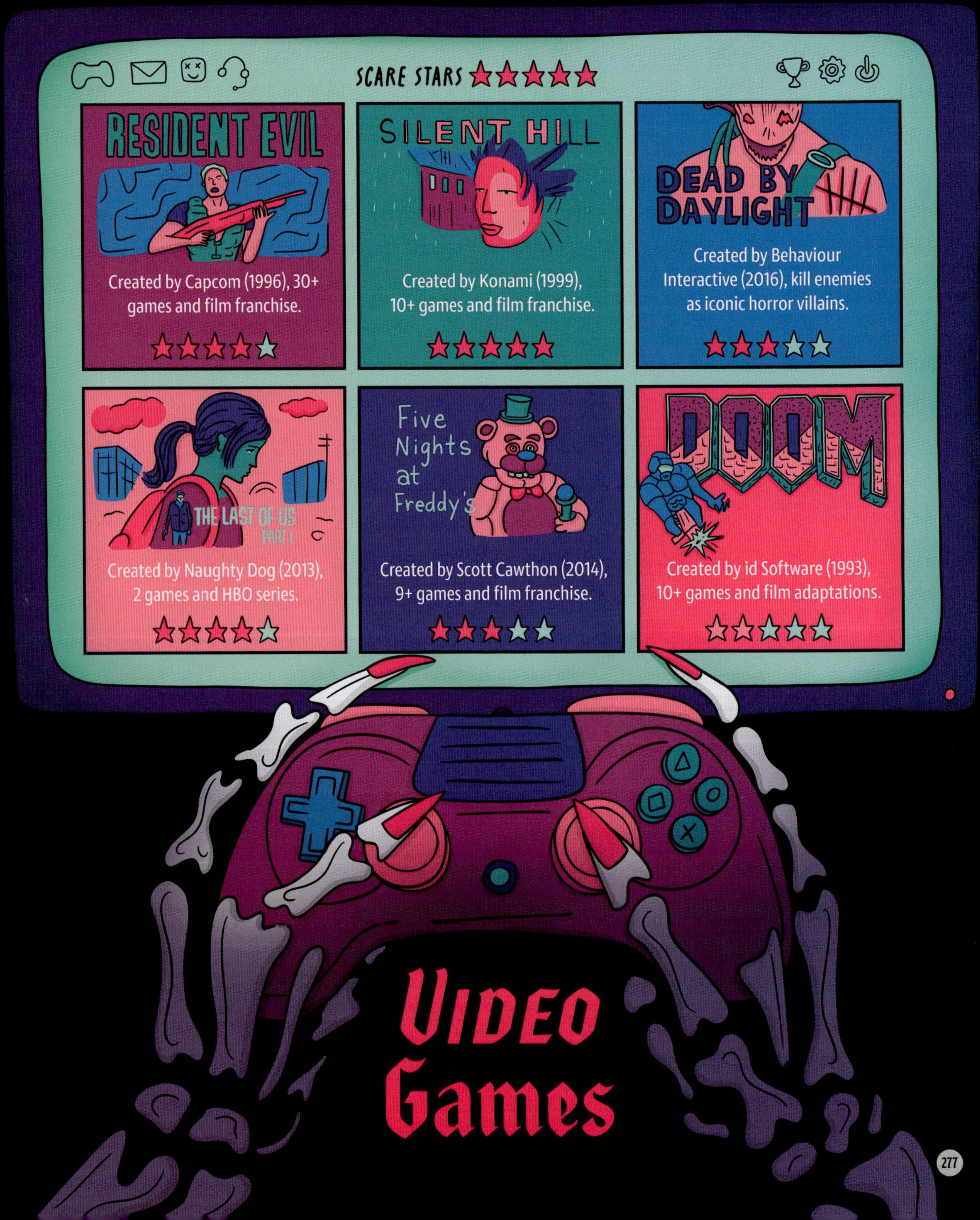
SCARE STARS
RESIDENT EVIL
Created by Capcom (1996), 30+ games and film franchise.
SILENT HILL
Created by Konami (1999), 10+ games and film franchise.
DEAD BY DAYLIGHT
Created by Behaviour Interactive (2016), kill enemies as iconic horror villains.
THE LAST OF US PART I
Created by Naughty Dog (2013), 2 games and HBO series.
Five Nights at Freddy's
Created by Scott Cawthon (2014), 9+ games and film franchise.
DOOM
Created by id Software (1993), 10+ games and film adaptations.

Video Games

Primetime Chills
11:30 PM
12:00 AM
The Twilight Zone
The Munsters
Twin Peaks
American Horror Story
Elvira's Movie Macabre
The Last of Us
Wednesday
The Walking Dead
The X Files
The Vampira Show
Black Mirror
Midnight Mass

Welcome to Aired to Scare—the *screaming* service of your nightmares where you can invite a vampire into your home with just the click of your remote. Now, sit back and tune into the most iconic horror TV shows we've ever let flicker into our living rooms!

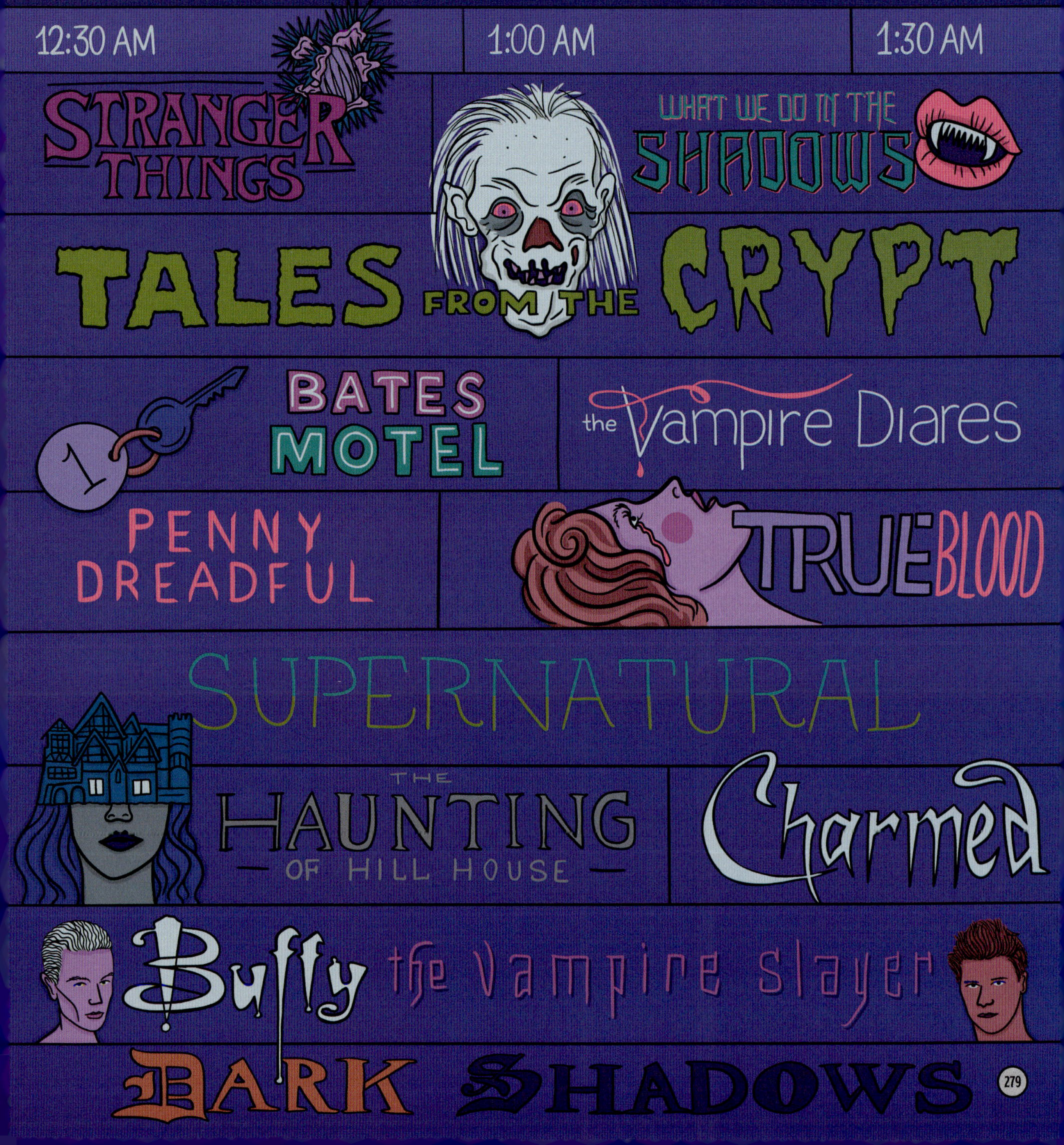

CHILD'S PLAY

Some of the world's most beloved horror was made for children. Growing up it filled our classrooms, campfires, and sleepovers. As kids, we wanted spooky. We wanted thrill and excitement, to levitate our friends after our parents went to sleep. We craved danger, and pop culture provided. Milton Bradley gave us the modern Ouija board planchette we swear moved on its own. General Mills baked it into snacks and cereal. R. L. Stein penned over two hundred Goosebumps books to devour, and Nickelodeon gave us kid-friendly shows to scream to. Whether these cultural staples were a gateway drug to becoming an adult horror addict, or led to nightmares and avoidance, you're invited to revisit them all tonight at my house. Will you RSVP yes? Or are you afraid of the dark?

Are You Afraid of the Dark?
Sabrina
The Teenage Witch
SCARY STORIES to Tell in the Dark
MORE SCARY STORIES to Tell in the Dark
THE WITCHES
Roald Dahl
THE GASHLYCRUMB TINIES
by Edward Gorey
THE FACE ON THE MILK CARTON
R.L. STINE
Goosebumps
THE MUMMY
Sleepy Hollow
Halloweentown
The Witches
GHOSTBUSTERS
Casper
The Addams Family
BEETLEJUICE
COUNT CHOCULA

CAN YOU FIND:

- 3 candy bars
- 5 spooky cats
- 5 spiderwebs
- Jason's mask
- 12 bats
- 2 witch hats
- 14 real pumpkins
- 2 Spirit Halloween bags

HAPPY Halloween

From pagan bonfires to pumpkin spice everything, All Hallows' Eve proves horror OWNS pop culture. Every year we make scary rituals mainstream, candy-coat our fears in fun-sized wrappers, and willingly conjure an entire spooky season industry to possess our happily haunted hearts. Pillowcase ready? Trick or treat!

THE END

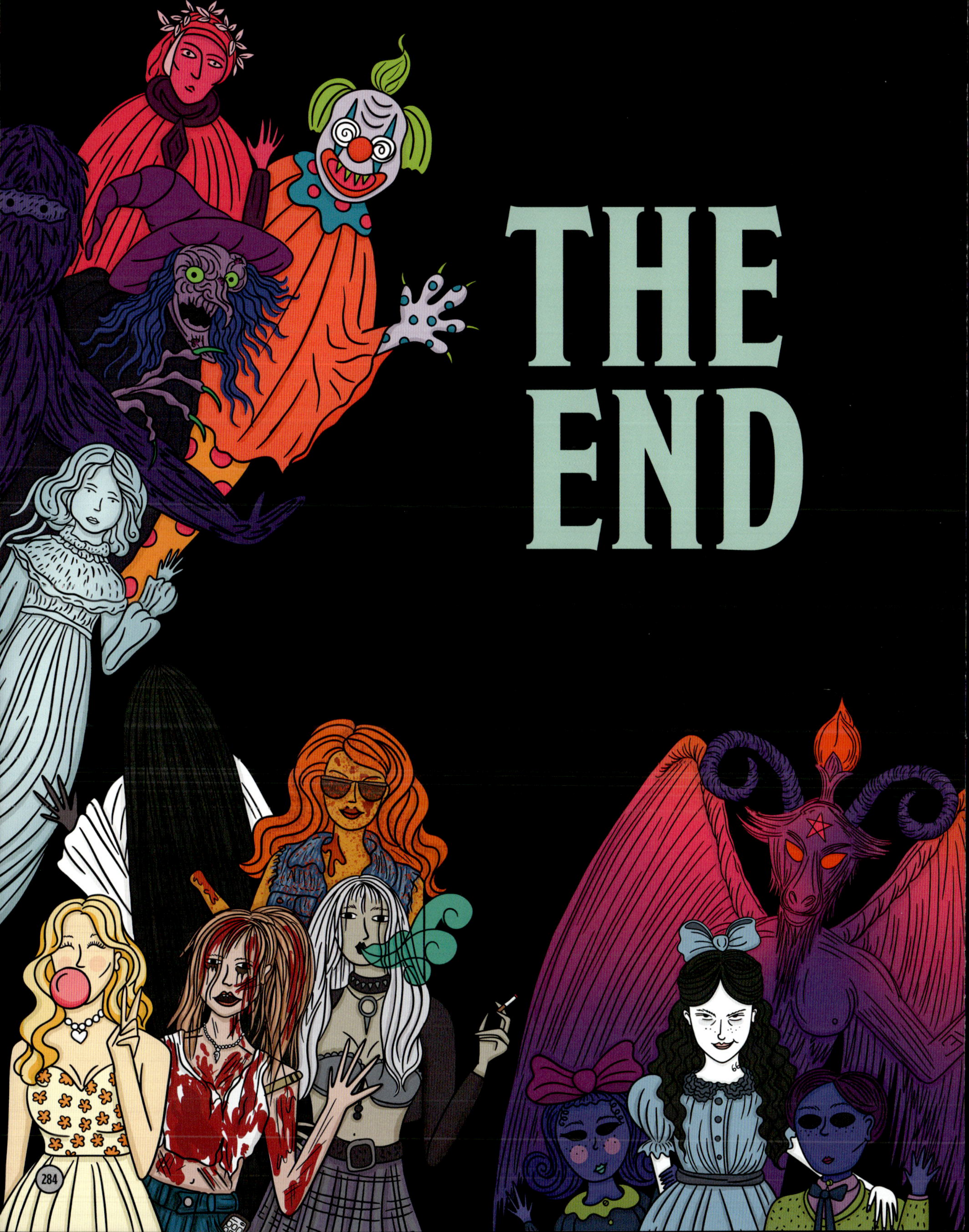

ACKNOWLEDGMENTS

To begin, this has by far been the hardest page of my book to write, for I don't believe the gratitude I have for the opportunity to write this book, or for the people that helped me do it, could ever be adequately expressed. Thank you from the bottom of my heart to the following:

Will, the constant antidote to my fears, and love of all loves. Your steadfastness in squashing every doubt, your willingness to look at every illustration and proofread pages no matter the hour, your honesty when something wasn't right, the meals cooked, the tears wiped, and the unwavering support of my dreams before, during, and after this book, all with your deep confidence in me, makes this book as much yours as it is mine. Mama, for your soulmate love, resolute reassurance, and lifelong support of my artistic ability. Thank you for being my medium to the spiritual world, and showing me that pursuing your passion is possible at any age. Daddio, even though you're no longer here in this world, I attribute so much of my success to you helping from wherever you are. I feel your pride, love, excitement, and support every day. Tarn, the greatest, most-loving sister, thank you for always including me, bestowing upon me a most thorough education in pop culture, and for sneaking a child into every 90s horror movie she wished. So much of this book came from these formative experiences you gave me. To my whole family for never censoring art and exposing me to as much of it as possible. For teaching me that whether it's high, low, unconventional, misunderstood, funny, sad, or scary, it is invaluable, critically important, and the spice of life. To Mom, Dad, Mary, and Charlie for letting us live in your houses while pursuing new careers. Without that time and space to freely create, experiment, fail, transition, heal, think, and rebuild, this book wouldn't have come to fruition as it did. To Sara and the girls, for making my life so full of constant fun, laughter, care and love. Thank you to my friends, aunties, and Bobbi Anchovy; a witch isn't a witch without her coven and familiar. To Leigh Eisenman, for being so wonderful to me, taking a chance on me, reminding me to rest, advocating for me, and always being there to chat whether about something work related, or just a great book. To the whole team at Simon Element for bringing this book to life and to Maria Espinosa, my champion, my collaborator, and my friend. Thank you for finding me, for trusting me; you made my dreams come true and I am eternally grateful. To say that meeting you and working with you has been an honor is selling the experience short. Whenever I felt doubt pursuing a career in art, I quelled it by knowing I just needed to continue to work hard, do what I love, and persevere because someday someone will see it and take a chance on me. You are that person. You changed my life. To my therapists, I wouldn't be here without you. Thank you to my mentors, Amanda Oleander and Victoria Venturi, and to all the artistic women in my life who showed me that having a career as an artist is possible. And finally, to all the subversive little creatures, freaks, others, outsiders, dissenters, and weirdos out there; without you, this beautiful genre wouldn't exist. The world is so lucky to have you.

Notes and Suggested Reading

Works Consulted

Dante Alighieri, *The Inferno*, trans. John Ciardi (New American Library, 2003).

Archive for Research in Archetypal Symbolism, ed., *The Book of Symbols: Reflections on Archetypal Images* (Taschen, 2010).

Ana Maria Bahiana, "The Blair Witches of Brazil," *BBC Culture*, July 6, 2017, https://www.bbc.com/culture/article/20170701-the-blair-witches-of-brazil.

Theresa Bane, *Encyclopedia of Vampire Mythology* (McFarland, 2010).

Dana Jan Bartelt, *Vampires: From Folklore to Fiction* (McFarland & Company, 2013).

Sandra Blakeslee, "A Small Part of the Brain, and Its Profound Effects," *The New York Times*, February 6, 2007, https://www.nytimes.com/2007/02/06/health/psychology/06brain.html.

The Book of Enoch, trans. R. H. Charles (SPCK Publishing, 2013).

Tim Brinkhof, "Horror Fiction: The Unexpectedly Ancient Origins of Ghost Stories," *Big Think*, October 31, 2021, https://bigthink.com/high-culture/horror-fiction-stories-ancient-history/.

Tim Brinkhof, "How the Vampire Myth Was Born and Evolved," *Big Think*, October 23, 2021, https://bigthink.com/high-culture/history-of-vampires/.

Raymond Buckland, *The Witch Book: The Encyclopedia of Witchcraft, Wicca, and Neo-Paganism* (Visible Ink Press, 2001).

Kit Carlson, *The Book of Killer Plants: A Field Guide to Nature's Deadliest Creations* (Cider Mill Press, 2022).

Carol J. Clover, *Men, Women, and Chain Saws: Gender in the Modern Horror Film* (Princeton University Press, 1992).

Loren Coleman and Jerome Clark, *Cryptozoology A to Z: The Encyclopedia of Loch Monsters, Sasquatch, Chupacabras, and Other Authentic Mysteries of Nature*, 2nd ed. (Fireside, 1999).

Zack Davisson, "What Are Kaidan?" *Hyakumonogatari Kaidankai*, August 18, 2010, https://hyakumonogatari.com/what-are-kaidan/.

Wheeler Winston Dixon, *A History of Horror* (Rutgers University Press, 2010).

The Epic of Gilgamesh, trans. N. K. Sandars (Penguin Books, 1972).

Thomas Fahy, ed., *The Philosophy of Horror: The Philosophy of Popular Culture* (University Press of Kentucky, 2012).

Rob Gilhooly, "Inside Aokigahara, Japan's 'Suicide Forest,'" *The Japan Times*, June 26, 2011, https://www.japantimes.co.jp/life/2011/06/26/general/inside-japans-suicide-forest/.

Raven Grimassi, *Encyclopedia of Wicca & Witchcraft* (Llewellyn Publications, 2000).

Jacob Grimm and Wilhelm Grimm, *Grimms' Fairy Tales*, trans. Margaret Hunt, ed. James Stern (Pantheon Books, 1972).

Nick Groom, *The Gothic: A Very Short Introduction* (Oxford University Press, 2012).

Rosemary Ellen Guiley, *The Encyclopedia of Demons and Demonology* (Facts On File, 2009).

Rosemary Ellen Guiley, *The Encyclopedia of Vampires, Werewolves, and Other Monsters* (Visionary Living, 2004).

J. A. Hernandez, "Coffin Joe of Brazil," *Into Horror History*, February 7, 2023, https://www.jahernandez.com/posts/coffin-joe-of-brazil.

Kate Hodges, *Warriors, Witches, Women: Mythology's Fiercest Females* (White Lion Publishing, 2020).

The Holy Bible: King James Version (Thomas Nelson, 1987).

Homer, *The Odyssey*, trans. Robert Fagles (Penguin Books, 1996).

Mitch Horowitz, *Occult America: White House Séances, Ouija Circles, Masons, and the Secret Mystic History of Our Nation* (Bantam, 2010).

History of the Occult, 3rd ed. (HISTORY Special Edition, 2022).

"How Trick-or-Treating Became a Halloween Tradition," *History*, October 3, 2019, https://www.history.com/articles/halloween-trick-or-treating-origins.

C. G. Jung, *Man and His Symbols* (Doubleday, 2023).

Darryl Jones, *Horror: A Very Short Introduction* (Oxford University Press, 2021).

Dawn Keetley, ed., *Jordan Peele's Get Out: Political Horror* (University Press of Mississippi, 2020).

Margee Kerr, *Scream: Chilling Adventures in the Science of Fear* (PublicAffairs, 2017).

Stephen King, *Danse Macabre* (Everest House, 1981).

Lisa Kröger and Melanie R. Anderson, *Monster, She Wrote: The Women Who Pioneered Horror and Speculative Fiction* (Quirk Books, 2019).

Tanika Koosmen, "The Ancient Origins of Werewolves," *The Conversation*, October 28, 2018, https://theconversation.com/the-ancient-origins-of-werewolves-104775.

Thomas W. Laqueur, *The Work of the Dead: A Cultural History of Mortal Remains* (Princeton University Press, 2015).

Maria Leach, ed., *Funk & Wagnalls Standard Dictionary of Folklore, Mythology, and Legend* (Harper & Row, 1984).

Murray Leeder, *Horror Film: A Critical Introduction* (Bloomsbury Academic, 2018).

David Leeming, *The Oxford Companion to World Mythology* (Oxford University Press, 2009).

India Marriott, "From Grimm to Gothic and Everything In Between: The Evolution of the Horror Genre," *The Gale Review*, February 2, 2023, https://review.gale.com/2023/02/02/the-evolution-of-the-horror-genre/.

Pam McKamey, "Monster Movies: The Origin of the Creature Feature," *Asgard Press*, October 4, 2022, https://www.asgardpress.com/monster-movies-the-origin-of-the-creature-feature/.

Peter Metcalf and Richard Huntington, *Celebrations of Death: The Anthropology of Mortuary Ritual* (Cambridge University Press, 1991).

John Milton, *Paradise Lost*, ed. John Leonard (Penguin Classics, 2003).

Moan Incorporated, "Medea," *Moan Inc.*, April 8, 2021, https://www.moaninc.co.uk/ancient-women/medea.

Melinda Wenner Moyer, "How Horror Stories Help Us Cope With Real Life," *The New York Times*, October 27, 2022, https://www.nytimes.com/2022/10/27/well/how-horror-stories-help-us-cope-with-real-life.html.

Mallory O'Meara, *The Lady from the Black Lagoon: Hollywood Monsters and the Lost Legacy of Milicent Patrick* (Hanover Square Press, 2019).

Michelle Park, "The Aesthetics and Psychology Behind Horror Films" (undergraduate honors thesis, Long Island University, 2018), https://digitalcommons.liu.edu/post_honors_theses/31.

W. Scott Poole, *Wasteland: The Great War and the Origins of Modern Horror* (Counterpoint, 2018).

Philip Pullman, ed., *Fairy Tales from the Brothers Grimm: A New English Version* (Viking, 2012).

Prop Store, https://www.propstore.com.

The Qur'an, trans. M. A. S. Abdel Haleem (Oxford University Press, 2005).

Andy Richards, *Asian Horror* (Oldcastle Books/Kamera Books, 2010).

Jonathan Risner, *Blood Circuits: Contemporary Argentine Horror Cinema* (SUNY Press, 2019).

SIMON
ELEMENT

An Imprint of Simon & Schuster, LLC
1230 Avenue of the Americas
New York, NY 10020

First Simon Element hardcover edition September 2026

SIMON ELEMENT and colophon are registered trademarks of Simon & Schuster, LLC

Manufactured in China

1 3 5 7 9 10 8 6 4 2

Library of Congress Control Number: 2026938422

ISBN 978-1-6680-9908-7
ISBN 978-1-6680-9909-4 (ebook)

Nicholas Rogers, *Halloween: From Pagan Ritual to Party Night* (Oxford University Press, 2003).

"Samhain," *Encyclopedia Britannica*, n.d., https://www.britannica.com/topic/Samhain.

Alex Savage, "The Grand-Guignol: A Dramaturgical Guide," *The Grand Guignol*, 2022, https://thegrandguignol.com/.

Steven Jay Schneider, ed., *Fear Without Frontiers: Horror Cinema Across the Globe* (FAB Press, 2003).

Steven Jay Schneider and Tony Williams, eds., *Horror International* (Wayne State University Press, 2005).

Mary Shelley, *Frankenstein* (Signature Editions, 2022).

David J. Skal, *The Monster Show: A Cultural History of Horror*, (Faber & Faber, 2001).

David J. Skal, *Screams of Reason: Mad Science and Modern Culture* (W. W. Norton & Company, 2005).

"The Science of Scare: The Scariest Movies According to Science," *MoneySuperMarket*, updated October 1, 2025, https://www.moneysupermarket.com/broadband/features/science-of-scare/.

Sylvia Stecher, "The Psychology of Fear: Exploring the Science Behind Horror Entertainment," *CSP Global*, July 13, 2020, https://online.csp.edu/resources/article/pyschology-of-fear/.

Elizabeth Svoboda, "Why We're Obsessed With Understanding Evil," *Greater Good Magazine*, February 21, 2017, https://greatergood.berkeley.edu/article/item/why_were_obsessed_with_understanding_evil.

Jon Towlson, *Global Horror Cinema Today: 28 Representative Films from 17 Countries* (McFarland & Company, 2021).

"Werewolf Legends," *History*, August 23, 2017, updated May 28, 2025, https://www.history.com/articles/history-of-the-werewolf-legend.

Barbara Weisberg, *Talking to the Dead: Séances, Mediums, and Spirit Photography in America* (HarperCollins, 2005).

The World's Most Haunted Places (Meredith Operations Corporation, 2022).

Haiyang Yang and Kuangjie Zhang, "The Psychology Behind Why We Love (or Hate) Horror," *Harvard Business Review*, October 26, 2021, https://hbr.org/2021/10/the-psychology-behind-why-we-love-or-hate-horror.

FURTHER READING

American Scary: A History of Horror, From Salem to Stephen King and Beyond by Jeremy Dauber

Carmilla by Sheridan Le Fanu

The Castle of Otranto by Horace Walpole

The Complete Tales and Poems of Edgar Allan Poe by Edgar Allan Poe

Dracula by Bram Stoker

Making Monsters: Inside Stories from the Creators of Hollywood's Most Iconic Creatures by Howard Berger and Marshall Julius

Necronomicon by H.R. Giger

Scared by the Bible: The Roots of Horror in Scripture by Brandon R. Grafius

The Scary Book of Christmas Lore by Tim Rayborn

Tell My Horse: Voodoo and Life in Haiti and Jamaica by Zora Neale Hurston

Uzumaki by Junji Ito

The Were-Wolf by Clemence Housman

The Witches by Roald Dahl

ART CREDITS

Unknown artist. *The Wolf Man*, 1941. Hand-painted studio poster illustration. Universal Pictures, Hollywood.

Ari Aster, *Hereditary*, 2018. Motion picture. A24, United States.

Quentin Blake, *The Witches* (book cover illustration), 1983. Ink and watercolor. Jonathan Cape, London.

Hieronymus Bosch, *The Garden of Earthly Delights*, c. 1490–1500. Grisaille, Oil on oak panel. Museo del Prado, Madrid.

Danny Boyle, *28 Days Later*, 2002. Motion picture. DNA Films, United Kingdom.

Mario De Berardinis, *Suspiria*, 1977. Theatrical film poster artwork. Italy.

John Carmack and John Romero, *Doom*, 1993. Video game design and development. id Software, United States.

Scott Cawthon, *Five Nights at Freddy's*, 2014. Video game design and development. Scottgames, United States.

Scott Derrickson, *Sinister*, 2012. Motion picture. Blumhouse Productions / Summit Entertainment, United States.

Neil Druckmann and Bruce Straley, *The Last of Us*, 2013. Video game design and development. Naughty Dog, United States.

Neil Druckmann and Craig Mazin, *The Last of Us*, 2023. Television series. HBO, United States.

Kyle Edward Ball, *Skinamarink*, 2022. Motion picture. IFC Midnight, Canada.

Henry Fuseli, *The Nightmare*, 1781. Oil on canvas. Detroit Institute of Arts, Detroit.

Stephen Gammell, *Scary Stories to Tell in the Dark*, 1981–1991. Pen and ink. Harper & Row, New York.

Artemisia Gentileschi, *Judith Beheading Holofernes*, c. 1620. Oil on canvas. Galleria degli Uffizi, Florence.

Robert Gleason, *Halloween*, 1978. Acrylic on board. Compass International Pictures, Los Angeles.

Edward Gorey, *The Gashlycrumb Tinies*, 1963. Pen and ink. G. P. Putnam's Sons, New York.

Francisco Goya, *Saturn Devouring His Son*, c. 1820–1823. Oil on plaster (transferred to canvas). Museo del Prado, Madrid.

Junji Ito, *Uzumaki* (detail), 1998–1999. Ink on paper. Shogakukan, Tokyo.

Tim Jacobus, *Goosebumps: Night of the Living Dummy* and *The Curse of Camp Cold Lake* (book cover illustrations), 1993–1997. Acrylic on illustration board. Scholastic, New York.

Carlo Jacono, *Il Delitto mi ha Vinto*, 1956. Painted book cover illustration. Arnoldo Mondadori Editore, Milan.

Alexander Juhasz, *The Babadook*, 2014. Character design for film. Screen Australia / Causeway Films, Australia.

Jennifer Kent, *The Babadook*, 2014. Motion picture. Causeway Films, Australia.

Shinji Mikami and Tokuro Fujiwara, *Resident Evil*, 1996. Video game design and development. Capcom, Japan.

Edvard Munch, *The Scream*, 1893. Tempera and oil on cardboard. National Gallery of Norway, Oslo.

Lanny Powers, *Dawn of the Dead*, 1978. Theatrical film poster artwork. United Film Distribution Company, New York.

Dave Richard, *Dead by Daylight*, 2016. Video game design and development. Behaviour Interactive, Canada.

Auguste Rodin, *The Gates of Hell*, c. 1880–1917. Bronze. Musée d'Orsay, Paris.

George A. Romero, *Night of the Living Dead*, 1968. Motion picture. Image Ten, United States.

Yeon Sang-ho, *Train to Busan*, 2016. Motion picture. Next Entertainment World, South Korea.

Rob Savage, *Host*, 2020. Motion picture. Shudder, United Kingdom.

Keiichiro Toyama and Team Silent, *Silent Hill*, 1999. Video game design and development. Konami, Japan.

Bob Wakelin, *Evil Dead: The Musical*, 2003. Theatrical poster artwork. New York.

James Wan, *Insidious*, 2010. Motion picture. Blumhouse Productions / FilmDistrict, United States.

Dirk Zimmer, *In a Dark, Dark Room and Other Scary Stories*, 1984. Ink and wash. Harper & Row, New York.